IRON NUTRITION
IN INFANCY AND CHILDHOOD

Iron Nutrition in Infancy and Childhood, Fourth Nestlé Nutrition Workshop, Manila, The Philippines, December 1982

Seated (from left to right): M. Certeza, V. Guzman, P. R. Guesry, F. S. Solon, A. Stekel, E. DeMaeyer. *Standing:* R. M. Guirriec, M. A. Siimes, Mrs. Siimes, H. Puruganan, P. R. Dallman, D. Karyadi, A. Marzan, R. F. Hurrell, S. G. Kahn, L. Hallberg, R. F. Florentino, B. Lönnerdal, S. J. Fomon, V. Doctor, L. Garby, J. D. Cook, C. A. Finch, R. K. Chandra.

Iron Nutrition
in Infancy and Childhood

Editor

Abraham Stekel, M.D.
Institute of Nutrition and Food Technology
University of Chile
Santiago, Chile

Nestlé Nutrition
Workshop Series
Volume 4

NESTLÉ NUTRITION, VEVEY

RAVEN PRESS ■ NEW YORK

Raven Press, 1140 Avenue of the Americas, New York, New York 10036

Made in the United States of America

Library of Congress Cataloging in Publication Data
Main entry under title:

Iron nutrition in infancy and childhood.

(Nestlé Nutrition workshop series; v. 4)
Paper presented at a conference sponsored by the Nutrition Center of the Philippines, held in Manila, Dec. 1982.
Includes bibliographical references and index.
1. Iron deficiency anemia in children—Etiology—Congresses. 2. Infants—Nutrition—Congresses. 3. Children—Nutrition—Congresses. I. Stekel, Abraham. II. Nutrition Center of the Philippines. III. Series. [DNLM: 1. Child nutrition—Congresses. 2. Infant nutrition—Congresses. 3. Anemia, Hypochromic—Prevention and control—Congresses. 4. Iron—Deficiency—Congresses. W3 NE468 v.4/WS 115 N468 1982i]
RJ416. I75I76 1984   618.92′152   83-27032
ISBN 0-89004-435-X (Raven Press)

Second Printing, June 1985

Preface

Iron deficiency is a widespread condition affecting hundreds of millions of people throughout the world. Although poorer populations suffer most, lack of iron remains one of the few nutritional deficiencies prevalent in affluent societies.

Severe iron deficiency is easy to recognize, and its effects on health have long been appreciated. However, as is true of other nutritional deficiencies, the milder forms are the most prevalent and difficult to diagnose. The negative effects on health of marginal iron deficiency, if any, have so far escaped a precise definition.

Infants, children, and women of childbearing age are the groups most affected by this condition. The focus of this book is on iron nutrition in infancy, an area in which considerable progress in our knowledge has been made in recent years. New laboratory techniques and the refinement of older methods have facilitated diagnosis of iron deficiency in individuals and populations. Developmental changes, not only in hemoglobin concentration but in other laboratory parameters, are now recognized. However, interpretation of results obtained with these new techniques is not always easy, and the precise diagnosis of mild iron deficiency is still difficult to establish.

Our understanding of factors affecting the availability of dietary iron has progressed steadily. The role of breast milk iron in the nutrition of the young infant is now well defined, and a better comprehension of the way infants absorb this iron may shed important light on factors determining dietary iron absorption.

Iron deficiency develops almost universally in low-birth-weight infants if preventive measures are not taken. The increasing survival rate of these infants, particularly very-low-birth-weight infants, is uncovering new problems and interesting new knowledge in this area of nutrition.

In recent years, international agencies and other groups have shown renewed interest in attacking the problem of iron deficiency. At the same time, the factors that determine dietary iron absorption have been better defined, resulting in new and more successful strategies for preventing iron deficiency. Food fortification has gained a central status among these strategies as technological advances have improved the absorbability and bioavailability of dietary supplements.

The recent interest in the health consequences of iron deficiency and the new information that has been generated hold great promise. However, much remains to be learned. The considerable costs of detecting and preventing the milder forms of this deficiency demand a rational basis for intervention. To make these decisions wisely, nutritionists and physicians need a more precise definition of the effects of iron deficiency on health. New knowledge of the kind presented in this volume undoubtedly will influence these decisions in the future.

v

This volume will be of interest to pediatricians, obstetricians, internists, and general practitioners, as well as specialists in nutrition and epidemiology.

I would like to express my gratitude to Professor Florentino S. Solon and the Nutrition Center of the Philippines, who were our hosts, and Nestlé Nutrition S.A., who initiated and made possible the development of this volume as part of the Nestlé Nutrition Workshop Series.

ABRAHAM STEKEL, M.D.

Foreword

The importance of iron deficiency in infancy and childhood is now well recognized. Methods of diagnosis and treatment are discussed in this fourth book in the *Nestlé Nutrition Workshop Series*. The key to prevention of iron deficiency in infancy begins with an adequate diet for pregnant and breast-feeding mothers. The food industry has a role to play in ensuring an adequate iron supply for children who are not breast-fed and for breast-fed children during the weaning period. Many technological advances have been made in the recent past, and work is under way to improve the absorbability of added iron in prepared foods. We hope that this volume will prove helpful to our colleagues confronted with this very widespread deficiency.

Among the many people responsible for making the meeting on which this book is based a success, I would especially like to thank Professor Florentino S. Solon of the Nutrition Center of the Philippines.

The Nestlé Nutrition Workshops concentrate on pediatric nutrition. Volumes already published in this series include *Maternal Nutrition in Pregnancy—Eating for Two?*, edited by J. Dobbing (Academic Press, 1981); *Acute Diarrhea: Its Nutritional Consequences in Children*, edited by J. A. Bellanti (Raven Press, 1983); *Nutritional Adaptation of the Gastrointestinal Tract of the Newborn*, edited by N. Kretchmer and A. Minkowski (Raven Press, 1983); and *Chronic Diarrhea in Children*, edited by E. Lebenthal (Raven Press, 1984). Forthcoming volumes are *Human Milk Processing and the Nutrition of the Very-Low-Birth-Weight Infant*, edited by J. D. Baum and A. F. Williams; and *Nutritional Needs and Assessment of Normal Growth*, edited by F. Faulkner and M. Gracey.

PIERRE R. GUESRY, M.D.
Vice-President
Nestlé Nutrition S.A.

Contents

Contributors

T. H. Bothwell
Department of Medicine
University of the Witwatersrand
    Medical School
Hospital Street
Johannesburg 2001, South Africa

*R. K. Chandra
Janeway Child Health Care Centre
St. John's, Newfoundland
Canada A1A 1R8

*J. D. Cook
Division of Hematology
Department of Medicine
University of Kansas Medical Center
Rainbow Boulevard
Kansas City, Kansas 66103, U.S.A.

*Peter R. Dallman
Department of Pediatrics
University of California
San Francisco, California 94143, U.S.A.

*Rodolfo F. Florentino
Nutrition Center of the Philippines
Metro Manila
P.O. Box 653, MCC
Makati, Philippines 3116

*Romualda M. Guirriec
Nutrition Center of the Philippines
Metro Manila
P.O. Box 653, MCC
Makati, Philippines 3116

*Richard F. Hurrell
Nestlé Products Technical
    Assistance Co. Ltd.
CH-1814 La Tour-de-Peilz, Switzerland

*Bo Lönnerdal
Department of Nutrition
University of California
Davis, California 95616, U.S.A.

Jerry D. Reeves
Department of Pediatrics
David Grant Medical Center
Travis Air Force Base
California 94535, U.S.A.

*Martti A. Siimes
Pediatric Hematology Division
Children's Hospital
University of Helsinki
Stenbäckinkatu 11
SF-00290 Helsinki 29
Finland

*Abraham Stekel
Institute of Nutrition and Food
    Technology
University of Chile
Casilla 15138
Santiago 11, Chile

Devhuti Vyas
Department of Pediatrics
Memorial University of Newfoundland
St. John's, Newfoundland
Canada A1A 1R8

*Conference participants.

Invited Attendees

Martina Certeza/*Manila, Philippines*
Edouard DeMaeyer/*Geneva,*
　Switzerland
Victor Doctor/*Quezon City, Philippines*
Clement A. Finch/*Seattle, Washington,*
　U.S.A.
Samuel J. Fomon/*Iowa City, Iowa,*
　U.S.A.
Lars Garby/*Odense, Denmark*
Virginia Guzman/*Manila, Philippines*
Leif Hallberg/*Göteborg, Sweden*

Samuel G. Kahn/*Washington, D.C.,*
　U.S.A.
Darwin Karyadi/*Bogor, Indonesia*
Miriam Kuizon/*Manila, Philippines*
Anita Marzan/*Quezon City, Philippines*
Miguel L. Noche, Jr./*Manila,*
　Philippines
Hermogenes Purugganan/*Manila,*
　Philippines
Florentino S. Solon/*Makati, Philippines*
Mrs. M. A. Siimes/*Helsinki, Finland*

Nestlé Participants

Pierre R. Guesry
Medical and Scientific Director
Nestlé Nutrition S.A.
Vevey, Switzerland

Richard F. Hurrell
Research Laboratories
Nestlé Products Technical Assistance
　Co. Ltd
La Tour-de-Peilz, Switzerland

IRON NUTRITION
IN INFANCY AND CHILDHOOD

Iron Nutrition in Infancy and Childhood,
edited by A. Stekel. Nestlé, Vevey/Raven Press,
New York © 1984.

Iron Requirements in Infancy and Childhood

Abraham Stekel

*Institute of Nutrition and Food Technology, University of Chile,
Casilla 15138, Santiago 11 Chile*

A critical characteristic of iron nutrition in infancy, as compared to adults, is the greater dependency of the infant on external sources of iron for daily red cell production. Dallman et al. (1) have calculated that in a 1-year-old, 10-kg infant, dietary iron must provide 30% of the needs for hemoglobin iron turnover as compared to only 5% in the adult male (Table 1). This imposes disproportionate requirements of iron to the infant. In addition, infants may (a) consume diets with a low iron content or poor iron availability; (b) be born with decreased iron reserves, as is the case with premature infants; (c) grow too rapidly and have excessive demands; or (d) have increased iron losses. The sum of these factors explains the high occurrence of iron deficiency observed at this age.

The main factors determining iron requirements in infants and children are the iron endowment at birth, the requirements for growth, and the need to replace losses.

IRON ENDOWMENT AT BIRTH

The human fetus has been described as a good parasite with respect to iron nutrition. Most studies, based either on the measurement of ferritin in the newborn (2,3) or the later development of anemia (4,5), suggest that iron status at birth is little dependent on the iron nutrition status of the mother. It is only under the most unusual circumstances of severe iron deficiency in the mother that the iron endow-

TABLE 1. *Greater dependence on dietary iron in the infant compared to the adult male[a]*

	1-year-old infant (Wt: 10 kg)	Adult male (Wt: 70 kg)
Hemoglobin iron (mg)		
In circulation	270.0	2.200
Turnover/day	2.3	18
Dietary iron		
Assimilated/day (mg)	0.7	0.9
Hgb iron turnover (%)	30	5

[a]From Dallman et al. (1).

1

ment of the newborn may be affected (6). It must be remembered, however, that severe maternal iron deficiency can be associated with intrauterine growth retardation or premature delivery, thus indirectly affecting the iron reserves of the newborn (6,7).

Chemical analysis of fetuses and stillborn term infants have shown a linear relationship between body weight and total body iron, so that premature and term infants have an average of 75 mg/kg iron at birth (8) (Fig. 1). An important feature about the distribution of this iron is that about 75% of it is in circulating hemoglobin, constituting a true iron reserve due to the fact that hemoglobin concentration is much higher in the newborn than later in infancy. Thus fetal bleeding during delivery or bleeding during the postnatal period will have a marked effect on iron reserves and on subsequent susceptibility to development of iron deficiency.

REQUIREMENTS FOR GROWTH

Calculations of iron requirements for growth are based on estimations of total body iron of normal infants and children at different ages. Growth is maximum during the first year of life when a term infant triples his birth weight. However, not all iron compartments increase their size proportionally during this period. As already mentioned, the physiologic fall in hemoglobin concentration in the first 2 months of life and the redistribution of this iron to storage compartments is of great significance. Iron stores, however, become depleted at about 4 months of age in term infants and at 2 to 3 months in preterm infants. At this time the infant becomes dependent on external iron sources for maintenance of an adequate iron nutrition status. These different postnatal stages of iron balance and erythropoiesis are depicted in Fig. 2 (1).

Based on existing data on the iron content of various tissues, blood volume, and weight of organs, calculations can be made of the total body iron content and the

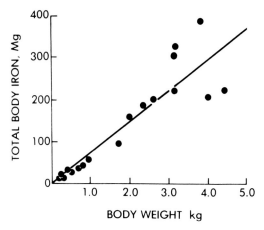

FIG. 1. Total body iron and body weight in the fetus and the newborn. (From Widdowson and Spray, ref. 8.)

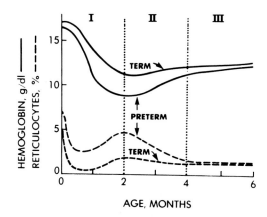

FIG. 2. Three postnatal stages of iron balance and erythropoiesis. Mean values for concentration of hemoglobin and reticulocyte count are shown for term infants and preterm infants. The duration of the stages is shown for term infants. I: Immediately after birth, the rate of erythropoiesis (reticulocyte count) and the concentration of hemoglobin decrease in response to increased availability of oxygen. Storage iron is augmented. II: At about 2 months of age, the concentration of hemoglobin has fallen to its lowest point and the rate of erythropoiesis is increased. Storage iron gradually decreases. III: Iron stores become depleted by about 3 months of age in preterm infants and by 4 months in term infants unless replenished by an adequate exogenous supply of iron. (From Dallman et al., ref 1.)

iron present in various compartments at different ages. An example of such calculations made by Smith and Ríos (9) is shown in Fig. 3. Although these estimations may be subject to some error, they provide a solid basis for calculating requirements for growth (Table 2). The main source of uncertainty in these calculations lies in the definition of a normal or optimal level of iron stores at different ages. The error introduced in the final results, however, may be of relatively little importance since the size of the main iron compartment, circulating hemoglobin, can be accurately calculated from existing data. Mean requirements of absorbed iron for growth calculated in this manner are about 0.4 mg/day from 0 to 12 months of age. Requirements are higher in the second semester (6–12 months), when the infant needs about 0.53 mg/day of iron for growth (Table 3). Growth rate decreases after the first year of life, resulting in decreased requirements for growth of 0.29 mg/day between 1 and 2 years and 0.23 mg/day between 2 and 8 years of age.

Adolescence is another critical period in the growth process. During this period there is a rapid expansion of the blood volume and an increase in hemoglobin concentration in boys. The mean iron requirement in an adolescent boy can amount to about 1 mg/day during the year of peak growth (1).

IRON LOSSES

Physiologic iron losses in man are small. Studies in adult men have shown mean daily losses of about 0.9 mg (10). Mechanisms for regulating iron excretion are very limited, so that even under extreme circumstances of iron deficiency or iron

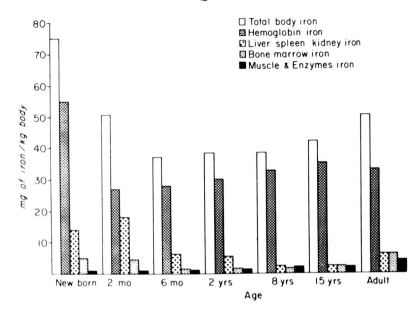

FIG. 3. Distribution of body iron at different ages. Values were calculated from data in the literature for body weight and length, organ weight, hemoglobin levels, blood volume, and amount of iron in different tissues. (From Smith and Ríos, ref. 9.)

TABLE 2. *Estimated total body iron content at different ages*

Age	Weight[a] (kg)	Body iron mg/kg[b]	mg
Birth	3.27	75	245
6 months	7.85	37	290
1 year	10.15	38	386
2 years	12.59	39	491
8 years	25.30	39	987

[a]50th percentile values for boys, from data of the National Center for Health Statistics.
[b]From estimations by Smith and Ríos (9).

overload, excretion does not vary more than two- or threefold (10). Most iron is lost in the gut as a consequence of physiological bleeding and cell desquamation (11).

Information on iron losses in infants and children is very limited. Garby et al. (12) measured iron lost in the feces using a radioisotopic method in 3 infants and obtained a mean value of 0.03 mg/kg. Elian et al. (13) determined the apparent blood loss in the feces of 25 normal infants 2 to 17 months of age using ^{51}Cr-labeled red cells and found a mean value of 0.64 ml/day (range: 0.17–2.5 ml).

TABLE 3. *Estimated requirements of absorbed iron for boys (mg/day)*

Age:	0–6 months	6–12 months	1–2 years	2–8 years
Requirements for growth[a]	0.25	0.53	0.29	0.23
Iron losses[b]	0.24	0.37	0.46	0.56
Total requirements	0.49	0.90	0.75	0.79

[a]Calculated from data by Smith and Ríos (9).
[b]Estimated at 0.04 mg/kg from 0–2 years and 0.03 mg/kg from 2–8 years.

This corresponds to approximately 0.25 mg of iron per day. Values of the same order were obtained by Hoag et al. (14) using ^{59}Fe-labeled red cells. Smith and Ríos (9) estimated mean total iron losses during the first 2 years of life at 0.04 mg/kg, which seems reasonable if one adds to the measured intestinal losses the small amounts lost through the skin and urine.

Physiological iron losses in infancy are frequently dismissed as an unimportant factor in the calculations of iron requirements, when in fact they account for approximately one-half of the iron needs during the first 2 years of life (Table 3). Losses in some cases may be much higher because of the wide variation in the amount of blood lost through the gut by normal infants (13). In addition, iron losses can be increased markedly by such common events as the feeding of fresh cow's milk to young infants (15,16) or the occurrence of diarrhea (13).

REQUIREMENTS OF ABSORBED IRON

Requirements of absorbed iron can be calculated on the basis of the requirements for growth and the need to replace iron losses. An example based on the previous discussion is shown in Table 3. Requirements of absorbed iron are estimated at approximately 0.5 mg/day from 0 to 6 months of age, 0.9 mg/day from 6 to 12 months, and 0.7 to 0.8 mg/day from 1 to 8 years.

Similar figures have been obtained by others. Schulman (17) estimated the needs of absorbed iron in the first year of life, after stores are depleted, to be 0.8 mg/day. Using a somewhat different method, Fomon (18) estimated these needs at 0.7 mg/day during the first year of life and 0.8 mg/day from 1 to 3 years of age, even though he probably underestimated iron losses.

All of these estimates are mean values. The somewhat higher recommendation by FAO/WHO (19) of 1 mg of absorbed iron throughout infancy and childhood is probably justified due to the considerable individual variation that can occur.

RECOMMENDED IRON INTAKES

Recommended intakes of iron should be those that can meet the needs of absorbed iron. Amounts needed will vary, depending on the bioavailability of the ingested iron. Absorption of food iron in infants and children can be as low as 1 to 2% or as high as 50%, as in the case of breast milk iron. Most existing recommendations

(20) are based on an estimated 10% absorption of food iron. In 1970, FAO/WHO (19) recognized the importance of animal tissues on food iron availability, estimating a mean iron absorption of 10% when animal tissues represented less than 10% of total calories, and a mean absorption of 20% when they represented more than 25%. In view of more recent information (21), these estimates of food iron availability appear too high and result in low recommended intakes of 5 to 10 mg/day in infants and children. In addition, it is only animal tissue (meat) that has an enhancing effect on nonheme iron absorption; other animal products of importance in pediatric nutrition such as eggs and milk lack this effect.

The Committee on Nutrition of the American Academy of Pediatrics recommends intakes of 1 mg/kg/day for term infants, up to a maximum of 15 mg, and 2 mg/kg/day for low-birth-weight infants (22). Recommendations based on body weight for infants and children have been justifiably questioned (18) on the basis that requirements of absorbed iron are not dependent on body weight.

Based on the detailed calculations of Monsen et al. (21), it can be estimated that infants and children will absorb about 10% of the iron in a good availability diet and about 5% in a poor availability diet. On this basis it would appear that, depending on the quality of the diet, intakes of 10 to 20 mg/day are needed to meet the requirement of 1 mg absorbed iron throughout most of infancy and childhood.

REFERENCES

1. Dallman PR, Siimes MA, Stekel A. Iron deficiency in infancy and childhood. Am J Clin Nutr 1980;33:86–118.
2. Fenton V, Cavill I, Fisher J. Iron stores in pregnancy. Br J Haematol 1977;37:145–9.
3. Ríos E, Lipschitz DA, Cook JD, Smith NJ. Relationship of maternal and infant iron stores as assessed by determination of plasma ferritin. Pediatrics 1975;55:694–9.
4. Murray MJ, Murray AB, Murray NJ, Murray MB. The effect of iron status of Nigerian mothers on that of their infants at birth and 6 months, and on the concentration of Fe in breast milk. Br J Nutr 1978;39:627–30.
5. Sturgeon P. Studies of iron requirements in infants. III. Influence of supplemental iron during normal pregnancy on mother and infant. B. The infant. Br J Haematol 1959;5:45–55.
6. Singla PN, Chand S, Khanna S, Agarwal KN. Effect of maternal anaemia on the placenta and the newborn infant. Acta Paediatr Scand 1978;67:645–8.
7. Roszkowski I, Wojcicka J, Zaleska K. Serum iron deficiency during the third trimester of pregnancy: maternal complications and fate of the neonate. Obstet Gynecol 1966;28:820–5.
8. Widdowson EM, Spray CM. Chemical development in utero. Arch Dis Child 1951;26:205–14.
9. Smith NJ, Ríos E. Iron metabolism and iron deficiency in infancy and childhood. In: Schulman I, ed. Advances in pediatrics, Vol. 21. Chicago: Year Book Medical Publishers, 1974.
10. Green R, Charlton R, Seftel H, Bothwell T, Mayet F, Adams B, Finch C, Layrisse M. Body iron excretion in man: a collaborative study. Am J Med 1968;45:336–53.
11. Bothwell TH, Charlton RW, Cook JD, Finch CA. Iron metabolism in man. Oxford: Blackwell Scientific Publications, 1979.
12. Garby L, Sjölin S, Vuille JC. Studies on erythro-kinetics in infancy. IV. The long-term behaviour of radioiron in circulating foetal and adult haemoglobin, and its faecal excretion. Acta Paediatr 1964;53:33–41.
13. Elian E, Bar-Shani S, Liberman A, Matoth Y. Intestinal blood loss: a factor in calculations of body iron in late infancy. J Pediatr 1966;69:215–9.
14. Hoag MS, Wallerstein RO, Pollycove M. Occult blood loss in iron deficiency anemia of infancy. Pediatrics 1961;27:199–203.

15. Wilson JF, Lahey ME, Heiner DC. Studies on iron metabolism. V. Further observations on cow's milk-induced gastrointestinal bleeding in infants with iron deficiency anemia. J Pediatr 1974;84:335–44.

16. Woodruff CW, Clark JL. The role of fresh cow's milk in iron deficiency. I. Albumin turnover in infants with iron deficiency anemia. Am J Dis Child 1972;124:18–23.

17. Schulman I. Iron requirements in infancy. JAMA 1961;175:118–23.

18. Fomon SJ. Infant nutrition. 2nd ed. Philadelphia: WB Saunders, 1974.

19. FAO/WHO. Requirements of ascorbic acid, vitamin D, vitamin B_{12}, folate and iron. Geneva: FAO/WHO; 1970; Technical report series no. 452.

20. Food and Nutrition Board, National Research Council. Recommended dietary allowances. 9th ed. Washington, D.C.: National Academy of Sciences, 1980.

21. Monsen ER, Hallberg L, Layrisse M, Hegsted DM, Cook JD, Mertz W, Finch CA. Estimation of available dietary iron. Am J Clin Nutr 1978;31:134–41.

22. Committee on Nutrition, American Academy of Pediatrics. Iron supplementation for infants. Pediatrics 1976;58:765–8.

DISCUSSION

Dr. Finch: Quantitative studies of placental iron procurement in the rat (American Journal of Clinical Nutrition, *in press*) have shown the limits of fetal iron supply. Fetuses of iron-deficient mothers were iron-deficient and many died and were resorbed *in utero*. However, considering that the rat has about 10 fetuses, and extrapolating these results to the one human fetus, it would seem most unlikely that there could be a deficient iron supply to the human fetus despite the most severe maternal iron deficiency.

Dr. Chandra: Dr. Finch, you mentioned fetal resorption, but you didn't tell us about the fetuses in whom the intrauterine growth was affected and whether there was higher incidence of congenital malformations among them. Such observations have been made in a number of other nutrient deficiencies.

Dr. Finch: The fetuses that were examined on the 20th day of pregnancy were as anemic and iron-deficient as the mother. The fetuses that were reduced in number were also small. In this current study we do not have information concerning fetal abnormalities, but in a previous report (Teratology 1980;22:329), Shepard et al. did note some defects. It was quite apparent, however, that the imposition of iron deficiency in the rat was far more detrimental to the fetus than to the mother. In the human, because of the difference in levels of iron requirements, it will be the mother who suffers rather than the fetus.

Dr. Chandra: Dr. Stekel, you have mentioned that the requirements of iron might be dependent, among other factors, on the mode of feeding. You have hinted that untreated cow's milk, for example, increases fecal losses of iron and therefore increases the requirements. At a previous conference on this topic, a statement was made that exclusively breast-fed infants have never been shown to have developed iron deficiency. I don't know if such a strong statement can be upheld.

Dr. Stekel: As it will be surely discussed in greater detail during this workshop, there is some evidence that availability of iron from breast milk is higher than that from cow's milk. Still, the relatively low iron concentration in breast milk, even with 100% absorption, is not enough to support indefinitely the iron requirements of the infant. Thus, I think that statement is quite strong and probably relates only to the young healthy term infant during the first 4 to 6 months of age. I think that after this age even the breast-fed infant will require an extra source of iron.

Dr. Fomon: The data of Smith and Ríos (1974) [ref. 9, *this chapter*] presented in your Table 2 and Fig. 3 estimate body iron to be 37 mg/kg at age 6 months and 39 mg/kg at age 8 years. This is an increase in quantity of iron per unit of body weight of 5%. I believe this is too small an increase. Iron in circulating hemoglobin and storage iron are almost certainly greater per unit of fat-free body mass in the 8-year-old than in the 6-month-old and fat-free body mass comprises a substantially greater percentage of body weight at age 8 years than at age 6 months.

Dr. Dallman: Dr. Stekel mentioned two areas that are possibly controversial. The first problem is, what constitutes normal iron reserves for an infant or child? One's first reaction might be to regard the usual circumstance of almost absent iron stores in rapidly growing children as pathological. Yet, we find this in healthy, well-nourished populations of children that only very rarely go on to develop anemia. It therefore seems that rapidly growing children may be considered to have adequate iron nutrition despite the virtual absence of stores.

The other topic deals with the guidelines of Monsen et al. (1978) [ref. 21, *this chapter*] for estimating iron absorption from adult diets on the basis of their meat and ascorbic acid content. Perhaps these values need to be increased for the child in the view of studies that suggest that infants and children absorb a greater percentage of dietary iron than adults.

Dr. Stekel: First, a short comment on Dr. Fomon's intervention. I know that he has made his own calculations for requirements based on estimations of the iron content of the body per kilogram of fat-free body mass at different ages. I really do not know what is the right answer. I do not know of any experimental data that can support either way of making these calculations. I don't think we have the gold standard, which would be data on total body chemical analysis of children at different ages.

Regarding Dr. Dallman's comment, I think this is really one of the main problems in trying to determine what are the requirements for growth. We have a fairly good idea of what a normal hemoglobin concentration is, but we have very little idea of what normal iron stores in infants should be. As Dr. Dallman just commented, the fact is that apparently normal infants in affluent countries, being fed what can be considered very good diets, have relatively low iron stores. Whether higher levels would be desirable is not known.

Dr. Cook: We should discuss desirable iron stores in the population rather than in the individual. In the individual person, there is no difference of clinical relevance between iron stores of 100 and 1,000 mg; in both cases, there is enough iron to supply the needs of the bone marrow. A desirable level of storage iron in the population should ensure that the vast majority have some iron reserves. In adult women in the United States, estimates of storage iron suggest that if the median store in the population is 300 mg, then maybe 20% have absent stores. Perhaps a desirable level is one at which no more than 10 to 15% of the population have absent stores.

Dr. Dallman: Judging from the low serum ferritin values in groups of children that are virtually free of anemia, it seems that iron stores can fall into a lower and narrower range than in women without necessarily having a substantial risk of anemia and the associated physiological consequences.

Dr. Stekel: In calculating requirements, I believe that the variation imposed by the normal range of iron losses may be more important than that derived from variations in growth, since most children will grow within a relatively narrow range. I think we need to learn a lot more about what is the normal range of iron losses. This may help explain why requirements in different individuals in a population can differ so much and why 20 to 30% of children who appear to have similar growth and a similar diet will develop iron deficiency anemia. We know very little about iron losses in children; it has been a very neglected area.

Dr. Dallman: I would like to ask Dr. Cook or Dr. Hallberg whether the difference between absorption in children and adults is due solely to lower iron reserves in children or whether there may be a difference in gastrointestinal function.

Dr. Cook: When extrapolating from adult to childhood absorption levels, one may need to assume higher absorption values for the infant and child. The question is whether differences in absorption between children and adults is due solely to a difference in iron status or whether there is some difference in gastrointestinal function. We have observed in studies of food iron absorption in adults that there is an age-dependent fall-off in absorption over the range of 20 to 60 years. This observation was first reported with inorganic iron by the Cardiff group and we have confirmed it with both heme and nonheme iron absorption. We are not able to determine why—whether it is a fall-off in mucosal cell function or perhaps related to a change in gastrointestinal secretion. I know of no data that would help sort out whether in the age range of 1 to 20 years there is a similar decline in gastrointestinal function, although I doubt this. I think the major difference in absorption levels between children and adults relates to differences in iron status.

Dr. Stekel: In this respect, Dr. Cook, I notice that in your presentation and in your recent publication on the absorption of iron from soya formulas in infants, you relate results to a reference dose absorption of 60%, which in a way would bear in this discussion. I would like to ask you if you used this figure because you think that infants with iron stores similar to adults absorb more iron or because you think that infants are more iron-deficient than adults.

Dr. Cook: When we select a single figure for the reference dose absorption, we defeat our purpose because the reference does allow an estimate of absorption at all levels of iron status. We should get away from the system of using 40 or 60 or 20% and simply express absorption of the test dose as a ratio of the reference dose. Then everyone can make their own conversions. If I remember correctly, the choice of 60% reference dose in our paper was to reflect that, in general, children are more iron-deficient than adults. This is not, however, a very solid basis for using a reference value of 60% in infants versus 40% in adults.

Dr. Dallman: These issues assume practical importance when recommended allowances for iron are calculated. If one assumes an iron absorption of 10% for infants in the United States, as was done some years ago, estimates of dietary iron needs are probably excessive. I don't have any better percentage to substitute, but I think that the validity of recommended allowances has to be verified whenever possible by experimental data, i.e., by actually determining what intakes of iron in various diets are successful in preventing iron deficient hematopoiesis and the associated handicaps of iron deficiency.

Dr. Stekel: You may be thinking about the kind of figures that one comes up with in these calculations, with the higher values in the range of 20 mg, which is a very high figure. On the other hand, if one considers children living in countries where the diet contains little meat and poor vegetable-iron sources, 20 mg of iron may be necessary to absorb 1 mg, i.e., 5%. Therefore, it is difficult to come up with fixed figures for recommended intakes. One should consider rather the amount that needs to be absorbed and calculate intakes depending on the type of diet available.

Dr. Guesry: I should like to come back to the point raised by Dr. Finch concerning the regulatory mechanisms controlling the passage of iron from the mother to the fetus. In rats, this mechanism does not appear to exist and mothers suffering from iron deficiency give birth to iron-deficient offspring. In humans, however, there is a mechanism which regulates the passage of iron, and iron-deficient mothers give birth to babies with fair iron stores. Could Dr. Finch comment on this mechanism.

Dr. Finch: It is likely that the supply to the fetus is a simple matter of a very large transferrin receptor mass in the placenta which can take up as much as one-third of the plasma iron with which it comes into contact. If we assume that maximum iron requirements of the human fetus are 6 mg/day and assume a cardiac output of 5 liters/min and 10% of this going to the placenta, it is apparent that there would be no difficulty in the fetus obtaining its needed iron even if maternal plasma levels are 5 or 10 mg/100 ml plasma.

Dr. Fomon: I understand that there is a large difference between the rat fetus and the human fetus, and Dr. Finch seems to indicate quite clearly the reasons why the human fetus may be to a large degree protected.

Dr. Finch: I think that the studies that have been carried out are reassuring in terms of the safety that the human fetus appears to have. If a number of fetuses were appreciably increased, obviously the human would have increased requirements approaching that of the rat. While there may be some point where increasing human requirements due to multiple pregnancies along with a marked restriction in plasma-iron content by the mother would cause a limitation in iron supply, there appears to be a greater margin of safety than we would have suspected.

Dr. Dallman: In regard to Dr. Fomon's earlier questions about the reasons for variability in iron stores in newborn infants, there was an interesting recent paper by MacPhail et al. (Scand. J. Haematol. 1980;25:141) showing a reciprocal relationship between hemoglobin concentration and serum ferritin in the newborn. Those infants that had the highest hemoglobin concentration tended to have the lowest serum ferritin and vice versa. The implication of these results was that the amount of iron crossing the placenta to the fetus tended to bear a constant relationship to the fetal weight. However, the distribution of iron in the fetus between stores and hemoglobin seemed to be partly regulated by other factors such as adaptation to altered oxygen availability.

Dr. Chandra: We know that iron deficiency is a problem principally of developing countries. I should like to mention another factor, infection, which might complicate any of the calculations that are being discussed. We recognize that the incidence of infection in the maternal-placental-fetal unit in developing countries is very high. Are there any studies that have looked at this question? We should also examine iron absorption in relationship to changes in gut microflora.

Dr. Hallberg: It is difficult to establish what is "normal" iron absorption in infants and children from studies made in adults. Infants and children are growing and their iron stores are proportionally less than in adults. If we want to compare the ability of a child and an adult to absorb food iron, we need to use the reference doses and the same level, e.g., 40%. However, to calculate the amount of iron absorbed from a diet by a child, one must take into account the facts of growth and lower iron stores.

Dr. Finch: To extend the discussion further, a change in iron requirements has a marked effect on iron stores. The male individual who gives one unit of blood a year has his "normal stores" dropped to half of their initial value. Blood donors who give more frequently may have no anemia, but may have a virtual absence of iron stores. The dynamics of iron balance at higher requirements as you are dealing with in infancy needs to be further examined.

Iron Nutrition in Infancy and Childhood,
edited by A. Stekel. Nestlé, Vevey/Raven Press,
New York © 1984.

Laboratory Diagnosis of Iron Deficiency

*Peter R. Dallman and **Jerry D. Reeves

*Department of Pediatrics, University of California, San Francisco, California 94143,
U.S.A.; and **Department of Pediatrics, David Grant Medical Center, Travis Air Force
Base, California 94535, U.S.A.*

INTRODUCTION

Until about 20 years ago, the diagnosis of iron deficiency was justifiably considered a simple matter. The focus of attention was then on hospitalized patients with a severe or moderate degree of anemia. When iron deficiency was suspected, the diagnosis could be substantiated by a decrease in serum iron, an elevation in the total iron-binding capacity (TIBC), and the typical changes of microcytosis, anisocytosis, and hypochromia on the blood smear. After the initiation of iron treatment, a rise in the reticulocyte count after 1 to 2 weeks and a slower, more gradual correction of the hemoglobin or hematocrit after about 2 months would confirm the diagnosis.

During the last 20 years, however, attention has shifted to the more common, milder cases of iron deficiency that are typically seen in an outpatient setting. Mild cases, in which the concentration of hemoglobin may be no more than 1 g/dl below the reference range, have proven to be an unexpectedly difficult diagnostic challenge. This is partly because textbook recommendations for diagnosis are often based on severe iron deficiency anemia and cannot be successfully extrapolated to the mild cases. The two types of patients require different diagnostic approaches.

In mild iron deficiency, the initial laboratory tests are less reliable in predicting a hemoglobin response than with severe iron deficiency because there is a substantial overlapping of results between iron-deficient and iron-sufficient populations (1–3). In contrast to severe iron deficiency, the blood smear cannot be distinguished from that of a normal individual (4). Furthermore, after treatment is initiated, the reticulocyte count does not usually rise sufficiently to allow a response to be detected.

In partial compensation for these inherent difficulties in diagnosing mild iron deficiency, there have been many technical improvements in established laboratory tests and a broader application of additional laboratory tests (5,6). Laboratory tests that have come into widespread use include the mean corpuscular volume (MCV), erythrocyte protoporphyrin (EP), and serum ferritin. Progress has also been made in automating and standardizing each of these laboratory tests as well as serum iron, TIBC, and hemoglobin analysis. The availability of more reproducible methods has led to increasingly reliable normative data for age and sex which are based on

11

healthy populations and which facilitate the interpretation of laboratory analyses, particularly in children (7).

Mild iron deficiency is very common, but it is not life threatening or even overtly symptomatic. Furthermore, in contrast to the adult man or elderly woman, iron deficiency in infants and children is usually of nutritional origin (7) and is rarely indicative of a serious occult disease, such as a peptic ulcer or intestinal carcinoma. It is therefore difficult to justify any routine for laboratory diagnosis unless it is safe, inexpensive, and simple for both the patient and the health worker. This means making a choice from among the many available laboratory tests, because using all of them is not a practical or realistic option. Fortunately, it is possible to select at least one regimen from among several simple combinations of laboratory tests that suits each clinical setting. In many situations, a therapeutic trial will be the most appropriate means of establishing a diagnosis.

In this review, we shall discuss both the therapeutic trial and the clinical application of the laboratory tests for mild and severe iron deficiency. A detailed discussion of the analytic procedures appeared in two recent reviews (5,6). Factors that influence the selection of laboratory tests include their local cost and availability, the technical difficulty of the analysis, the prevalence of iron deficiency, and the type of blood sample that can be obtained. However, it is necessary to emphasize at the outset that diagnostic routines are likely to change if the rapid pace of technical advances continues.

Groups That Are Most Likely to Develop Iron Deficiency

Because the clinical manifestations of iron deficiency are rarely apparent, the diagnosis is usually suspected on the basis of laboratory tests done at the time of a routine examination. Groups in whom laboratory screening for iron deficiency has the highest yield include infants, children, adolescents, and women between menarche and menopause (5,7,8).

Among infants, the prevalence of iron deficiency is highest between about 6 months (when neonatal iron stores become depleted) and 3 years of age. In the first few months after birth, the rapid rate of growth with the corresponding increase in red cell mass is the most important factor in the development of iron deficiency. Premature infants and twins who do not receive supplemental iron or iron-fortified formula are at particular risk because their neonatal iron stores are smaller and weight gain proportionately greater than in term infants; the former two groups may develop iron deficiency anemia as early as 2 or 3 months after birth (9). In term infants, whose postnatal weight gain has been greater than average, iron deficiency is also apt to develop by about 6 months because of the increased iron requirements imposed by rapid growth.

After neonatal iron stores have been mobilized for hemoglobin production, dietary factors gradually assume an increasingly important role. Infants whose diet consists of formulas without added iron or who are given whole cow's milk at an early age may develop iron deficiency by 6 months of age (10). Milk not only contains very little iron, but can actually decrease the absorption of this mineral from other foods eaten in the same meal (see Cook and Bothwell, *this volume*). Furthermore, some infants who consume more than a liter of cow's milk a day develop occult intestinal blood loss, occasionally leading to severe iron deficiency anemia (11,12). The introduction of a weaning food that is based on cereal or legumes may predispose to iron deficiency (13). Although such foods may contain substantial amounts of iron, the percentage absorbed may be low (Bothwell and Cook, *this volume*) unless the diet also contains meat and/or ascorbic-acid-rich foods that enhance iron assimilation.

Between about 3 years of age and adolescence, iron deficiency in industrialized countries becomes far less common because the rate of body growth decreases while the diet becomes more diversified. However, in developing countries where hookworm infestation is common, the prevalence and severity of iron deficiency may be almost as high in this age group as in infants. Other parasitic infestations that are associated with blood loss, such as schistosomiasis, may also predispose to iron deficiency.

Adolescents constitute another high-risk group, but relatively little epidemiologic information is available about their iron status. Boys in industrialized countries gain an average of 10 kg/year at the peak of their growth spurt (14). At about the same age as the growth spurt, and concurrent with sexual maturation, the concentration of hemoglobin increases between 0.5 and 1.0 g/dl/year toward values that are characteristic of men (7). These changes require an increase of about 25% in total body iron during the year of peak growth. The iron needs of adolescent girls are similarly large but are more evenly spread out over several years. The average weight gain at the peak of the growth spurt—9 kg/year—is almost as great as in boys (14); however, the concentration of hemoglobin changes very little during this time (7). The onset of menses, which usually occurs well after the adolescent growth spurt, requires additional absorption of iron to balance the menstrual losses of iron. The caloric intake of females drops substantially below that of males in adolescence. Because the iron/1,000 kcal is similar for males and females, consumption of iron by females is substantially below that of males. One of the few detailed studies of adolescents dealt with menstruating high school girls in Helsinki, Finland that were randomly divided into a group receiving iron tablets and another group that was given a placebo (15). After 2 months, a significant response in hemoglobin had occurred in about 75% of the iron-treated group. This represented a surprisingly high prevalence of iron deficiency for a relatively affluent population.

In women, the last half of pregnancy is associated with the highest prevalence of iron deficiency (8). One can anticipate that the risk would be even greater among pregnant teenagers, since even at the beginning of pregnancy their iron stores are likely to be depleted by a recent growth spurt.

Stages of Iron Deficiency

When a person progresses from adequate iron balance to overt iron deficiency anemia, as in experimental protocols involving repeated phlebotomy, the deficiency may be considered to develop in a sequence of three stages (5). The first stage consists of a depletion of storage iron. This stage is characterized by a decrease in the concentration of serum ferritin, which reflects the declining concentration of iron stores in the liver, spleen, and bone marrow. An alternative to the analysis of serum ferritin is to obtain a bone marrow aspirate and stain it for iron to make a qualitative estimate of the amount present. Because it is much simpler to obtain a blood specimen, the analysis of serum ferritin is supplanting bone marrow aspiration for estimating the amount of storage iron.

A second stage of iron deficiency that is likely to be transient consists of a decrease in transport iron. This is characterized by a declining concentration of serum iron and an increase in the iron-binding capacity. These changes result in a decrease in the transferrin saturation, which is calculated from the ratio of the serum iron to the TIBC. The term "latent iron deficiency" is sometimes used to refer to these first two, preanemic stages of iron deficiency.

A third stage develops when the supply of transport iron decreases sufficiently to restrict hemoglobin production. This stage is characterized by an elevation of erythrocyte protoporphyrin and the gradual development of detectable anemia and microcytosis. An alternative definition of the third stage is in terms of a hemoglobin concentration that has decreased sufficiently to fulfill the laboratory definition of anemia. Iron therapy is usually directed at the correction or prevention of the anemia that characterizes the third stage of iron deficiency.

Iron Deficiency as a Steady State Condition

Although it is conceptually convenient to classify laboratory tests according to stages of iron deficiency, laboratory results do not consistently conform to this pattern among individual patients with mild iron deficiency (2,3). This is probably because the mild deficiency has developed very gradually, and is almost in equilibrium, due to conditions that have been present for many months and often for years. Under such circumstances of a mild iron deficiency that is virtually in steady state, the analytic and biologic variability of the laboratory tests may be relatively large in relation to the degree of deviation from normal. Thus, individual patients often prove to have an iron-responsive anemia (third stage) despite having a normal value for serum ferritin or transferrin saturation (3).

SCREENING TESTS

The laboratory tests that are used in the diagnosis of iron deficiency can be conveniently grouped into screening tests and confirmatory tests. Screening tests are most commonly used in the initial evaluation of those populations who are most likely to have iron deficiency. The usual goal is to identify persons with anemia whose hemoglobin concentration is likely to increase with administration of iron, an improved diet, or a combination of both.

Among term infants, laboratory testing to detect iron deficiency is commonly recommended at about 1 year of age; the corresponding age for preterm infants is between 6 and 9 months (16). In many populations, these ages are characterized by the highest prevalence of iron deficiency. Other suitable ages for the laboratory detection of anemia are between 2 and 3 years, at about 5 years, and in adolescence. The most appropriate times will differ according to the population. At all ages, iron deficiency is far more common among lower socioeconomic groups than in affluent populations.

Hemoglobin and Hematocrit

The hemoglobin and hematocrit (5,6) are the most widely used tests to screen for anemia and iron deficiency. The concentration of hemoglobin is most reliably measured after accurate dilution of the blood specimen in a solution that converts hemoglobin to cyanmethemoglobin, which is then quantitated spectrophotometrically. The analysis is done either with a simple spectrophotometer or as part of a complete blood count by a more elaborate electronic counter in a centralized laboratory. Blood counts obtained by electronic counter usually include red cell indices, which provide valuable additional information for the differential diagnosis of anemia, as will be discussed below. The electronic counter will also provide a calculated hematocrit; however, this determination is not considered as reliable a means of diagnosing anemia as is the hemoglobin concentration.

In office and clinic laboratories, the hematocrit is often measured by centrifugation of a minute amount of blood that has been collected in a heparinized capillary tube. The hematocrit is then calculated by comparing the height of the column of packed red cells with the height of the entire column of red cells and plasma. The total volume of blood in the capillary tube is therefore not critical. An advantage of this method is its technical simplicity, particularly when appled to skin puncture blood specimens. On the average, the hematocrit is equivalent to the hemoglobin concentration multiplied by 2.9.

It is essential to interpret either the hemoglobin or hematocrit determination in relation to age-specific and sex-specific reference standards (7). Table 1 shows reference values for hemoglobin concentration after 6 months of age; laboratory testing for iron deficiency is rarely done before this age. The reference values from 6 months to 5 years of age are based on the 95% range in venous blood from white, nonindigent populations living at sea level and exclude those who have other laboratory evidence of iron deficiency or thalassemia minor. Between 6 months and 5 years, the lower limit of the 95% range for hemoglobin is 11.0 g/dl. Subsequently there is a gradual rise in hemoglobin values that continues throughout childhood. The use of developmental curves for hemoglobin (Fig. 1) during this period decreases the errors that are inherent in the abrupt stepwise increases of 0.5 to 1.0 g/dl from one age range to the next in the tabulated values. At puberty there is a further increase in concentration of hemoglobin in boys, and during adult life the hemoglobin concentration in men is maintained at an average of about 2.0 g/dl higher than in women.

TABLE 1. *Estimated mean and lower limits of normal (95% range) for hemoglobin, hematocrit, and mean corpuscular volume in Caucasians*[a]

Age in years	Hemoglobin (g/dl)		Hematocrit (%)		Mean corpuscular volume (fl)	
	Mean	Lower limit	Mean	Lower limit	Mean	Lower limit
0.5–2	12.5	11.0	36	32	77	70
3–5	12.5	11.0	36	32	79	73
6–8	13.0	11.0	38	32	81	75
9–11	13.0	11.0	38	33	83	76
12–14						
female	13.5	11.5	39	34	85	78
male	14.0	12.5	40	35	84	77
15–17						
female	13.5	11.5	40.	35	87	79
male	15.0	13.0	43	39	86	78
18–44						
female	13.5	12.0	40	35	90	80
male	15.5	13.5	45	40	90	80

[a]For ages 2 and above, data for hemoglobin and hematocrit are in accord with the preliminary results of the United States Health and Nutrition Examination Survey II, 1976–80 (N-HANES II). Data for ages 0.5 through 2 years and MCV values are from Dallman et al. (7) and are in accord with the developmental curves shown on Figs. 1 and 2. The lower limit of hemoglobin values from N-HANES II are somewhat lower than the corresponding portions of the percentile curves between ages 6 and 11 years. The hemoglobin data were provided through the courtesy of Clifford Johnson of the National Center for Health Statistics.

The values in Table 1 for children and adults over the age of 3 years were derived from the United States Health and Nutrition Examination Survey, 1976–80 (N-HANES II) *(manuscript in preparation)*. These values are from a randomly selected population that excludes military personnel and institutionalized individuals. The total of 27,801 subjects were selected according to census data. For purposes of the tabulation, only values based on venipuncture in nonpregnant white individuals were utilized and all subjects with MCV < 80 fl, Fe/TIBC < 16%, or EP greater than 75 µg/dl packed red blood cells were excluded.

The laboratory definition of anemia is usually based on a hemoglobin value that is below the 95% reference range for age and sex. This definition is used in most clinical settings. An alternative operational definition of anemia is based on a rise in hemoglobin (such as 1.0 g/dl or more) or hematocrit during a therapeutic trial with iron. A hemoglobin response, despite an initial value within the normal 95% range, is common in populations that have a high prevalence of iron deficiency and indicates that the production of hemoglobin was restricted by a lack of iron. Of course, anemia by this operational definition can only be identified retrospectively, after a therapeutic trial. When serial hemoglobin values are available in the same individual, a decline in concentration of 1 g/dl or more may represent anemia because values normally remain relatively constant.

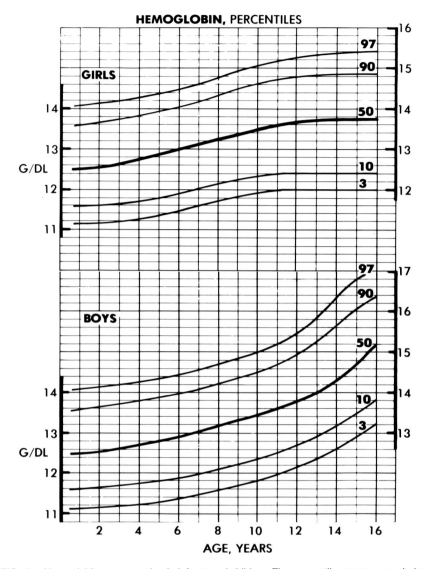

FIG. 1. Hemoglobin concentration in infants and children. The percentile curves were derived from nonindigent white children living at sea level or after exclusion of subjects with laboratory evidence of iron deficiency, thalassemia minor, and/or hemoglobinopathy. (From Dallman et al., ref 7.)

Anemia in Blacks

Numerous surveys have shown that hemoglobin concentrations in blacks are 0.3 to 1.0 g/dl lower than in white or other races. Although socioeconomic status and higher prevalence of iron deficiency may play a role, these factors cannot entirely explain the difference. In the United States, iron deficiency anemia appears to be more prevalent among black infants, children, and women during the childbearing years than among whites. The results of one study in infants indicated that the effect of a slight but significant inherent tendency to lower hemoglobin values in blacks was counterbalanced by a substantially higher prevalence of iron deficiency anemia (17). From the results of a therapeutic trial with iron, the use of uniform hemoglobin screening criteria seemed justified in this population. However, it may not be possible to extrapolate this conclusion to populations of blacks that are at lower risk of iron deficiency, such as black adult males in the United States.

Mean Corpuscular Volume

Electronic counters have made the MCV an accurate and practical laboratory test. The manual determination of the MCV was a time-consuming and poorly reproducible procedure because it was derived from the ratio of the hematocrit to a red blood cell count that was obtained microscopically with a counting chamber. The electronic determination of red cell volume is highly reproducible and is actually less subject to sampling error in skin puncture blood than the hemoglobin determination because dilution by tissue fluid does not affect red cell size. When a blood count is obtained by electronic counter, it is important to give full attention to the result of the MCV because this provides valuable help in the differential diagnosis. A low MCV with anemia favors the diagnosis of iron deficiency. Small red blood cells are also characteristic of thalassemia minor (8) and may sometimes be found with the anemia of infection and chronic disease. However, most other anemias are characterized by a normal or elevated MCV.

As in the case of hemoglobin and hematocrit determinations, the MCV normally changes during development, making it important to refer to age-specfic reference standards (7) (Table 1) (Fig. 2). Red cells are normally larger at birth than in adulthood, but red cell size decreases rapidly during the first 6 months of life. Cells are smallest during the remainder of infancy and gradually increase in size during childhood. There is little difference in red cell volume between sexes, and values increase only to a minor degree in adult life.

Other red cell indices obtained by electronic counter include mean corpuscular hemoglobin (MCH), which is derived by dividing the hemoglobin concentration by the red cell number and which undergoes similar changes in iron deficiency as the MCV, and the mean corpuscular hemoglobin concentration (MCHC), which is the least directly measured and least useful of the indices obtained by electronic counter. Because the MCHC can be calculated by dividing hemoglobin by hematocrit, it is the only red cell index that is readily obtained without electronic counters. However, it is the last of the indices to become abnormal during the progression of iron deficiency (9).

Abnormal Findings in Screening Tests

When the hemoglobin concentration (or the hematocrit) is below the lower limit of normal, the diagnosis of an iron-responsive anemia should be considered. If

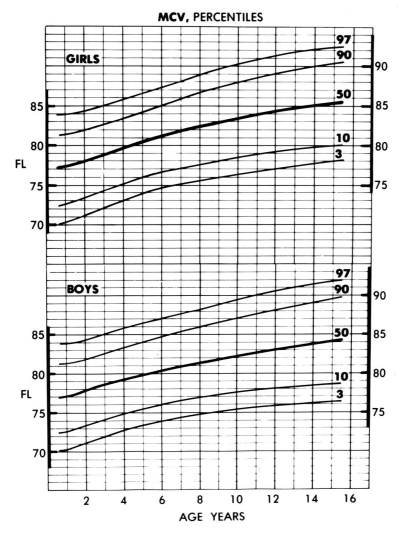

FIG. 2. Mean corpuscular volume (MCV) in infants and children. The percentile curves were derived from a portion of the same population as in Fig. 1. (From Dallman et al., ref. 7.)

blood specimens have been analyzed by an electronic counter, the presence of a low or low-normal MCV in conjunction with anemia increases the likelihood that the anemia is due to iron deficiency (20). If the anemia is mild (within 1 g/dl of the reference range), and iron deficiency is suspected but not yet confirmed, there are two choices: either additional laboratory tests should be obtained or, alternatively, a therapeutic trial with iron may be initiated. Our own practice is not to proceed with additional laboratory tests on the basis of a borderline hemoglobin value on skin puncture blood. We would first confirm the result on venous blood because of the relatively poor reproducibility of hemoglobin values obtained from skin puncture blood (see section entitled Skin Puncture and Venous Blood Sampling).

Relationship Between Prevalence and Diagnostic Criteria

Knowing the approximate prevalence of iron deficiency among the group of patients being screened will influence the selection of a cutoff value below which iron deficiency should be suspected. The importance of taking prevalence into account is familiar to epidemiologists, and it would scarcely warrant discussion here if it were not for the fact that prevalence is rarely considered in the clinical interpretation of laboratory tests. The mathematical methods for dealing with prevalence have been recently reviewed (21). A screening limit for anemia that is set too low will result in a high percentage of individuals with iron deficiency anemia as demonstrated by a high rate of response to a therapeutic trial. This superficially satisfactory state of affairs will provide no indication that a very large percentage of individuals with iron-responsive anemia is being missed by being classified as screen-negative. Conversely, when the screening limit is set too high, the proportion of individuals with iron deficiency anemia as demonstrated by response to treatment becomes unacceptably low because too many normal individuals are considered screen-positive.

For the purpose of this discussion, the two hypothetical examples in Fig. 3 may be helpful. The left portion of the figure represents a population of infants in whom about 15% would have a significant hemoglobin response if they were treated with iron. This responsive group is represented by the gray area under the dashed curve. The nonresponsive 85% of the population is represented by the larger open area

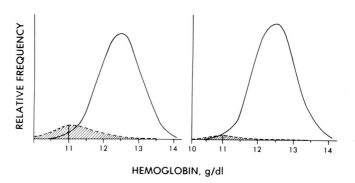

HEMOGLOBIN, g/dl

FIG. 3. The role of prevalence in the selection of screening criteria. The **left side** of the figure shows the frequency distribution of hemoglobin in a hypothetical population of infants in which 15% would have a hemoglobin response to iron treatment (represented by the *gray area* under the *dashed curve*) and 85% would not respond (the *open area* under the *solid curve*). The vertical line at 11.0 g/dl indicates the lower limit of the 95% range of normal. The **right side** of the figure illustrates a population in which only 2% would have a hemoglobin response to therapy. In the population with a high prevalence of iron deficiency shown on the **left**, the use of a screening criterion higher than the usual limit of 11.0 g/dl would be justified.

under the solid curve. These conditions are analogous to those described in a later section entitled Diagnosis of Iron Deficiency in Healthy Infants in the United States, in which only about half of those subjects with a hemoglobin response of at least 1 g/dl would have been detected by the traditional approach of treating only those infants with a hemoglobin value below the lower limit of the 95% range of normal (shown by a vertical line) (22). Consequently, it could be argued that raising the hemoglobin criteria for further laboratory evaluation or for treatment by about 0.5 g/dl would be worthwhile in screening this population for iron deficiency anemia. However, this degree of relaxation of the treatment criteria would be totally inappropriate for a population with a 2% prevalence of iron deficiency. This population might correspond to infants who have received an adequate supply of dietary iron. In this group, the use of the traditional 95% reference range would be more appropriate. If a higher hemoglobin cutoff value were used, too many normal infants would be considered screen-positive for every one that is iron-deficient. Thus, laboratory cutoff values used in screening have to be adjusted to suit local conditions. In the case of hemoglobin, the usual convention of using the lower limit of the 95% range will be appropriate where iron-responsive anemia is relatively rare, but a somewhat higher value can be justified when iron deficiency is common.

DIAGNOSIS BY THERAPEUTIC TRIAL

Dietary iron deficiency is by far the most common cause of anemia in otherwise healthy infants and children. A relatively brief therapeutic trial of iron for about 1 month is therefore often justified on the basis of anemia alone. An iron dose of 3 mg/kg/day as ferrous sulfate is well tolerated by infants as a single before-breakfast dose (22). This is equivalent to about 30 mg/day in a representative 1-year-old infant. In older children, the 3 mg/kg/day may be divided into two or three doses. The medication is far better absorbed between or before meals than with meals (23). In the relatively rare case of gastrointestinal intolerance, however, symptoms may resolve when the dose is given with meals. It should be emphasized that a therapeutic trial should rarely continue for more than 1 month.

In an otherwise healthy individual, the recovery from anemia is about two-thirds complete after 1 month (24). If the concentration of hemoglobin has increased significantly during the month, as will be the case with most anemic subjects, an expensive workup will have been avoided. Medication can then be continued for 3 to 5 months to replenish iron reserves. More prolonged treatment will provide no additional benefit and might lead to iron overload in individuals with thalassemia.

If there has been no hemoglobin response after 1 month, the decision on how to proceed will depend on the posttreatment hemoglobin value in relation to the 95% reference range for age and sex. If anemia persists, a more extensive diagnostic workup is probably indicated, especially if the value remains more than 0.5 g/dl below the reference range. The 1-month delay in diagnosis in otherwise healthy infants and children with mild anemia is unlikely to be harmful and is outweighed by the substantial initial savings in additional laboratory tests.

If a borderline anemia persists after a therapeutic trial (a value within 0.5 g/dl of the reference range), there is a possibility that the individual's hemoglobin is normally in the lowest part of the frequency distribution curve. On the other hand, there may be a condition, such as thalassemia minor or hereditary spherocytosis, which would be detected by further laboratory tests. Decisions on how to proceed in this situation are difficult and will be swayed by the characteristics of the population, the laboratory resources that are available, and the history of the individual child. Whatever the specific situation, it is important to be alert to causes of anemia other than iron deficiency while also avoiding the extreme of an expensive and elaborate workup for every child with a borderline anemia.

If the posttreatment hemoglobin value is within the low-normal range, it is probable that the individual did not have an iron-responsive anemia and that no further treatment or diagnostic workup is indicated.

Regression to the mean is an important statistical phenomenon that affects the interpretation of the results of a therapeutic trial (21), particularly if it has been based on a hemoglobin value from skin puncture blood. If an individual is singled out on the basis of a low laboratory value, simply repeating that laboratory test is likely to yield a result that is closer to the normal mean for that test. This so-called regression to the mean is due to a composite of random factors, such as sampling and laboratory errors and biologic variations, that could have been partly responsible for the initial outlying value. Thus a therapeutic trial might seem successful when it actually resulted from random events. In the case of a venous hemoglobin, both biologic variations and analytic variations are relatively low with coefficients of variation under 3%. However, sampling error is very large when skin puncture blood is used (see section entitled Skin Puncture and Venous Blood Sampling).

The alternative to a therapeutic trial is a more extensive initial laboratory workup to strengthen the presumptive diagnosis of iron deficiency. The confirmatory tests that are most commonly used are the EP, serum ferritin, and serum iron/TIBC. Each of these tests has certain advantages and disadvantages to be discussed below.

CONFIRMATORY TESTS FOR IRON DEFICIENCY

Serum Ferritin

Ferritin is normally present in the serum but in such small quantities that it was undetectable prior to the recent development of a radioimmunoassay. Under most circumstances, the concentration of serum ferritin is roughly proportional to the abundance of storage iron (25). Thus, the serum ferritin is the only blood determination that is helpful in allowing an evaluation of iron status within the normal range, as well as in the diagnosis of iron deficiency. For example, the developmental changes in serum ferritin levels reflect normal changes in iron stores with increasing age (7).

High values in newborn infants reflect the abundant iron stores that exist at birth. Values fall rapidly during early infancy and remain low throughout later infancy and childhood. The serum ferritin remains low in women of childbearing age but rises after menopause. In men, a rise in serum ferritin occurs after adolescence and continues at a more gradual rate throughout adult life. At all ages, a serum ferritin value of <10 or 12 μg/liter (or ng/ml) indicates depletion of iron stores.

A low concentration of serum ferritin is indicative of depleted iron stores. However, values may be in the normal range despite the presence of iron deficiency, particularly in association with infection or inflammatory disease. Even mild upper-respiratory infections are associated with an elevation in serum ferritin (26). With severe infections, the serum ferritin elevation often persists for several weeks beyond the symptomatic period (7). It is possible that enteritis and parasitic infestation, which are common in many parts of the developing world, may involve sufficient inflammation to modify serum ferritin values. Liver disease, even if it is mild, can result in major elevations of serum ferritin (28). Consequently, the serum ferritin is of little use in diagnosing iron deficiency in patients with suspected or proven liver disease.

The serum ferritin determination may be useful in diagnosing iron deficiency anemia in the presence of inflammatory diseases that do not affect the liver if a lower limit of 25 or 50 μg/liter is used. For example, anemia in patients with rheumatoid arthritis cannot be assumed to be due to their chronic disease unless iron deficiency has been excluded as a contributing factor (29). Iron deficiency anemia due to blood loss is common among patients with rheumatoid arthritis who are chronic users of aspirin. A serum ferritin value below 25 μg/liter in such persons makes it very likely that there will be a hemoglobin response to iron therapy. However, a higher value is less helpful because it does not exclude the possibility of response.

In patients with chronic renal disease who are on hemodialysis regimens, the blood loss that occurs at the time of each dialysis makes the eventual development of iron deficiency virtually inevitable. In such patients, serum ferritin determinations obtained at approximately 3-month intervals will show a gradual decline in values. When the serum ferritin concentration falls below about 50 μg/liter, the initiation of iron prophylaxis is appropriate. However, when values are higher than 100 μg/liter, iron treatment is unnecessary.

Serum Iron and Iron-Binding Capacity

Almost all of the iron in the serum is bound to the iron-binding protein, transferrin (5,6). Serum iron and TIBC are generally measured by spectrophotometric techniques. The assay, when done manually, is time consuming and subject to errors due to contamination by iron from the environment. Automated techniques make it possible not only to obtain results more rapidly but to achieve greater reproducibility. A disadvantage of the serum iron is its large biologic variability compared to the other laboratory tests. One component of this variability is a pronounced diurnal fluctuation, after about 3 years of age (30), usually with high values in the morning and low values at night (31). It is therefore easiest to interpret results from blood specimens drawn in the morning or early afternoon because a low value (less than 30 μg/dl or 5.4 μmoles/liter) is most likely to represent iron deficiency at this time of day.

The TIBC is less subject to biologic variations than the serum iron, but its analytic error is greater than that of serum iron. The normal range for the TIBC is 250 to 400 μg/dl (or 45–72 μmoles/liter). Because the serum iron decreases whereas the TIBC is likely to increase in iron deficiency, the transferrin saturation, which is the ratio of the two values, is more consistently helpful than either value alone. The transferrin saturation is calculated by dividing the concentration of serum iron by the TIBC and multiplying by 100 to express the results as a percentage. Thus, transferrin saturation will reflect the biologic variability and laboratory errors of both the serum iron and TIBC. In adults, a transferrin saturation below 16% is considered indicative of iron deficiency (5). In infants and children, the corresponding value is about 10% (32,33).

Transferrin saturation may decrease in inflammatory disease (34) as well as in iron deficiency. In some instances the TIBC is useful in distinguishing between the two conditions. A TIBC of more than 400 μg/dl strongly suggests iron deficiency, whereas a value below 200 μg/dl is characteristic of inflammatory disease. Unfortunately, the overlapping of laboratory values between these two conditions is considerable, and most values will be in the intermediate range between 200 and 400 μg/dl.

Erythrocyte Protoporphyrin

There is an accumulation of protoporphyrin in red blood cells when insufficient iron is available to combine with protoporphyrin to form heme. The recent interest in the diagnostic use of this test can be largely attributed to the availability of a simplified method for extracting EP from small samples of blood and measuring it fluorometrically (35). In addition, specialized fluorometers have been developed that provide a result directly from a thin film of whole blood (36). The use of such instruments requires little technician time or training and makes it practical to diagnose and initiate treatment for iron deficiency on a single clinic visit. The EP is elevated in both iron deficiency and lead poisoning and is therefore used to screen infants and young children in urban, low-income areas where both conditions are common. In such settings, an elevated EP value will warrant a follow-up analysis for blood lead before it can be attributed to possible iron deficiency. The EP is also increased in infection and inflammatory disease. An advantage of the EP is that it is unaffected by recent iron medication, in contradistinction to serum iron and, in the case of very high iron doses, serum ferritin (37).

There is a strong association between lead toxicity and iron deficiency that appears to be due to a shared mechanism for the intestinal absorption of lead and iron (38). In iron-deficient individuals, the homeostatic increase in absorption of iron is accompanied by a similar increase in absorption of ingested lead. Thus, iron deficiency appears to predispose to lead toxicity. Indeed, anemia in the presence of lead intoxication may be primarily or entirely attributable to iron deficiency.

Marked elevations in EP are most likely to be due to lead exposure, whereas moderate increases can be associated with iron deficiency, lead exposure, or both. The upper limit of normal for EP is considered to be about 3 μg/g Hgb (or 30 μg/dl whole blood or 100 μg/dl red cells). In mild iron deficiency, the EP is rarely more than two times higher than these upper limits. In infants, EP is normally somewhat higher than in adults, but normative developmental data remain to be established.

SELECTION OF LABORATORY TESTS

Factors that will influence the selection of laboratory tests include the type of blood sample obtained, the experience of laboratory personnel, the availability of equipment, the proximity of laboratory facilities, and the rapidity with which results can be provided. Another important consideration is the prevalence of conditions that may complicate the diagnosis, such as thalassemia minor, acute infections, chronic inflammatory disease, and nutritional deficiencies other than iron lack.

Skin Puncture and Venous Blood Sampling

It is technically much simpler to obtain skin puncture blood from a fingertip, particularly during infancy, but also throughout childhood. However, the use of skin puncture blood substantially decreases the diagnostic reliability of some laboratory tests. Probably the most important problem is the variability of skin puncture hemoglobin and hematocrit values. In the case of hemoglobin, sequential venous values in the same individual usually remain within 0.6 g/dl (39). In contrast, the discrepancy between skin puncture and venous values is often 0.5 to 1.0 g/dl (20). Such a sampling discrepancy that approaches 10% of the hemoglobin concentration is a serious problem when the degree of anemia in the population rarely involves more than a 10% depression below the normal range. The difficulties created by skin puncture sampling was recently highlighted for us by a study in which 1-year-old infants were considered potentially iron-responsive if their capillary hemoglobin value was less than 11.5 g/dl (20). When the determination in these 122 infants was repeated on venous blood within a 2-week period, the finding was confirmed in only 53%. We concluded that the diagnosis of mild anemia on the basis of a skin puncture sample is more tentative than with a venous sample.

In the case of other laboratory tests, the consequences of a sampling error approaching 10% would be less serious than with hemoglobin. This is particularly true of the MCV, since red cell size is unaffected if the sample is diluted by tissue fluid. In the case of serum ferritin and EP, skin puncture sampling appears to pose no major problems because only a few drops of blood are required, and the clinically significant deviations from the normal range usually exceed 10%. Serum iron and TIBC are rarely determined in capillary blood because of the larger volume of blood required.

To obtain the best possible skin puncture sample, it is important to warm the extremity in order to facilitate a free flow of blood and to avoid any squeezing of the finger so that contamination of blood with tissue fluid is minimized. Samples of blood can be obtained in larger volume from an antecubital vein and with no more pain than skin puncture samples from a fingertip, where there is a denser network of nerve endings. However, venipuncture in infants and small children has the distinct disadvantage of requiring a second person to immobilize the extremity. Health workers with limited experience will also have more difficulty in placing a needle into the vein, particularly in children between 6 months and 2 years of age whose veins are likely to be obscured by subcutaneous fat. In this age group, the external jugular vein may be the easiest site for venous blood sampling. However, use of the external jugular may arouse more parental anxiety than venipuncture of an antecubital vein and may therefore be impractical for screening purposes.

Time Required for Analysis

In the outpatient management of iron deficiency, the eventual goal is to establish the diagnosis and to start treatment in a single, brief visit. This requires laboratory tests that can be performed quickly and in close proximity to where the patient is seen. In the past few years, technical improvements have made it possible to have the result of any of the tests that have been discussed within a few hours. Of the established and generally available methods, those that can be done most rapidly and with the least expensive equipment include the hemoglobin, hematocrit, and the EP. In addition, cheaper electronic counters for MCV and automated methods for serum iron may make these assays more attractive in the future for use in small clinic laboratories. Even the serum ferritin assay, which until recently was perhaps the most expensive and time-consuming test, can be simplified to serve as a 90-min screening test (40).

DIFFERENTIAL DIAGNOSIS

Problems of differential diagnosis fall into two categories. The simpler of the two involves distinguishing among different conditions that may result in similar laboratory findings, e.g., the anemia and microcytosis that characterize both iron deficiency and thalassemia minor. The second and more difficult type of problem is the detection of iron deficiency in the presence of another condition which may confuse the interpretation of laboratory results, e.g., iron deficiency in the presence of acute infection or chronic inflammatory disease. We will discuss both types of situations with an emphasis on the most common problems in differential diagnosis.

Chronic Inflammatory Diseases

Chronic inflammation is commonly associated with a mild anemia that can either mimic or be partially caused by iron deficiency (34). Factors that predispose to the anemia include a decreased red blood cell survival and a decreased erythropoietic response to anemia. In addition, there are major changes in iron metabolism that include a diminished reutilization of iron from senescent red cells and decreased intestinal absorption of iron. Both of these changes result in a redistribution of iron from hemoglobin to iron stores and help to account for a decline in serum iron.

In some instances, medications can aggravate the anemia of chronic inflammatory disease. An example is aspirin treatment of polyarticular rheumatoid arthritis.

Chronic aspirin use often results in iron deficiency due to prolonged occult loss of blood from the intestine. However, the diagnosis of iron deficiency is likely to be obscured by the effects of chronic inflammation. Both iron deficiency and inflammation are often characterized by mild anemia, an elevated EP, and a low serum iron. The MCV is only occasionally decreased with inflammatory conditions.

The two laboratory tests that may sometimes, but not always, show divergent results in chronic inflammatory disease and iron deficiency are the TIBC and the serum ferritin. In chronic disease, the TIBC is often depressed, whereas in iron deficiency it is frequently elevated. Conversely, a depressed serum ferritin (below 10 to 12 μg/liter) is diagnostic of iron deficiency, whereas infection and chronic disease are associated with normal or elevated values. A serum ferritin below 25 μg/liter in anemic patients with rheumatoid arthritis (29), chronic renal disease, or other chronic disorder suggests coexisting iron deficiency anemia. A therapeutic trial of iron is likely to decrease the degree of anemia in such cases. However, some patients will also have a hemoglobin response to iron therapy despite a serum ferritin value of greater than 50 μg/liter. This seems to be in part due to impaired mobilization of iron stores with inflammatory disease but also due to a serum ferritin that is disproportionately elevated in relation to iron stores. Because of the often confusing pattern of laboratory results, a 1-month therapeutic trial of iron may prove to be more worthwhile than an extensive laboratory workup for mild anemia accompanying chronic disease.

Acute Infection or Inflammation

These conditions are common among infants and children and complicate the diagnosis of iron deficiency. Indeed, the patient is frequently brought to medical attention for the acute illness, and the anemia is merely an incidental finding. In some instances, the anemia proves to be related to the infection or inflammation, whereas in others there is a coexisting iron deficiency. One of us (J.D.R.) recently did a prospective study of 9 children who were hospitalized for an acute infection or inflammatory illness. During the period of active illness, which averaged 5 days, there was a mean decline in hemoglobin concentration of 1.7 g/dl. This was far in excess of what could be explained by changes in hydration or removal of blood for laboratory studies. Subsequently, during recovery there was a mean rise in hemoglobin concentration of 2.4 g/dl over a period of follow-up that averaged 4 weeks.

The changes in laboratory results in acute infection are similar to those in chronic inflammatory disease. However, it is noteworthy that at least some of the abnormalities persist for several weeks after the disappearance of the clinical manifestations. This is the case with elevated serum ferritin (41). If the elevation of serum ferritin that occurs with mild infections (26) proves to be similarly persistent, it might explain the fact that infants often have an iron-responsive anemia despite having had a normal serum ferritin (42).

Thalassemia Minor

Aside from iron deficiency, thalassemia minor is the most common cause of mild anemia accompanied by microcytosis. In thalassemia minor, the MCV is usually well below the normal range, even when the concentration of hemoglobin is in the low-normal range or only slightly depressed (18). Thus, a disproportionately low MCV suggests thalassemia minor. However, the presence of one condition does not exclude the other; individuals with thalassemia minor are just as likely to be iron-deficient as nonthalassemic individuals.

If an individual is anemic, the ratio of the MCV to the red blood cell (RBC) count in millions (the Mentzer Index) is helpful in distinguishing iron deficiency from thalassemia minor (43). In thalassemia minor, the RBC count tends to be high for the degree of anemia. Thus an MCV/RBC of 13 or less is found in about 85% of subjects with thalassemia minor, whereas a similar percentage of patients with iron deficiency anemia have higher values. The Mentzer Index has been proposed only for use in differential diagnosis of anemia. Its effectiveness is uncertain when the hemoglobin is in the low-normal range.

In beta-thalassemia minor, hemoglobin electrophoresis reveals an elevation in hemoglobin A_2. Alpha-thalassemia minor is suspected if one parent also has microcytosis. In thalassemia minor without iron deficiency, serum iron, TIBC, serum ferritin, and EP are normal.

Combined Nutritional Deficiencies

Iron deficiency is often found in combination with other nutrient deficiences, particularly in developing countries. Combinations that are common and that have been well studied include iron lack with either protein-calorie or folate deficiency. Each of these deficiencies not only results in anemia but also obscures the diagnosis when found in combination with iron deficiency.

Protein-Calorie Malnutrition

Anemia is common in severe protein-calorie malnutrition. The concentration of hemoglobin is often of the order of 10 g/dl in infants between the ages of 1 and 3. In Thailand (Fig. 4), groups of infants and young children who were treated with a regimen designed to correct protein-calorie malnutrition had an encouraging reticulocyte response, but their hemoglobin concentration reached a plateau well before the anemia was corrected (44). Bone marrow iron became depleted as the concentration of hemoglobin reached the plateau. When iron was added to the rehabilitation regimen at that time, there was a prompt second reticulocytosis and a further rise in the concentration of hemoglobin. The diagnosis of iron deficiency was not initially evident by laboratory studies. Indeed, the infants did not become overtly iron-deficient until their rapid growth and hemoglobin production outstripped their limited supply of storage iron. On the basis of such findings, many

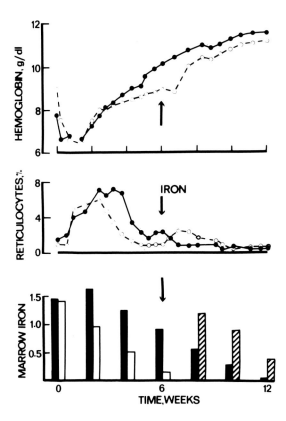

FIG. 4. Correction of anemia with treatment of protein-calorie malnutrition (44). One group of patients initially received supplemental iron with its treatment regimen (*closed circles* and *solid bars*). A second group received supplemental iron only after 6 weeks (*open circles* and *striped bars*). A complete response in hemoglobin was obtained only after addition of iron to the regimen (*arrows*). The fall in concentration of hemoglobin during the first few days of treatment was due to an expansion of the blood volume.

treatment centers routinely add iron to the nutritional rehabilitation regimen after about 2 weeks. Laboratory evaluation of iron status is also more reliable after general malnutrition has been treated for about 2 weeks and when infection, dehydration, and other acute and life-threatening problems have been resolved.

Folate Deficiency

Folate deficiency combined with iron deficiency may occur in preterm infants who are fed unsupplemented formulas based on evaporated milk and among infants who are fed goat's milk. Infants with diarrhea, malnutrition, infection (45), and hemolytic anemia (46) are at increased risk of developing folate deficiency. Combined folate and iron deficiencies are also common in women during the last half of pregnancy.

Mild folate deficiency is often overshadowed by a more dominant and severe iron deficiency. In this situation, the detection of hypersegmentation of the neutrophils is diagnostically useful. Hypersegmentation of the neutrophils is a familiar characteristic of vitamin B_{12} and folate deficiency, but it was previously believed that it could also occur with simple iron deficiency. However, more recent studies showed evidence of covert folate deficiency among most patients in whom an apparently uncomplicated iron deficiency was associated with hypersegmentation (47). The importance of detecting these subtle manifestations of folate deficiency was underscored by the development of megaloblastic bone marrow changes in some of these patients when they were treated with iron alone. The appearance of more overt folate deficiency after treatment of iron deficiency suggested that the patient's body pool of folate was marginally adequate to sustain the lower red cell mass present during iron deficiency but not adequate for the increased erythropoiesis that occurred in response to iron treatment.

Other Nutrient Deficiencies

Vitamin B_{12} deficiency in strict vegetarians and in patients with malabsorption of the vitamin (pernicious anemia) may result in megaloblastic anemia. The interaction of vitamin B_{12} deficiency with iron deficiency is similar to that of folic acid in that the milder of the two deficiencies comes to prominence only after the more severe one is treated.

Other nutrients that have been associated with anemia in humans and experimental animals include vitamins A, E, and B_1 (thiamine). The role of each of these nutrients in the anemia that is prevalent in various developing countries is not yet clear. Possibly, a lack of one or more of these or other nutrients will explain the fact that treatment with iron sometimes results in a plateau of hemoglobin concentration somewhat below what is considered normal in industrialized countries.

CLINICAL STUDIES

Diagnosis of Iron Deficiency in Healthy Infants in the United States

At the present time, 1-year-old infants are probably at a higher risk of developing iron deficiency than any other group in the United States (3,20,22). For this reason, screening for anemia at about 1 year of age has become routine practice. About 4 years ago we decided to examine various laboratory tests and screening criteria for iron deficiency in terms of their value in predicting a hemoglobin response to treatment with iron. We studied a group of 1-year-old infants who were dependents of military personnel and who were being screened at Travis Air Force Base. The experimental protocol was designed to fit as closely as possible into routine screening procedures. The data described below pertain to 1,128 infants who had a well-baby visit at 1 year of age between 1978 and 1980.

Skin puncture blood was initially obtained for Coulter counter determination of hemoglobin and red cell volume. Any infant who had a hemoglobin below 11.5 g/dl or a red cell volume below 72 fl (criteria that intentionally included the lower portion of the normal ranges) was considered screen-positive and was asked to return for a venipuncture. Hemoglobin and MCV determinations were then repeated on venous blood and, in addition, serum ferritin, EP, serum iron, iron-binding capacity, and hemoglobin electrophoresis were done. All screen-positive infants were then treated with a 3-month course of 3 mg/kg/day of iron as ferrous sulfate given orally before breakfast. Three months later, they were seen again for a repeat determination of the hematologic and biochemical measures on venous blood.

This population was probably fairly representative of infants in the United States, except that extremes of affluence and poverty were not included. Mild anemia was quite common, but severe anemia was rare. Twenty-five percent of the infants had a capillary hemoglobin value below 11.5 g/dl, the estimated 10th percentile of a healthy, iron-suffucient population of infants. Eleven percent had concentrations below 11.0 g/dl, the lower limit of the normal 95% range, and could therefore be considered anemic. Only 2% had a hemoglobin concentration below 10.0 g/dl, however.

All of the laboratory tests for iron deficiency were reasonably accurate in identifying those few infants who were most severely iron-deficient. The laboratory values for those infants who had initial hemoglobin values below 10 g/dl and who responded to iron therapy with more than a 2.0-g/dl rise in venous hemoglobin are shown in Table 2. Since these infants had values that were at least 1 g/dl below the lower limit of the reference range, they were easily identified as anemic. In addition, the results of all of the four additional laboratory tests (MCV, EP, transferrin saturation, and serum ferritin) were abnormal in all but one of these most anemic infants. Thus, the laboratory diagnosis of moderate to severe iron deficiency seemed relatively straightforward in that any single one of the confirmatory tests for iron deficiency would have been diagnostically useful.

The situation became more complicated when the hemoglobin concentration was within 1.0 g/dl of the reference range and the definition of response to iron therapy was broadened to include all infants with a rise in venous hemoglobin equal to or greater than 1.0 g/dl. This degree of response is significant from the public health point of view and would also be considered clinically meaningful in individual patients. About half of the infants who were anemic (hemoglobin below 11.0 g/dl) had at least a 1.0-g/dl response. The rate of response would probably have been even greater if a smaller increase in hemoglobin concentration had also been considered a response or if compliance had been more complete.

Perhaps of greater interest than the response of the anemic group was the high rate of response in infants whose hemoglobin values were in the lower part of the 95% reference range, between 11.0 and 11.5 g/dl, and who might therefore have been classified as normal. As would be expected, the rate of response in this group was lower than in the anemic infants; slightly less than one-third of this group had an increase in venous hemoglobin of at least 1.0 g/dl. Although the average response

TABLE 2. *Diagnosis of moderate and severe iron deficiency*[a]

Patient identification number	Pretreatment Hgb (g/dl)	Posttreatment Hgb (g/dl)	MCV (fl)	Pretreatment values		
				Protoporphyrin (μg/g Hgb)	Transferrin saturation (%)	Serum ferritin (mg/liter)
75	6.3	13.2	48	19.4	3.4	1.8
86	9.5	11.8	64	3.6	5.2	6.9
104	8.0	12.0	48	—	1.9	2.0
122	6.0	14.1	48	19.3	24.7	2.4
177	8.2	12.9	59	16.7	3.2	0.5
203	7.7	11.1	54	18.8	2.3	1.7
204	9.7	11.8	62	—	5.3	4.8
273	6.4	13.1	46	45.9	2.2	5.8
Mean	7.7	12.5	54	20.6	6.0	3.2
Normal cutoff	≥11.0	≥11.0	≥70	≥3.0	≥10.0	≥10.0

[a]With a single exception (transferrin saturation, 24.7%), all laboratory tests were abnormal in the 8 infants with an initial hemoglobin concentration of less than 10 g/dl who subsequently had a hemoglobin rise of at least 2 g/dl after treatment with iron for 3 months.

was 1.6 g/dl compared to 2.3 g/dl in the anemic group, the absolute number of responses was equal to that in the anemic group. Thus, by restricting treatment only to the anemic infants, we would have missed treating half of the potential responders. These results illustrate the clinical dilemma posed by the overlapping of hemoglobin values in normal and mildly iron-deficient individuals.

The same problem of overlapping values was also evident with the other laboratory tests of iron nutrition, as illustrated in Fig. 5. The hatched bars designate infants who had a hemoglobin response equal to or greater than 1.0 g/dl and the open bars indicate infants whose response, if any, was less than 1.0 g/dl. With each of the tests, an abnormal value (to the left of the diamonds) was associated with a rate of response greater than 50%, a result that is clinically acceptable, although far from ideal. What is of far greater concern is that over half of the potentially responsive infants would have been falsely classified as normal by any one of the tests. This problem of overlapping laboratory values in infants with mild iron deficiency is likely to be representative of other populations in which iron deficiency is common but most cases are mild.

Because of the difficulties in applying the standard hematologic or biochemical tests to individual infants with mild iron deficiency, we concluded that the diagnosis of iron deficiency could be established much more inexpensively and conclusively by doing a therapeutic trial based on the initial measurement of hemoglobin (or hematocrit) with or without the MCV. This applied particularly to the vast majority of individual infants whose values were in the low-normal range or no more than 1 g/dl below normal. On the other hand, all of the laboratory tests were useful in characterizing the iron status of the infants as a group. Mean values of MCV, EP, transferrin saturation, and serum ferritin were all substantially and significantly different in the iron-responsive and nonresponsive groups.

Evaluating the Iron Status of Chilean Infants in Response to a Fortification Program

In January 1982, Chile embarked on a national program of iron fortification using as a vehicle the powdered milk that is distributed to most of the infants in the country. During one of the preparatory pilot studies, laboratory tests of iron status were used to monitor the effectiveness of this type of program in the prevention of iron deficiency, as described elsewhere (Stekel, *this volume*). In one phase of these studies, 280 infants received an iron-fortified milk and 278 in a control group received the regular unfortified milk. Acceptance of the milk was very good, with about 90% of infants still taking it at 15 months of age. Analysis of laboratory data showed significant and substantial differences between the two groups in hemoglobin, serum iron, TIBC, transferrin saturation, free EP, and serum ferritin at 15 months of age. Anemia was present in only 1.6% of infants receiving the fortified milk. The corresponding figure in the control group was 27.8%. Only 6.4% of infants in the fortified group had a transferrin saturation below 9% versus

35.2% in the control group. Erythrocyte protoporphyrin values over 100 μg/dl whole blood were present in 22.4 and 4.6% of the cases, respectively. Thus, all three laboratory tests were helpful in showing a marked difference between the groups that would be ascribed to iron fortification.

In another of the pilot studies, infants who had received either unfortified or fortified milk were given iron medication under the supervision of a health aide for 75 days. The purpose was to determine the degree of iron-responsive anemia present in the two groups. The dose was 45 mg of iron as ferrous sulfate per day. The results showed very little hemoglobin response in the group that had received the iron-fortified milk; of the total of 43 infants, none had a concentration of hemoglobin below the lower limit of the normal 95% reference range (11.0 g/dl), and only 5 infants had an increase equal to or greater than 1.0 g/dl in hemoglobin concentration. In contrast, in the unfortified group of 43 infants, 12 had a hemoglobin concentration below 11.0 g/dl and 28 had an increase of at least 1.0 g/dl in hemoglobin concentration. These findings were impressive in verifying the effectiveness of iron fortification. They also provided additional data for the interpretation of hemoglobin values in infants. As in the Travis Air Force Base study, there was a clear demonstration that hemoglobin values in individual iron-responsive and unresponsive infants overlap to a marked degree. Among the 43 infants that received the unfortified milk, 13 had a hemoglobin response despite an initial hemoglobin value that was within the normal reference range.

Estimating Prevalence of Anemia and Iron Deficiency Among Children

In a healthy, well-nourished population, hemoglobin values approximate a Gaussian distribution. When there is a high prevalence of anemia, some estimate of the prevalence and severity of the anemia is provided by the extent to which a frequency distribution curve for hemoglobin is skewed to the left. The degree of skew is easiest to appreciate when the familiar frequency distribution plot is converted to a plot of the cumulative distribution of values on a probability scale. This scale results in a linear plot when values show a Gaussian distribution, but when there is a high prevalence of anemia, the values show a deviation to the left of linearity in the lower portion of the curve. This approach, which has been termed "distribution analysis," can provide a relative estimate of the prevalence of anemia. Unfortunately, the results are unreliable when the size of the population is under about 100, when the prevalence of iron deficiency is low, or when children within a broad age range are being evaluated.

————————————————————————►

FIG. 5. Distribution of MCV, EP, transferrin saturation, and serum ferritin values in infants with a skin puncture hemoglobin concentration below 11.5 g/dl who subsequently had at least a 1-g/dl rise in venous hemoglobin in response to iron therapy *(hatched bars)*. Values for infants who had no response or a less than 1-g/dl response are shown by *open bars.* The estimated limits of the normal range are indicated on the *horizontal axes (diamond symbol)*; values to the left of the symbol are considered indicative of iron deficiency. FL = femtoliters. (From Dallman et al., ref. 3.)

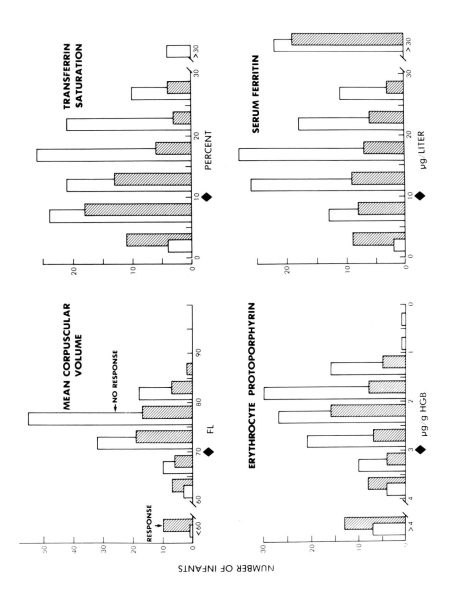

Black and White Infants at Travis Air Force Base

Some of the advantages and limitations of distribution analysis are illustrated in Fig. 6. The left portion of the figure shows the frequency distributions of hemoglobin for 159 black and 800 white infants. The same data are shown as probability plots on the right side of the figure. Values for white infants were distributed in a linear fashion consistent with a Gaussian distribution. Values for blacks were parallel in the middle and upper parts of the distribution, with a median value that was 0.3 g/dl lower than that for whites. The identical difference of 0.3 g/dl was found when the groups were matched socioeconomically by comparing values from only those infants whose paternal military rank was in the middle range. The hemoglobin in the middle and upper portions of the distribution is in accord with an inherently, slightly lower hemoglobin concentration in blacks than in whites but was of smaller magnitude than the 0.5 to 1.0 g/dl in previous reports (17).

The other point illustrated by Fig. 6 is that hemoglobin values in blacks showed a substantial skew from a normal, Gaussian distribution in the lower portion of the hemoglobin range, a finding that was not evident in the data for whites. This marked deviation from linearity at the lower end of the curve in blacks indicated a higher prevalence of anemia that was substantiated by therapeutic trial.

The limitations of distribution analysis become evident on considering that more than a third of the 22% of white infants with a hemoglobin concentration below 11.5 g/dl had a venous hemoglobin response of at least 1.0 g/dl with iron treatment.

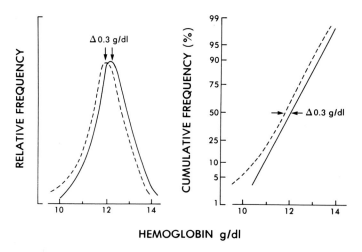

HEMOGLOBIN g/dl

FIG. 6. Distribution analysis. The **left side** of the figure shows the frequency distribution of hemoglobin values in black *(dashed line)* and white *(solid line)* infants at Travis Air Force Base. On the **right**, the same data are plotted as cumulative distribution curves on a probability scale. The median hemoglobin concentration was 0.3 g/dl lower in blacks than in whites. The linearity of the plot for whites indicates a Gaussian distribution. The deviation to the **left** of the lower portion of the plot for black infants shows a skew of the distribution toward anemic values. (From Reeves et al., ref. 17.)

Thus, an 8% prevalence of iron-responsive anemia would have been missed on the basis of finding a Gaussian distribution for hemoglobin concentration by distribution analysis.

Eskimo Children in Alaska

Margolis et al. (48) recently evaluated the effect of iron therapy on the distribution of hemoglobin values among a group of Alaskan Eskimo children whose ages ranged from 2 to 16 years. Although the total population of 533 children in the pilot study was large, conventional analysis of the data was hampered by the fact that there are major changes in normal hemoglobin concentration within the age span of the group, including the divergence of male and female values after 10 years of age. If the population had been divided into smaller age groups to correspond to tabulations of hemoglobin concentration by age and sex, many of the advantages of a large study group would have been lost.

A high prevalence of mild anemia that affected all ages and both sexes to a similar degree became evident when hemoglobin concentrations from individual children were plotted on percentile curves (Fig. 7). Twenty-one percent of the group had hemoglobin concentrations below the third percentile of normal. After 277 of the children had been treated with iron for a 3-month period, 43% had an increase in venous hemoglobin of 1.0 g/dl or more, whereas only 31% had a rise of less than 0.5 g/dl increase. The change in hemoglobin distribution could be best appreciated by using an approach that would take into account normal developmental changes in the concentration of hemoglobin. This was done by converting the hemoglobin concentrations to standard deviation scores for age and sex, based on the percentile curves for hemoglobin. The standard deviation (SD) scores allowed an evaluation of the change in distribution of age-normalized hemoglobin values for the group as a whole, as well as a comparison with an ideal Gaussian distribution (Fig. 8). There was a marked skew toward low hemoglobin values among the 533 children in the pilot study and the 277 children in the treatment group prior to iron administration. After treatment, values approximated a Gaussian distribution for hemoglobin concentration in a healthy population.

Several conclusions emerged from Fig. 8. First, in accord with other laboratory data, iron lack was the major cause of anemia since only 5% of the children had hemoglobin values below -2 SD for the reference population after they had been treated with iron. Second, there was an impressive overall shift in the distribution curve. Before treatment, very few of the individual SD scores were above the reference mean, and 42% were below the normal distribution curve, whereas after treatment the number of values above the reference mean was close to normal. The change in distribution indicated not only that the pretreatment group had a high prevalence of anemia but that marginal iron reserves were a virtually universal finding. It would be conceptually misleading to conceive of this group as being composed of distinctly iron-deficient or iron-sufficient individuals. Instead, the

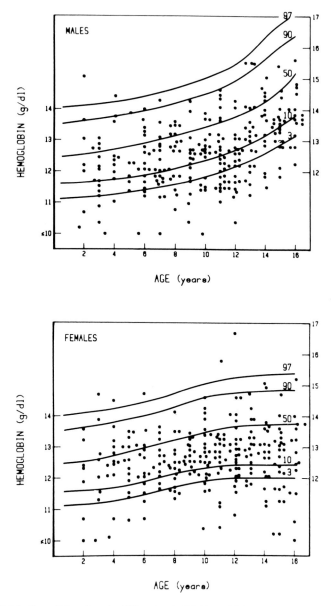

FIG. 7. Distribution of Hb values for 533 untreated Eskimo children studied during a pilot study in August 1977 as compared to reference curves obtained from an iron-sufficient population (7). (From Margolis et al., ref. 48.)

population appeared to consist of varying gradations from mild iron deficiency anemia to marginal iron sufficiency. This is probably a common characteristic of groups in which there is a high prevalence of iron deficiency anemia.

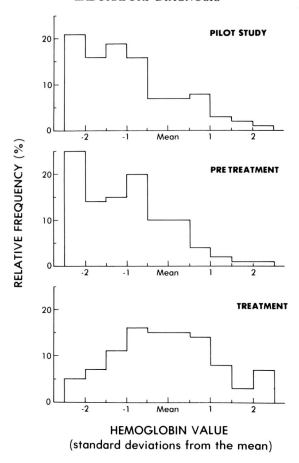

FIG. 8. Frequency distribution of SD scores before the iron-supplementation trial (pilot study in August 1977 and pretreatment results from December 1977) compared with posttreatment results (May 1978). After treatment, the distribution of hemoglobin values approximated a normal Gaussian distribution. (From Margolis et al., ref. 48.)

Mexican School Children

The results of a treatment trial with iron- and copper-supplemented milk in a group of Mexican school children between 6 and 15 years of age were depicted in a different manner (49). The study was designed to include a placebo group and two iron-treatment groups, each receiving different forms of supplemental iron. Change in concentration of hemoglobin is depicted in a bar graph diagram (Fig. 9). This method of presenting the data also lends itself to studies involving children of a broad age range. Both iron groups showed a response that was highly significant in relation to the placebo group. However, supplementation with iron as ferrous chloride was much more effective in raising the hemoglobin concentration than ferric lactobionate, a more stable iron chelate. As in the Alaskan Eskimo population,

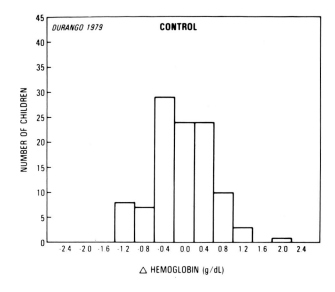

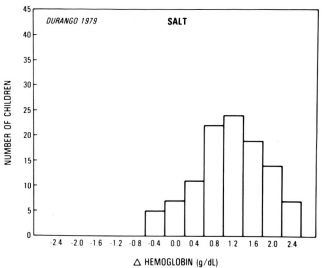

FIG. 9. Treatment trial with iron- and copper-supplemented milk in Mexican school children. The response is shown in terms of change in hemoglobin concentration. This illustrates the marked contrast between the response in children who received a placebo (control) and those who were given ferrous chloride and cupric chloride (salt). (From Rivera et al., ref. 47.)

almost all of the individuals in the latter group had some rise in the concentration of hemoglobin.

CONCLUSIONS

The initial step in the diagnosis of iron deficiency is a determination of the concentration of hemoglobin or, as a second choice, the hematocrit. Venipuncture samples are preferable, but when circumstances allow only skin puncture sampling, it is important to obtain a free flow of blood from a warm extremity. If the patient is found to be anemic (the hemoglobin or hematocrit is below the 95% range for a healthy population), the next steps to be taken are relatively straightforward. If the anemia is severe (the hemoglobin is more than 1 g/dl below the lower limit of normal), one or two further diagnostic tests will usually be indicated, and in most cases they will help either to establish or to exclude a diagnosis of iron deficiency. These additional tests could include MCV, serum iron/TIBC, EP, or serum ferritin. Which of these tests are selected will depend on the differential diagnosis and the specific clinical setting. When severe iron deficiency is diagnosed among low-risk populations (e.g., adult males or postmenopausal females), causes of pathologic intestinal blood loss must be investigated. This is also true when the anemia in infants and children is so severe that it becomes difficult to attribute the iron deficiency to dietary factors alone.

Patients with mild anemia present a more difficult problem because they tend to be either passed off as normal or evaluated with an excessive number of laboratory tests. When mild anemia is diagnosed on the basis of a skin puncture sample, it is helpful if the diagnosis of anemia can be confirmed by repeating the hemoglobin analysis on the venous blood. The next steps to be taken should then be influenced by factors such as the age, sex, and socioeconomic group of the patient. When such factors suggest a greater likelihood of iron deficiency, as in infants and adolescents from a poverty group, a therapeutic trial of iron may be more appropriate than further laboratory studies, especially if previous experience in the same population has shown the anemia to be due primarily to nutritional iron deficiency. A more extensive workup can then be reserved for the relatively small number of patients whose anemia is unresponsive to a 1-month course of iron therapy. However, further laboratory tests would be much more useful among patients in whom anemia is normally rare (e.g., men in industrialized countries). The development of mild iron deficiency anemia in such groups often signals a serious underlying disease that requires prompt attention.

The most difficult problem is the detection of the relatively mild cases of iron-responsive anemia in individuals who have a screening hemoglobin that is in the lower part of the normal range. In populations that rarely develop iron deficiency, such patients are so vastly outnumbered by healthy individuals that it is impractical to seek them out unless the history or physical examination suggests a reason to do so. In contrast, in a population known to have a high prevalence of iron deficiency (e.g., 1-year-old infants), a therapeutic trial of iron may be justified because there may be about as many iron-responsive infants with low-normal hemoglobin values as there are anemic ones. Because other laboratory tests were not of much value in distinguishing iron-responsive from unresponsive individuals in the low-normal hemoglobin group, a therapeutic trial would be a more cost-effective means of identifying iron-responsive subjects.

When populations are monitored for iron deficiency for the purpose of guiding health policy or planning fortification programs, it is essential to rely on more than one laboratory test. In addition to the hemoglobin determinations, the MCV will be helpful because it can be obtained at little extra cost if an electronic counter is available. Of the other tests, the serum ferritin has the clear advantage of allowing an estimate of iron reserves, as well as identification of iron deficiency. However, serum iron/TIBC and EP also provide information that may be helpful and may offer advantages in certain settings. If funds permit, the most reliable information is obtained by obtaining a broad battery of these tests on an appropriately selected sample population. Thus, multiple tests should be emphasized in the evaluation of populations, whereas a simpler approach of few tests and reliance of a brief therapeutic trial can be the basis for management of individual patients.

ACKNOWLEDGMENTS

This work was supported in part by Contract 200-70-09100, Centers for Disease Control and National Institutes of Health Grant No. AM13897, United States Public Health Service.

REFERENCES

1. Garby L, Irnell L, Werner I. Iron deficiency in women of fertile age in a Swedish community III. Estimation of prevalence based on response to iron supplementation. Acta Med Scand 1969;185:113–7.
2. Cook JD, Finch CA, Smith NJ. Evaluation of the iron status of a population. Blood 1976;48:449–55.
3. Dallman PR, Reeves JD, Driggers DA, Lo EYT. Diagnosis of iron deficiency: the limitations of laboratory tests in predicting response to iron treatment in 1-year-old infants. J Pediatr 1981;99:376–81.
4. Fairbanks VF. Is the peripheral blood film reliable for the diagnosis of iron deficiency anemia? Am J Clin Pathol 1971;55:447–51.
5. Bothwell TH, Charlton RW, Cook JD, Finch CA. Iron metabolism in man. Oxford: Blackwell Scientific Publications, 1979.
6. Cook JD ed. Methods in hematology: iron. New York: Churchill Livingstone, 1980.
7. Dallman PR, Siimes MA, Stekel A. Iron deficiency in infancy and childhood. Am J Clin Nutr 1980;33:86–118.
8. Bothwell TH, Charlton RW. Iron deficiency in women: a report of the international nutritional anemia consultative group. New York: Nutrition Foundation, 1981.
9. Lundström U, Siimes MA, Dallman PR. At what age does iron supplementation become necessary in low-birth-weight infants? J Pediatr 1977;91:878–83.
10. Saarinen UM. Need for iron supplementation in infants on prolonged breast feeding. J Pediatr 1978;93:177–80.
11. Woodruff CW, Clark JL. The role of fresh cow's milk in iron deficiency. I. Albumin turnover in infants with iron deficiency anemia. Am J Dis Child 1972;124:18–23.
12. Wilson JF, Lahey ME, Heiner DC. Further observations on cow's milk-induced gastrointestinal bleeding in infants with iron deficiency anemia. J Pediatr 1974;84:335–44.
13. International Nutritional Anemia Consultative Group. Iron absorption from cereal and legumes. New York: Nutrition Foundation, 1982.
14. Tanner JM, Whitehouse RH, Takaishi M. Standards from birth to maturity of height, weight, height velocity, and weight velocity: British children 1965. Arch Dis Child 1966;41:454–71.
15. Vartiainen E, Widholm O, Tenhunen P. Iron prophylaxis in menstruating teenage girls. Acta Obstet Gynecol Scand 1967; 46(suppl 1, part 2):49–54.
16. Committee on Standards of Child Health Care. Standards of child health care. 2nd ed. Evanston, Illinois: American Academy of Pediatrics, 1972:10.
17. Reeves JD, Driggers DA, Lo EYT, Dallman PR. Screening for anemia: evidence in favor of using identical hemoglobin criteria for Blacks and Caucasians. Am J Clin Nutr 1981;34:2154–7.
18. Berman BW, Ritchey AK, Jekel JF, Schwartz AD, Guiliotis DK, Pearson HA. Hematology of β-

thalassemia trait-age-related developmental aspects and intrafamilial correlations. J Pediatr 1980;97:901–5.

19. Conrad ME and Crosby WH. The natural history of iron deficiency induced by phlebotomy. Blood 1962;20:173–85.

20. Reeves JD, Driggers DA, Lo EYT, Dallman PR. Screening for iron deficiency anemia in one-year-old infants: hemoglobin alone or hemoglobin and mean corpuscular volume as predictors of response to iron treatment. J Pediatr 1981:98:894–8.

21. Galen RS, Gambino SR. Beyond normality: the predictive value and efficiency of medical diagnoses. New York: John Wiley & Sons, 1975:236.

22. Driggers DA, Reeves JD, Lo EYT, Dallman PR. Iron deficiency in one-year-old infants: comparison of results of a therapeutic trial in infants with anemia or low-normal hemoglobin values. J Pediatr 1981;98:753–8.

23. Hallberg L, Björn-Rasmussen E, Ekenved G, Garby L, Rossander L, Pleehachinda R, Suwanik R, Arvidsson B. Absorption from iron tablets given with different types of meals. Scand J Haematol 1978;21:215–24.

24. Norrby A. Iron absorption studies in iron deficiency. Scand J Haematol 1974;(Suppl)20:1–125.

25. Worwood M. Ferritin in human tissue and serum. Clin Haematol 1982;11:275–306.

26. Siimes MA, Addiego JE, Dallman PR. Ferritin in serum: the diagnosis of iron deficiency and iron overload in infants and children. Blood 1974;43:581–90.

27. Birgegard G, Hallgren R, Killander A, Strömberg A, Venge P, Wide L. Serum ferritin during infection. Scand J Haematol 1978;21:333–40.

28. Lipschitz DA, Cook JD, Finch CA. A clinical evaluation of serum ferritin as an index of iron stores. N Engl J Med 1974;290:1213–6.

29. Koerper MA, Stempel DA, Dallman PR. Anemia in patients with juvenile rheumatoid arthritis. J Pediatr 1978;92:930–3.

30. Schwartz E, Baehner RL. Diurnal variation of serum iron in infants and children. Acta Paediatr Scand 1968;57:433–5.

31. Hamilton LD, Gubler CJ, Cartwright GE, Wintrobe MM. Diurnal variation in the plasma iron level of man. Proc Soc Exp Biol Med 1950;75:65–8.

32. Saarinen UM, Siimes MA. Developmental changes in serum iron, total iron-binding capacity, and transferrin saturation in infancy. J Pediatr 1977;91:875–7.

33. Koerper MA, Dallman PR. Serum iron concentration and transferrin saturation in the diagnosis of iron deficiency in children: normal developmental changes. J Pediatr 1977;91:870–4.

34. Cartwright GE, Lee GR. Annotation. The anemia of chronic disorders. Br J Haematol 1971;21:146–52.

35. Piomelli S, Brickman A, Carlos E. Rapid diagnosis of iron deficiency by measurement of free erythrocyte porphyrins and a hemoglobin: the FEP/hemoglobin ratio. Pediatrics 1976;57:136–41.

36. Blumberg WE, Eisinger J, Lamola AA, Zuckerman DM. Zinc protoporphyrin level in blood determined by a portable hematofluorometer: a screening device for lead poisoning. J Lab Clin Med 1977;89:712–23.

37. Thomas WJ, Koenig HM, Lightsey AL, Green R. Free erythrocyte porphyrin : hemoglobin ratios, serum ferritin, and transferrin saturation levels during treatment of infants with iron deficiency anemia. Blood 1977;49:455–62.

38. Yip R, Norris TN, Anderson AS. Iron status of children with elevated blood lead concentrations. J Pediatr 1981;98:922–5.

39. Statland BE, Winkel P, Harris SC, Burdsall MJ, Sanders AM. Evaluation of biologic sources of variation of leukocyte counts and other hematologic quantities using very precise automated analyzers. Am J Clin Pathol 1978;69:48–54.

40. Pintar J, Skikne BS, Cook JD. A screening test for assessing iron status. Blood 1982;59:110–3.

41. Birgegard G, Hällgren R, Killander A, Strömberg A, Venge P, Wide L. Serum ferritin during infection. A longitudinal study. Scand J Haematol 1978;21:333–40.

42. Saarinen VM, Siimes MA. Serum ferritin in assessment of iron nutrition in healthy infants. Acta Paediatr Scand 1978;67:745–51.

43. Mentzer WG. Differentiation of iron deficiency from thalassemia trait. Lancet 1973;1:882.

44. Kulapongs P. The effect of vitamin E on the anemia of protein-calorie malnutrition in Northern Thai children. In: Olsen RE, ed. Protein calorie malnutrition. New York: Academic Press, 1975:263–8.

45. Matoth Y, Zamir R, Bar-Shani S, Grossowicz N. Studies on folic acid in infancy. II. Folic and

folinic acid blood levels in infants with diarrhea, malnutrition and infection. Pediatrics 1964;33:694–9.

46. Gandy G, Jacobson W. The influence of folic acid on birthweight and growth of the erythroblastic infant. III. Effect of folic acid supplementation. Arch Dis Child 1971;52:16–21.

47. Das KC, Herbert V, Colman N, Longo DL. Unmasking covert folate deficiency in iron-deficient subjects with neutrophil hypersegmentation; dU suppression test on lymphocyte and bone marrow. Br J Haematol 1978;39:357–75.

48. Margolis HS, Hardison HH, Bender TR, Dallman PR. Iron deficiency in children; the relationship between pretreatment laboratory tests and subsequent hemoglobin response to iron therapy. Am J Clin Nutr 1981;34:2158–68.

49. Rivera R, Ruiz R, Hegenauer J, Saltman P, Green R. Bioavailability of iron- and copper-supplemented milk for Mexican schoolchildren. Am J Clin Nutr 1982;36:1162–9.

DISCUSSION

Dr. Finch: One variation that we tend to overlook is that plasma volume may change rapidly. If the venipuncture is painful, hemoglobin concentration can increase by 1g as blood is drawn. If you then leave the needle in the vein for 5 or 10 min, you may get a hemoglobin concentration change due to the positioning of the individual, whether standing or lying down.

Iron Nutrition in Infancy and Childhood,
edited by A. Stekel. Nestlé, Vevey/Raven Press,
New York © 1984.

Functional Implications of Iron Deficiency

Devhuti Vyas and R. K. Chandra

*Department of Pediatrics, Memorial University of Newfoundland, St. John's,
Newfoundland, Canada A1A 1R8*

Iron undernutrition is the most common single nutrient deficiency worldwide. Iron deficiency has often been presumed to have few deleterious effects unless severe enough to compromise cardiovascular function. Whereas the effect of reduced iron availability on hemoglobin levels and other hematopoietic indices has been well recognized for a long time, it is only recently that the association between iron deficiency itself, with or without anemia, on immunocompetence, cognition, physical work capacity, and other functions has been documented (1,2). A number of organs and systems show variable changes in structure and function, often before any drop in hemoglobin occurs. This is not surprising because iron is an integral component or an essential cofactor of several enzymes that play an important role in metabolic processes and cell proliferation; these include aconitase, catalase, cytochrome C, cytochrome C reductase, cytochrome oxidase, formiminotransferase, monoamine oxidase, myeloperoxidase, peroxidase, ribonucleotidyl reductase, succinic dehydrogenase, tyrosine hydroxylase, tryptophan pyrrolase, and xanthine oxidase (3,4). These enzymes are involved in a number of key pathways such as DNA synthesis, mitochondrial electron transport, catecholamine metabolism, neurotransmitter levels, detoxification, and other functions. Many iron-containing proteins, e.g., myoglobin, serve important functions. It is not surprising then, that iron deficiency results in a variety of functional abnormalities.

In this selective review, the effects of iron deficiency on immune responses and susceptibility to infection, muscle function and physical work capacity, cognitive function and behavior, gastrointestinal structure and function, and thermogenesis are briefly described.

IMMUNOCOMPETENCE AND INFECTION

On the one hand, free iron is essential for the multiplication of all bacteria, with the exception of *Lactobacillus*. *In vitro* studies showed that iron depletion of medium inhibits bacterial growth and iron excess promotes it (5), but the extent of *in vivo* saturation does not affect bacterial growth rate (6). On the other hand, iron is essential for the normal development and functional integrity of lymphoid tissues; iron deficiency may be expected to impair immune response mediated by lymphocytes and granulocytes (7,8).

Immune Responses

Iron deficiency results in a mild but detectable reduction in cell-mediated immunity. The proportion and absolute number of rosette-forming T cells is slightly decreased (Fig. 1), but normal figures may be seen. More consistent is a reduction in lymphocyte proliferation response to mitogens—phytohemagglutinin (PHA), Concanavalin A—and antigens (8–12) (Fig. 2). Impaired response is seen also in individuals with "latent" iron deficiency without anemia. The discrepant observations reported in one study of 8 patients with anemia from chronic blood loss due

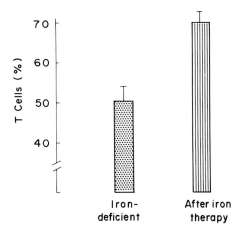

FIG. 1. Proportion of rosette-forming T cells in iron-deficient children and iron-replete controls.

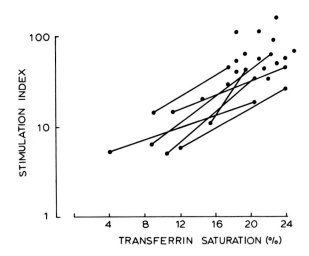

FIG. 2. Lymphocyte stimulation response to phytohemagglutinin in relation to transferrin saturation. In some patients, the test was repeated after 4 weeks of oral iron therapy. (From Chandra, ref. 37.)

to hookworm disease (13) may reflect differences in the cause of iron deficiency and in laboratory techniques. In another report (14), only 5 patients were investigated and iron deficiency was marginal (mean iron 54 μg/dl, range up to 88 μg/dl); the two subjects restudied after iron therapy showed a 44 to 55% increase in lymphoctye response to PHA. Hershko et al. (15) showed that, in chronic iron deficiency, the incorporation of radiolabeled thymidine into DNA was reduced together with decreased content of cellular DNA and impaired utilization of iron and glycine for heme and protein synthesis. The production of lymphokines, e.g., macrophage migration inhibition factor (MIF), in response to previously experienced antigens is reduced (9). Iron-deficient individuals may respond less often to recall antigens, e.g., candida, trichophyton, streptokinase-streptodornase, mumps, purified protein derivative (PPD); however, it must be emphasized that it is rare to encounter complete anergy in this group, unlike patients with protein-energy malnutrition.

Opsonization, ingestion, and chemotaxis are generally normal in iron deficiency in humans but intracellular bacterial and fungal killing is often reduced (16) (Fig. 3). It is important to employ an appropriate phagocyte:bacteria ratio, perhaps 1:5, and to construct kinetic curves of bacterial killing. In chronically iron-deficient rabbits, impaired uptake of opsonized *Staphylococcus aureus* by neutrophils was observed; the rate of phagocytosis could not be increased by autologous leukophilic α-globulin (17). Impaired reduction of nitroblue tetrazolium was observed when a quantitative test was conducted (16) but the result of the qualitative test in which the number of neutrophils with the reduced dye are counted was reported to be within the normal range (11,18). These apparently conflicting data are not incompatible since it is quite possible that the amount of dye reduced by each cell was

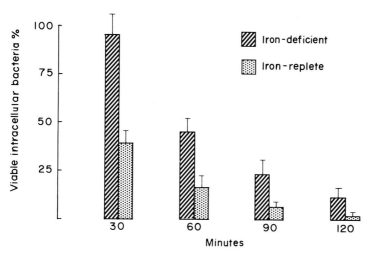

FIG. 3. Microbicidal capacity of neutrophils in iron deficiency and controls. *S. aureus* was used as the test organism at a ratio of five bacteria to one phagocyte and the results were expressed as the percentage of viable intracellular bacteria.

decreased in the iron-deficient group. The molecular basis of reduced microbicidal activity in iron deficiency is not clear, but decreased peroxidase activity and iodination may be contributory.

Serum immunoglobulin concentrations are within the normal range in iron-deficient subjects and increase after infection. The number of B lymphocytes and specific antibody responses to tetanus toxoid and S. typhi, and serum complement activity and levels, was also found to be comparable in iron-deficient and healthy children (10,11). Although salivary IgA level may be normal, specific IgA antibody to measles virus was reported to be reduced (8,19). These changes in immune responses occur early in the evolution of iron depletion (11,20). Similarly, in those with iron deficiency anemia, treatment with iron improves immunocompetence prior to increase in hemoglobin levels (16). These data suggest that reduction in tissue and cellular iron concentration and not the anemia is the primary cause of altered immunity associated with lack of iron.

The differences in the results of various studies on immune responses in iron deficiency may well be due to a number of confounding variables, including variations in methodology of various immunity function tests, e.g., dose of antigen or mitogen, or number of microorganisms (21,22). In some reports, the number of subjects examined was very small: 5 to 8 (13,14). A second important variable is the presence of concomitant or recent infection and parasitic disease. Thirdly, the cause of iron deficiency is a significant factor; reduced dietary intake of iron produces more prominent effects on immunity than deficiency resulting from blood loss, including hookworm disease. The diagnosis of iron deficiency is often suspect and appropriate controls may not be used.

Iron-Binding Capacity

The growth needs of microbes and animal cells for iron are similar. Bacteria have the ability to produce "siderophores," such as phenolate or hydroxamate compounds, to solubilize and assimilate the metal (5). Fever, a host protective mechanism, suppresses the ability of pathogens to synthesize iron ligands. The control of iron concentration and temperature are widely employed in industry to modulate the amount of toxin and antibiotic formation in fermentation processes.

In vitro, the ability of added ionic iron to reduce the microbiostatic function of serum has been demonstrated with a variety of bacteria and fungi. Based on iron dependency for virulence and the nature of the infection produced, bacteria have been arbitrarily classified into four categories (23). Transferrin saturation in excess of 70% is generally necessary to achieve this effect, a condition rarely encountered in clinical practice. Lactoferrin present in large amounts in human milk may contribute to the anti-infective properties of breast milk, particularly in protection against enterobacterial diarrhea (24). Bacteriostasis achieved by lactoferrin is markedly potentiated by specific antibody (Fig. 4). This iron-binding compound may also have a bactericidal action (25).

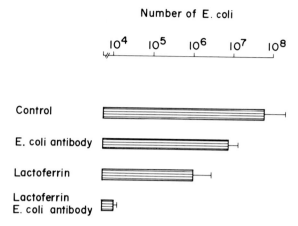

FIG. 4. Bacterial growth in 18 hr and the effect of lactoferrin and specific antibody.

Iron Status and Incidence of Infections

Observations in Humans

Studies on the incidence of infections in relation to iron status are difficult to control and conduct. One can fault most of the published literature on this topic on the grounds of inaccurate diagnosis (of iron deficiency and infection), retrospective analyses, inadequate controls, observer bias, and frequency of observations. However, it can be stated with confidence that iron supplementation within physiological needs to prevent anemia or in doses necessary to correct anemia may reduce, but certainly not increase, the risk of infection. Moreover, oral iron intake generally does not increase the availability of free iron that is necessary for bacterial multiplication.

Infection is the most common disease for which iron-deficient children seek medical advice. An Expert Group of the World Health Organization (26) commented that individuals with nutritional anemia tend to have more frequent infection. MacKay (27) observed a modest decrease in the number of episodes of bronchitis and gastroenteritis in iron-supplemented infants from low-income families in London. Andelman and Sered (28) found that respiratory infections were significantly less in infants who were given an iron-fortified milk formula. Other studies have not demonstrated any beneficial effects (29,30). A. Stekel and G. Heresi *(personal communication)* found decreased prevalence of diarrhea in some seasons in iron-supplemented infants. We have observed a reduced frequency of upper- and lower-respiratory infections in infants given iron supplements.

Iron deficiency and impaired cellular immunity are common findings in patients with chronic mucocutaneous candidiasis (31). The skin lesions as well as immunologic abnormalities reverse rapidly on administration of iron. Fletcher et al. (32) reported *Candida albicans* infection in the mouth lesions seen in iron-deficient individuals; the patients' saliva supported fungal growth better than control samples.

A local factor, such as changes in microflora consequent to iron lack, was postulated to be important.

We have examined a group of medical students with recurrent herpes simplex infection and found a higher prevalence of iron deficiency in them compared with other students without herpes (Fig. 5). Moreover, the response of lymphocytes to herpes simplex antigen and tetanus toxoid improved significantly 4 weeks after oral iron therapy (Fig. 6) and was associated with clinical remission monitored over a period of 1 year.

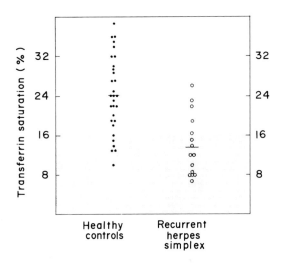

FIG. 5. Transferrin saturation of individuals with recurrent herpes labialis and those without such history. A cutoff point of ≤16% defines iron deficiency.

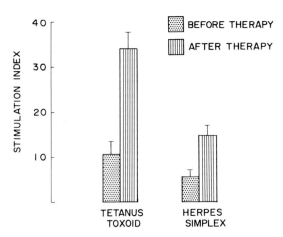

FIG. 6. Lymphocyte stimulation response to tetanus toxoid and herpes simplex antigens in iron-deficient individuals before and after iron therapy.

The assertion that "iron deficiency protects against infection" is not supported by a critical analysis of observations. The data of one report (33) often cited as evidence for this hypothesis must be correctly viewed in detail. This study looked at the presence of infection on admission among 110 adults with hemoglobin less than 10 g/dl; of the 67 with severe iron deficiency or dimorphic anemia, five (7%) were diagnosed to have bacterial infection and 16 (24%) malaria. It was stated that the "malarial attacks in the iron-deficiency group usually developed after iron treatment was started." The workers concluded that, "the low frequency of bacterial infections in the iron-deficient group suggests that patients with iron-deficiency anemia are not as vulnerable to infections as has hitherto been suspected, but they are susceptible to malaria." These conclusions are not justified on the basis of the observations made. Firstly, no control group of nonanemic subjects was examined. What was being compared was the prevalence of infection among patients with different etiologic types of anemia. Secondly, those with positive bone marrow iron included patients with sickle cell disease and trait and other conditions known to change susceptibility to disease. Thirdly, the diagnosis of iron deficiency was based on blood and bone marrow smears; serum iron and transferrin saturation were not done. Fourthly, blood cultures to document bacterial infection were set up only in those patients (34 of 110) who had fever. It is well known that protein-calorie malnutrition present in many of the study subjects can suppress febrile response. In others, bacterial infection was diagnosed on the basis of response to antibiotics; the self-limited course of many infectious illnesses, especially viral, makes the therapeutic response an unsatisfactory diagnostic criterion. Similarly, malaria was diagnosed by demonstration of the parasite only in 6 patients; in the remaining 12, it was based on response to chloroquine. Also, the nature of iron supplements and their duration are not stated, and posttherapy data are provided for malaria but not for bacterial infections. The impact of other associated nutrient deficiencies (33 had swelling of the legs), protein deficiency, or a malarial nephrotic syndrome was not considered. These limitations detract seriously from the conclusions reached. Similarly, Murray's observations (36) that symptomatic disease was evident more often in Somali nomads after a period of iron supplementation may mean that the prevalence of clinical diseases in which cell-mediated immunity plays a role of clinical expression may be more apparent because iron therapy has improved cellular immunity, but these data do not imply that the incidence or the outcome of infectious illness is adversely affected by treatment of iron deficiency. Lack of documentation of infection, effects of season, overcrowding, and other variables present major difficulties in interpretation of these data.

Some reviews on the topic (35,36) have failed to emphasize these limitations of reported data, implying that iron deficiency in humans protects from infections, and thus have wavered on the question of iron status and susceptibility to infection.

Chronic iron overload, as in thalassemia and hemochromatosis, is not characterized by frequent infections. This is further supported by the observation that *in vivo* iron saturation of serum does not impair its bacteriostatic properties (6).

Observations in Animals

The infectious consequences of dietary iron deficiency have been evaluated in several animal models and the data have been reviewed (7,37,38). In young swine rendered iron-deficient and exposed to *E. coli* endotoxin, the mortality was extremely high in the experimental anemic group. Antibody production in response to tetanus toxoid immunization was significantly reduced in rats that received inadequate dietary iron. The susceptibility to infective challenge with *S. typhi* or *Strep. pneumoniae*, assessed by morbidity and mortality, was enhanced in iron-deficient animals. Preweaning iron deprivation impaired the rats' ability to resist the stress of infection, even if a period of nutritional rehabilitation had intervened. Inability to produce and deliver myeloperoxidase-containing cells was considered to be the pathogenesis of vulnerability to *S. typhi*. There is some evidence, on the other hand, that the parenteral administration of iron compounds reduces the number of bacteria necessary to produce disease or death. For instance, the growth of nonpigmented mutants of *Pasteurella pestis* was enhanced by injections of iron. In an experimental mouse model, changes in iron status, secondary to administration of endotoxin or iron, mediated the susceptibility of animals to challenge with *C. albicans*. Thus the route of administration and the nature of iron compound used may be important in host-bacteria interactions. A recent report (39) describes the effect both of oral iron and intramuscular iron-dextran on incidence of pneumonia and diarrhea in calves. Iron-dextran administration reduced the frequency of anemia but oral iron produced a more distinct benefit than intramuscular therapy, the effect being more evident in the duration of pneumonia.

Iron Administration and Infection

A report of a high incidence of gram-negative septicemia in Polynesian newborn infants given a series of iron-dextran injections (40) has evoked concern about the use of iron in the prevention of iron deficiency in infants. However, newborns may have a relatively inefficient mechanism for dealing with large quantities of complexed iron. Macrophage blockade may impair host defense. The use of moderate doses of iron-dextran after the neonatal period did not predispose infants to infections (41). Certainly, the use of the conventional preventive or therapeutic doses of oral iron has not been associated with increased risk of infection; if at all, this may decrease such common illnesses as otitis, upper- and lower-respiratory infections, and diarrhea.

Children suffering from protein-calorie malnutrition present a special problem since they have reduced levels of iron-binding proteins (42), which correlate with chances of survival. Large doses of iron in the initial stages of nutritional management may predispose malnourished children to bacteremia and high mortality. However, this risk is minimized if iron administration is delayed by a few days, giving opportunity for repair of transferrin synthesis (Table 1).

TABLE 1. *Timing of iron therapy and mortality
in well-nourished and malnourished children
with iron therapy*[a]

	After 72 hr of admission	Within 72 hr of admission
Well nourished	2/50	1/41
Kwashiorkor	3/18	5/12
Marasmus	2/35	1/16

[a]Number of deaths/total number of patients.

GASTROINTESTINAL SYSTEM

Iron deficiency is associated with a variety of clinical manifestations pertaining to the gastrointestinal tract. These can be both the cause and the effect of iron deficiency. Histological studies have shown changes in epithelial morphology, including metaplasia of buccal and esophageal mucosae. Surface epithelial cells in tissues obtained from iron-deficient subjects have a reduced content of cytochrome and other enzymes. Hypo- and achlorhydria may occur. A few studies have shown variable dysfunction of absorptive processes, including reduced uptake of ingested D-xylose and of fat. Jejunal biopsies have revealed morphologic changes in villus structure and enzyme content in iron deficiency; the extent of such changes varied from mild to severe (43,44). In some patients, the investigations have been repeated after appropriate iron therapy and a partial or complete recovery of gastrointestinal structure and function was observed. Fecal occult blood is detected more often in iron-deficient subjects than in controls. Iron deficiency in young puppies and rats is associated with reduced activity of sugar-splitting enzymes, but the mucosal architecture is preserved (45,46). The subject of small intestinal structure and function in nutritional deficiency has been recently reviewed (47).

THERMOREGULATION

It has been reported that iron-deficient rodents cannot maintain normal core body temperature when stressed with cold, and that the conversion of T4 to T3 is impaired (48). The serum and urinary levels of catecholamines are increased. Iron deficiency alters mitochondrial electron transport systems both in adipose tissue and in brown fat. Body insulation is not changed since hair thickness is unaltered and cutaneous vasoconstriction is intact. Oxygen consumption at 4°C is reduced. Treatment with iron results in reversal to normal T3 levels in 1 week. The modulating influence of thyroid function in thermoregulation has been shown also by the observations that thyroidectomized iron-deficient rats injected with T3 do not show cold stress-induced hypothermia whereas T4 administration fails to prevent hypothermia and increases catecholamines at 4°C (48).

PHYSICAL WORK CAPACITY

Latent iron deficiency without anemia may be expected to alter cellular metabolism and tissue function by decreasing the availability of various iron-containing and iron-dependent enzymes and other proteins, including cytochromes, and mitochondrial enzymes for oxidative phosphorylation and energy production. Iron deficiency anemia leads to decreased oxygen delivery to the tissues, such as skeletal muscle. The effect of anemia would be obviously more pronounced in laborers doing physically demanding tasks than in domestic or sedentary workers. Decreased oxygen affinity and increased cardiac output are the adaptive physiological measures of the body in response to anemia. This adaptation can cover the metabolic needs of the body at rest or for sedentary work but it cannot cope with the metabolic needs of the body for work involving physical endurance.

In humans, physical work capacity studied by the Harvard step test has been shown to be proportional to the hemoglobin concentration of the subject (49). An analysis of work time, percentage of the people reaching the maximal work load, heart rate response to work, and postexercise blood lactate levels has led to the conclusion that anemic subjects have a lower work capacity than healthy nonanemic controls (50). Subjects with hemoglobin concentrations between 11.0 and 11.9 g/dl showed a 20% decrease in work tolerance when compared to those with levels above 13.0 g/dl. In a study carried out in Indonesia on rubber plantation workers it has been shown that anemia, even at the high cutoff level of 13.0 g/dl, affected a worker's ability to perform the Harvard step test (51). Income from rubber tapping was directly proportional to the hemoglobin concentration. Treatment with ferrous iron and a small incentive payment resulted in improved work output and hence productivity. Our data corroborate such findings relating anemia to physical work capacity (Fig. 7). Furthermore, we differentiated the ability to perform short bursts of activity from endurance; the latter was affected much more in iron deficiency (Fig. 8). Work performance may increase as early as 4 days after initiation of iron treatment (52). A significant improvement in the productivity of

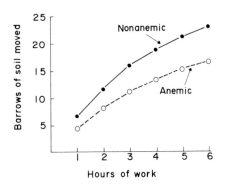

FIG. 7. Physical work performance related to the presence of anemia. The differences were more marked as the duration of work increased. (From Chandra and Vyas, ref. 2.)

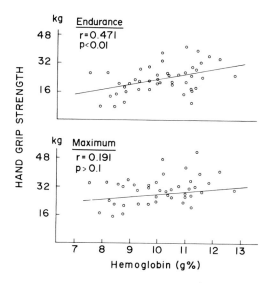

FIG. 8. Hand grip strength related to hemoglobin concentration. Short burst of activity for 10 sec (maximum strength) was not dependent on hemoglobin level but endurance calculated as an average of 10-sec strength over 1 min was significantly correlated with severity of anemia. (From Chandra and Vyas, ref. 2.)

iron-deficient workers on a tea plantation was observed after 3 weeks of iron supplementation (53).

Animal studies support such observations. Finch et al. (54), using iron-deficient rats, have shown that work performance increased fivefold after 3 days of iron treatment prior to any detectable change in hemoglobin levels. Iron-deficient rats had lower exhaustive run time, elevated heart rate, and cardiomegaly (55).

These data suggest that iron deficiency anemia is related to decreased work capacity, leading to reduced productivity and poor individual income, which may aggravate the problem further by worsening undernutrition and consequent enhanced morbidity and mortality. Anemia per se reduces work capacity but improvement in this function after iron supplementation for a short period suggests that not only hemoglobin concentration but changes in tissue enzymes secondary to iron deficiency, e.g., α-glycerophosphate oxidase, and the resulting lactic acidosis also may be important in iron-deficient subjects.

COGNITION AND BEHAVIOR

In laboratory animal studies, iron deficiency has been shown to cause fetal resorption and decrease in body size and weight. Rats deprived of iron during early life have reduced amounts of nonheme iron in the brain, with behavioral and physiological consequences (56). Mackler et al. (57) have shown that the specific activity and tissue concentration of enzymes of oxidative phosphorylation in mitochondria from the brain were unaffected by iron deficiency while aldehyde oxidative activity was decreased. There was an accumulation of serotonin and 5-hydroxyindol compounds. Iron treatment restored the level of the enzymes and neurotransmitters to the normal range. Serotonin and tryptaminergic drugs have been reported to produce drowsiness and decreased attentiveness and ability to learn. Thus, it has been postulated that iron deficiency may lead to defects in cognitive development and function. There are several reports documenting impaired mental functions in iron-deprived animals and human subjects. Massaro and Widmayer (58) have shown that iron deficiency anemia in rats adversely affected some aspects of associative learning. Howell (59) reported that 3- to 5-year-old iron-deficient children with hemoglobins less than 10 g/dl showed decreased attentiveness, narrow attention span, and perceptual restriction. Sulzer et al. (60) have shown that anemic children of 4 to 5 years of age with hemoglobins less than 10 g/dl were poor in a vocabulary test, had lower IQ measures, and showed impaired performance in measures of the latency and associative reactions. Iron deficiency has adverse effects on attention and memory control processes, which return to normal after iron treatment. Iron-deficient young adolescent subjects were also shown to score comparatively lower on tests of academic performance—which included vocabulary, reading knowledge, use of reference material, arithmetic concepts, and problem solving—and were, moreover, found to be more disruptive, irritable, and restless in the classroom than other students. Oski and Honig (61) have shown that mental and developmental scores in infants 9 to 26 months old with hemoglobins less that 10.5 g/dl improved after iron treatment for 6 to 8 days. In addition, iron treatment also resulted in improved gross and fine motor coordination. Others did not find any relationship between IQ measures and degree of anemia among children (62), but the type of anemia investigated was of the hemolytic variety observed in sickle cell disease in which iron deficiency may not be seen. A recent report by Lozoff et al. (63) concluded that developmental deficits assessed by the Bailey method are more frequent in anemic children than in nonanemic controls and that there was little improvement after short-term oral iron therapy. The lack of improvement may be due to the need for long-term therapy, as seen also in experimental animals. Perhaps the cause of lower developmental scores in anemic children may be an intervening variable closely linked to iron deficiency; lead toxicity could be considered one such factor. Pollitt and Leibel (64) state that "it is unclear whether the poor performance, perceptual disturbance and conduct problems observed in anemic subjects were consequences of anemia, per se, of iron deficiency alone, or of a general nutritional inadequacy."

Iron deficiency may occasionally be associated with behavior disorders, such as pica, pagophagia, breath-holding spells, and temper tantrums (65,66). Abnormal eating behavior may both be the cause or the effect of iron deficiency. Iron therapy has been observed to accelerate the cessation of these generally self-limited aberrations of behavior.

The interesting results of these studies on iron deficiency and behavioral development suggest that iron is a critical element for the normal functioning of the central nervous system. Many methodologic problems, however, plague studies on this topic, not the least of which is the reliability of the testing procedures for young children; others are the problems of crosscultural transfer of techniques, retrospective analyses, inadequate controls, and definition of iron deficiency. Several investigations in progress are attempting to use improved assessment methods and should provide much-needed answers to the question of the effect of iron deficiency on cognitive ability and behavior.

REFERENCES

1. Jacobs A. Non-haematological effects of iron deficiency. Clin Haematol 1982;11:353–64.
2. Chandra RK, Vyas D. Functional consequences in iron deficiency: non-erythroid effects. In: Chandra RK, ed. Critical reviews in tropical medicine. Vol. 2. New York: Plenum Press, 1984.
3. Higashi O, Sato Y, Takamatsu H, Oyama M. Mean cellular peroxidase (MCP) of leukocytes in iron deficiency anemia. Tohoku J Exp Med 1967;93:105–13.
4. Wrigglesworth JM, Baum H. The biochemical functions of iron. In: Jacobs A, Worwood M, eds. Iron in biochemistry and medicine. London: Academic Press, 1980:29.
5. Weinberg ED. Iron and susceptibility to disease. Science 1974;184:952–6.
6. Baltimore RS, Shedd DG, Pearson HA. Effect of iron saturation on the bacteriostasis of human serum: in vivo does not correlate with in vitro saturation. J Pediatr 1982;101:519–23.
7. Chandra RK. Iron and immunocompetence. Nutr Rev 1976;34:129–32.
8. Chandra RK, Au B, Woodford G, Hyam P. Iron status, immune response and susceptibility to infection. In: Ciba Foundation Symposium on Iron Metabolism. Amsterdam: Elsevier Excerpta Medica North-Holland, 1977:249–61.
9. Joynson DHM, Jacobs A, Walker DM, Dolby AE. Defect of cell-mediated immunity in patients with iron-deficiency anaemia. Lancet 1972;2:1058–9.
10. Chandra RK, Saraya AK. Impaired immunocompetence associated with iron deficiency. J Pediatr 1975;86:899–902.
11. Macdougall LG, Anderson R, McNab GM, Katz J. The immune response in iron-deficient children: impaired cellular defense mechanisms with altered humoral components. J Pediatr 1975;86:833–43.
12. Bhaskaram P, Prasad J, Krishnamachary KAVR. Anaemia and immune response. Letter. Lancet 1977;1:1000.
13. Kulapongs P, Vithayasai V, Suskind R, Olson R. Cell-mediated immunity and phagocytosis-killing function in children with severe iron deficiency anaemia. Lancet 1974;2:689–91.
14. Gross RK, Reid JVO, Newberne PM, Burgess B, Marston R, Hift W. Depressed cell-mediated immunity in megaloblastic anemia due to folic acid deficiency. Am J Clin Nutr 1975;28:225–32.
15. Hershko CH, Karsai A, Eylon L, Izak G. The effect of chronic iron deficiency on some biochemical functions of the human hemopoietic tissue. Blood 1970;36:321–9.
16. Chandra RK. Reduced bactericidal capacity of polymorphs in iron deficiency. Arch Dis Child 1973;48:864–6.
17. Likhite V, Rodvien R, Crosby WH. Depressed phagocytic function exhibited by polymorphonuclear leucocytes from chronically iron-deficient rabbits. Br J Haematol 1976;34:251–5.
18. VanHeerden C, Oosthuizen R, VanWyk H, Prinsloo P, Anderson R. Evaluation of neutrophil and lymphocyte function in subjects with iron deficiency. S Afr Med J 1981;59:111–3.
19. Chandra RK. Mucosal immunity in nutritional deficiency. In: McGhee JR, Mestecky J, eds. Secretory immune system in health and disease. New York: New York Academy of Sciences, 1983:345–51.
20. Chandra RK. Immunocompetence in nutritional assessment. In: Levenson SM, ed. Nutritional assessment —present status, future directions and prospects. Columbus, Ohio: Ross Laboratories, 1981:111–3.
21. Buckley RH. Iron deficiency anemia; its relationship to infections and susceptibility and host defense. J Pediatr 1975;86:993–5.
22. Chandra RK. Immune response in iron-deficient children. J Pediatr 1976;88:698–9.
23. Payne SM, Finkelstein RA. The critical role of iron in host-bacterial interactions. J Clin Invest 1978;61:1428–40.

24. Bullen JJ, Rogers HJ, Leigh L. Iron-binding proteins in milk and resistance to Escherichia coli infection in infants. Br Med J 1972;1:69–75.
25. Arnold RR, Cole MF, McGhee JR. A bactericidal effect for human lactoferrin. Science 1977;197: 263–5.
26. WHO Expert Group. Control of nutritional anemia with special reference to iron deficiency. WHO Tech Rep Ser 1975;No.580.
27. MacKay HM. Anaemia in infancy; its prevalence and prevention. Arch Dis Child 1928;3:117–47.
28. Andelman MB, Sered BR. Utilization of dietary iron by term infants. Am J Dis Child 1966;111: 45–55.
29. Burman D. Hemoglobin levels in normal infants aged 3 to 24 months, and the effect of iron. Arch Dis Child 1972;48:863–6.
30. James JA, Combes M. Iron deficiency in the premature infant. Significance and prevention by the intramuscular administration in iron-dextran. Pediatrics 1960;26:368–74.
31. Higgs JM, Wells RS. Chronic mucocutaneous candidiasis; associated abnormalities of iron metabolism. Br J Dermatol 1973;86(suppl 8):88–94.
32. Fletcher J, Mather J, Lewis MJ, Whiting G. Mouth lesions in iron-deficient anemia: relationship to Candida albicans in saliva and to impairment of lymphocyte transformation. J Infect Dis 1975;131:44–50.
33. Masawe AEJ, Muindi JM, Swai GBR. Infections in iron deficiency and other types of anaemia in the tropics. Lancet 1974;2:314–7.
34. Editorial. Iron and resistance to infection. Lancet 1974;2:325–6.
35. Lukens JN. Iron deficiency and infection. Fact or fable. Am J Dis Child 1975;129:160–2.
36. Murray MJ, Murray AB, Murray MB, Murray CJ. The adverse effect of iron repletion on the course of certain infections. Br Med J 1978;1113–5.
37. Chandra RK. Immunology of nutritional disorders. London: Arnold, 1980.
38. Gross R, Newverne PM. Role nutrition in immunologic function. Physiol Rev 1980;60:188–302.
39. Bünger U, Pongé J, Schmoldt P. Zur oralen und intramuskulären Ferri dextranintervention bei männlichen Aufzuchtkälbern. 2. Morbiditätstraten und Behandlungshaüfigkeiten an Pneumonia und/oder Durchfall. Arch Tierernaehr 1982;32:673–84.
40. Barry DMJ, Reeve AW. Increased incidence of gram-negative neonatal sepsis with intramuscular iron administration. Pediatrics 1977;60:908.
41. Hesse HdeV. Iron status in South African mothers and infants. Perceptions, random thoughts and studies. In: Oski FA, Pearson HA, eds. Iron nutrition revisited: infancy, childhood and adolescence. Columbus, Ohio: Ross Laboratories, 1981:15.
42. Antia Au, McFarlane H, Soothill JF. Serum siderophilia in kwashiorkor. Arch Dis Child 1968;43: 459–62.
43. Naiman JL, Oski FA, Diamond LK, Vawter GF, Schwachman H. The gastrointestinal effects of iron-deficiency anemia. Pediatrics 1964;33:83–90.
44. Guha DK, Walia BNS, Tandon BN, Deo MG, Ghai OP. Small bowel changes in iron-deficiency anaemia of childhood. Arch Dis Child 1968;43:239–44.
45. Hoffbrand AV, Broitman SA. Effect of chronic nutritional iron deficiency on the small intestinal disaccharidase activities of growing dogs. Proc Soc Exp Biol Med 1969;130:595–602.
46. Sriratanaban S, Thayer WR. Small intestinal disaccharidase activities in experimental iron and protein deficiency. Am J Clin Nutr 1971;24:411–5.
47. Vyas D, Chandra RK. Small intestinal structure and function in nutritional deficiency. In: Booth CC, ed. Disorders of small intestine. London: Blackwell, 1984.
48. Dillman E, Gale C, Green W, Johnson DG, Mackler B, Finch C. Hypothermia in iron deficiency due to altered triiodothyronine metabolism. Am J Physiol 1980;238:R377–81.
49. Viteri F, Torun B. Anaemia and physical work capacity. Clin Haematol 1974;3:609–26.
50. Gardner GW, Edgerton VR, Senewiratne B, Barnard RJ, Ohira Y. Physical work capacity and metabolic stress in subjects with iron deficiency anemia. Am J Clin Nutr 1977;30:910–7.
51. Basta SS, Soekirman, Karyadi D, Scrimshaw NS. Iron deficiency anemia and the productivity of adult males in Indonesia. Am J Clin Nutr 1979;32:916–25.
52. Ohira Y, Edgerton VR, Gardner GW, Barnard RJ, Senewiratne B. Work capacity, heart rate and blood lactate responses to iron treatment. Br J Haematol 1979;41:365.
53. Edgerton VR, Gardner GW, Ohira Y, Barnard RJ, Senewiratne B. Iron deficiency anemia and its effect on worker productivity and activity patterns. Br Med J 1979;2:1546.

54. Finch CA, Miller LR, Inamdar AR. Iron deficiency in the rat: Physiological and biochemical studies of muscle dysfunction. J Clin Invest 1976;58:447.
55. Koziol BJ, Ohira Y, Edgerton Ur, Simpson DR. Changes in work tolerance associated with metabolic and physiological adjustment to moderate and severe iron deficiency anemia. Am J Clin Nutr 1982;36:830–9.
56. Weinberg J, Dallman PR, Levine S. Iron deficiency during early development in the rat: behavioral and physiological consequences. Pharmacol Biochem Behav 1980;12:493–9.
57. Mackler B, Person R, Miller LR, Inamdar AR, Finch CA. Iron deficiency in the rat: biochemical studies of brain metabolism. Pediatr Res 1978;12:217–20.
58. Massaro TF, Widmayer P. The effect of iron deficiency on cognitive performance in the rat. Am J Clin Nutr 1981;34:864–70.
59. Howell D. Significance of iron deficiencies. Consequences of mild deficiency in children. Extent and meaning of iron deficiency in the United States. Washington, DC: National Academy of Sciences, 1971.
60. Sulzer JL, Wesley HH, Leonig F. Nutrition and behavior in head start children: results from the Tulane Study. In: Kallen DJ, ed. Nutrition, development and social behavior. Washington, DC: DHEW publication no. (NIH-)73-242, 1973;87–99.
61. Oski FA, Honig AS. The effects of therapy on the developmental scores of iron-deficient infants. J Pediatr 1978;92:21–5.
62. Chodorkoff J, Whitten CF. The intellectual status of children with sickle cell anemia. J Pediatr 1963;63:29.
63. Lozoff B, Brittenham GM, Viteri FE, Wolf AW, Urrutia JJ. The effects of short-term oral iron therapy on developmental deficit in iron-deficient anemic infants. J Pediatr 1982;100:351–7.
64. Pollitt E, Leibel RL. Iron deficiency and behavior. J Pediatr 1976;88:372–81.
65. Coltman CA Jr. Pogophagia and iron lack. JAMA 1969;207:513–6.
66. Chandra RK. Association of breath-holding attacks with anaemia and their treatment. Indian Pediatr 1965;2:411–6.

Iron Nutrition in Infancy and Childhood,
edited by A. Stekel. Nestlé, Vevey/Raven Press,
New York © 1984.

Prevalence of Nutritional Anemia in Infancy and Childhood with Emphasis on Developing Countries

Rodolfo F. Florentino and Romualda M. Guirriec

Nutrition Center of the Philippines, Metro Manila, Makati, Philippines 3116

Even a rapid review of the literature reveals that millions of people around the world, especially in developing countries, suffer from nutritional anemia despite advances in detection as well as in methods of prevention and treatment. This high prevalence is due to multiple and complex factors that abound in developing countries. In these countries, there is a low standard of living with a high prevalence of malnutrition, poor environmental sanitation, high morbidity among children, and unequal distribution of wealth leading to extremes of wealth and poverty; all these conditions favor the onset of anemia. Although the major causes of nutritional anemia are, firstly, of dietary origin due to low intake and low bioavailability of iron and, secondly, due to blood loss caused by parasitism, these two factors are basically the result of interaction of other deep-seated factors linked to underdevelopment.

It is imperative therefore that the causes of iron deficiency and of anemia be viewed beyond the immediate environment of the affected individual. The disease can be traced to its basic social, economic, and political environment. Figure 1 summarizes the underlying and immediate causes of iron deficiency.

Not only is iron deficiency caused by a low amount of iron in the diet but also by its poor absorbability. The poor absorption of iron from cereal-vegetable-based diets is well known. Economic factors often limit the intake of meat and ascorbic-acid-rich foods that would enhance the absorption of iron. There are also socio-cultural practices that directly or indirectly affect dietary intake. Some religions prohibit the intake of certain meats. Preschool children, girls, and women are often at a disadvantage; cultural taboos and superstitious beliefs may prohibit the intake of certain foods at certain times, especially during infancy and childhood or during pregnancy and lactation.

Parasitic infection is the second leading cause of iron deficiency anemia, and hookworm is the most notorious in this regard. Hookworm assumes greater significance among older children, but fortunately not much in infants. Parasitic infection thrives in an unsanitary environment, and transmittal is enhanced by poor sanitary habits, inadequate health facilities, ignorance, poverty, and poor agricultural practices.

The hidden losses become significant when iron stores are depleted because of increased physiological requirements, making infants and children particularly vul-

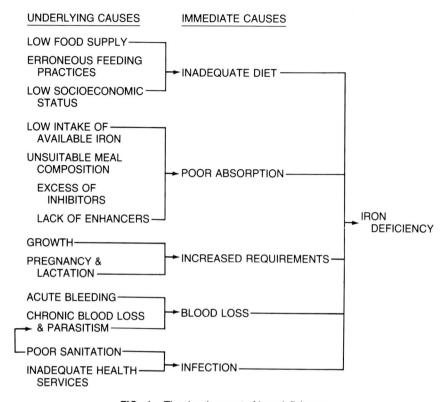

FIG. 1. The development of iron deficiency.

nerable. The iron requirements of infants and children, despite their much smaller body size, are almost as high or higher than those of the adult male. This situation is responsible for the high prevalence of nutritional anemia during infancy and childhood.

DIAGNOSTIC PARAMETERS/PROCEDURES FOR ESTIMATING IRON DEFICIENCY

Iron deficiency may be defined as a condition when the iron supply is inadequate for the normal synthesis of essential iron compounds (1). With the advancement of technology, new laboratory tests have become available; these have made possible a clearer definition of iron deficiency and a recognition of the limitations inherent in the traditional methods. The various tests have been thoroughly discussed, including their applications and limitations in several publications (2–6).

Several factors influence the selection of diagnostic tests; it is important to realize that their usefulness for defining iron deficiency depends on the objectives for which they are being used. Thus nationwide surveys, for example, are designed to obtain data on prevalence and to identify populations at risk as targets of intervention strategies, whereas to a clinician the focus is on the individual diagnosis, therapy, and follow-up. One factor affecting the selection of a test procedure, especially among infants and young children, is the volume of the blood sample required and the manner in which it is obtained. With the exception of transferrin saturation, the various tests can be performed on a very small amount of blood that can easily be obtained by finger prick. The selection of tests will also depend on the equipment available and the level of expertise or training of laboratory technicians. The time required to obtain results of analysis is also a factor to consider. It should be pointed out that in most developing countries, where manpower and material resources are limited, the diagnostic tests generally used are the simplest and least expensive ones.

Our present knowledge of the extent of iron deficiency has been dependent on the parameters used in laboratory diagnoses. Infants and children, however, pose certain problems in the use of such parameters. The laboratory diagnosis of iron deficiency in this age group, for example, requires the use of age-specific reference standards (5,6). There are marked developmental changes in normal values for hemoglobin, hematocrit, mean corpuscular volume (MCV), mean corpuscular hemoglobin (MCH), erythrocyte protoporphyrin, serum ferritin, and transferrin saturation. Dallman (5) has discussed the "physiological anemia of infancy" wherein there is a decline in the concentration of hemoglobin during the first 2 months after birth from the highest to the lowest levels observed at any period of development. This is independent of nutritional factors and is primarily attributed to an abrupt decrease in erythropoiesis in response to increased postnatal delivery of oxygen to the tissues. Special attention must therefore be taken when interpreting data from infants and children.

Ideally, reference standards for "normal" values should be obtained from healthy populations that have been screened to exclude individuals with mild iron or folate deficiencies or with conditions such as thalassemia minor. The nature of the population from which normative data are derived will greatly influence estimates of prevalence of iron deficiency, especially in infants and children (6).

The parameters for the diagnosis of iron deficiency may be considered within the framework of the three stages occurring in its development. The first stage is the depletion of stored iron, and this is detected by the concentration of serum ferritin. The second stage involves transport of iron to the bone marrow, and deficiency is reflected in an increase in iron-binding capacity, decrease in transferrin saturation, decrease in serum iron, and increase in concentration of free erythrocyte protoporphyrin. The third stage is a decrease in erythropoiesis, resulting in a fall in hemoglobin and the presence of hypochromic microcytic red cells as reflected in a low hematocrit.

Hemoglobin determination is the traditional method used for diagnosis, treatment, and follow-up of iron deficiency. Where the prevalence of iron deficiency is high, hemoglobin remains the best parameter for use in prevalence surveys.

The concept of distribution analysis is very useful in public health practice (2,4). This is particularly helpful where prevalence is high. By comparing the proportions of the population below an arbitrary standard at different times, the changes in the severity of the anemia problem can be clearly seen. At any given point in time, however, the problem of what arbitrary standard to use becomes the issue. Marzan and Ibe (7), for example, using distribution analysis, proposed a value for the Philippines of 8.8 g% hemoglobin for children 1 to 3 years old as a cutoff point between "deficient-low" and "acceptable" levels, and corresponding values of 10.5 and 10.8 g% for children 4 to 6 and 7 to 9 years, respectively. These values are somewhat different from those recommended by the World Health Organization. In any event, such standards or cutoff points are, by their nature, arbitrary because they depend on the objectives for which they have been set. In the planning of public health interventions, for example, one not only considers the number of iron responders vis-à-vis nonresponders that would be below the cutoff point, but also the logistical constraints and available resources for such interventions.

Since estimates of prevalence have critical implications on public health programs, they should ideally be determined through appropriate surveys with three important considerations: (a) well-defined criteria for diagnosis, (b) well-defined "normal" values, and (c) adequate representativeness of the population. Although this is hypothetically possible, most of the prevalence studies done so far have been conducted on the segment of the population most at risk from nutritional anemia. In practice also, data are obtained from infants and young children admitted to clinics or hospitals. Iron deficiency is therefore most commonly detected through the routine laboratory assessment of the population that comes into contact with health services for treatment or for routine check-up.

The figures cited in the following discussion of prevalence in the different countries by no means reflect the overall situation in each country because of lack of representativeness of the sample. Comparisons either among countries or between different periods of time are therefore difficult if not impossible.

PREVALENCE

From a review of available literature, iron deficiency and anemia appear to be widespread throughout the world. It is very difficult, however, to assess the overall situation in each country, particularly among infants and young children, because of the lack of national data. It is even more difficult to get estimates of iron deficiency with or without anemia because parameters other than hemoglobin are not measured on a large scale. Nevertheless, a brief review will give us a general picture of the prevalence, pinpointing the extensiveness of the problem and the need for action.

In *Asia*, the prevalence of anemia among the various countries is more or less similar, with the exception of Japan, Korea, and possibly Malaysia and Singapore (Table 1). The anemia is mainly due to iron deficiency. The most affected population groups are pregnant women, infants, and young children.

In *Bangladesh*, the prevalence of anemia is high, caused by multiple factors including dietary deficiencies and parasitic infestation. The majority of children 4

TABLE 1. *Prevalence of nutritional anemia among infants and children in some selected countries in Asia and the Pacific*

Population	N	Prevalence (%)	Method/parameter	Reference
Bangladesh				
0–4 yr		82	Hb < 11 g%	K. Ahmad *(personal communication)*
5–14 yr				
male		74	Hb < 12 g%	
female		75	Hb < 12 g%	
Indonesia				
6 mo–5 yr		37.8–73		Soemantro et al. (8)
India				
5–15 yr				
urban	617	33.8	PCV response to iron	Singla et al. (9)
rural	493	69.4	supplementation	
China				
Kindergarten/ nursery school	1148	23.0	Hb < 11 g%	Hsue-Cun Chen *(personal communication)*
Malaysia/Singapore	30	83	Hb < 11 g%	Chong (10)
Philippines				
0–6 yr	220	42.2	Hb < 10.8 g%	Marzan et al. (11,12)
6 mo–6 yr	1883	46.0	Hb < 11.0 g%	
6–9 yr	175	47.2	Hb < 12.5 g%	
10–13 yr				
male	108	21.1	Hb < 12.5 g%	
female	123	32.0	Hb < 12.5 g%	

years of age and under are affected (prevalence of 82%) but older children between 5 to 14 years show a prevalence of 74%. Over 90% of the children have helminths.

In *Indonesia*, the prevalence among children between 6 months and 6 years of age belonging to a low socioeconomic but well-nourished group ranged from 37.8 to 73%; it was 83% in those with mild protein-energy malnutrition, and between 85 to 100% (8) in those with severe malnutrition. The prevalence in the middle and high socioeconomic (well-nourished) groups was reported to be 24%. The most significant cause of anemia was iron deficiency, with some reported folate deficiency among low-birth-weight infants, and vitamin B_{12} and possibly protein deficiencies. Intestinal parasitism is apparently an important factor; the incidence of hookworm infestation ranged from 22 to 93%.

In *India*, the prevalence has remained essentially the same since the 1960s. In a recent study involving 1,110 children 5 to 15 years of age, the prevalence of anemia based on packed-cell volume (PCV) response to iron supplementation was 34% in urban areas and 69% in rural areas (9). Some 26.7% in urban and 65.3% in rural areas had *Giardia lamblia* and *Ascaris lumbricoides*.

Among *Malaysians* and *Singaporeans*, the study by Loh and Chang (13) underscores the influence of economic status on the prevalence of iron deficiency. Their study of liver specimens for iron concentration in relation to age and ethnic groups consisting of Chinese, Malays, and Indians showed that the Chinese, presumably because of better socioeconomic status, had larger iron stores than the Malays and Indians. High iron concentrations were found during the neonatal period (2 years and younger) and low concentrations were found in childhood (2–11 years) and in adolescence (12–15 years). In a small study (10) of infants, 83% had <11 g% of hemoglobin.

In the *Philippines*, a high prevalence of anemia among various population groups has been reported in a series of studies by the Food and Nutrition Research Institute (14). The most affected groups were pregnant women, infants, and preschoolers. Iron deficiency was clearly the most prevalent type. Based on hemoglobin concentrations, in a study by Marzan et al. (11) involving 600 children from a lower socioeconomic group, 45% of children 9 years of age and under were anemic; the prevalence of anemia in older children was much less. Folate deficiency was observed in only 5 to 6% of the children. Among children, the most affected groups appear to be infants and toddlers; thereafter, the prevalence of anemia steadily declines with increasing age.

In another study of 331 Filipino children 9 months to 7 years old, it was shown that 60% of the children below 4 years of age were anemic whereas older children had a lower prevalence of 20% (12). Furthermore, it appears that the frequency of nutritional anemia increases as the degree of malnutrition becomes worse. Thus, under the Philippine Nutrition Program, it is advocated that in areas where no laboratory analysis can be done, all second- and third-degree malnourished children should receive iron preparations together with food intervention.

In another study by the Nutrition Center of the Philippines covering 1,883 preschoolers, a 46% prevalence of anemia was found (F. S. Solon, R. F. Florentino, et al., *unpublished data*). The same study showed a strong association between nutritional status and anemia.

In *Thailand*, hemoglobin and hematocrit surveys in various localities showed an overall prevalence of about 35%. Iron deficiency seems to be the major cause of anemia. A study in Chiengmai reported that high-protein and calorie supplementation to kwashiorkor and marasmic children increased the hemoglobin concentration, which was further increased by administration of iron but not by folate, riboflavin, or vitamins E or B_{12}, leading to the conclusion that anemia in protein-energy malnutrition (PEM) is due to protein deficiency with secondary iron deficiency (15).

In *China*, very little information is available. A study involving 1,148 kindergarten and nursery school children in Peking showed that 23% of the children had a hemoglobin concentration below 11 g%. Iron deficiency anemia was suspected to be widespread on the basis of unpublished data from other parts of the country (Hsue Cun Chen, *personal communication*).

In *South Korea*, a collaborative study conducted from 1968 to 1977 involving 1,318 cases of nutritional anemia showed that the most common type was due to iron deficiency (96%), with a 3.4% prevalence of megaloblastic anemia. However, the pattern of etiology at least in adults is different from that in most Asian countries, with excessive blood loss resulting from upper gastrointestinal bleeding and menorrhagia as the most common causes. There has been a steady decrease in the prevalence of anemia in recent years in this country, most probably as a result of the rapid socioeconomic development (16). The urban industrialization was obviously accompanied by improvements in housing, hygiene, and sanitation.

In *Iran*, a study by Froozani et al. showed that socioeconomic status affects the mother's nutritional status and consequently that of her offspring (17). This study involving 194 pregnant women randomly selected from a public hospital (representing low socioeconomic status) showed that the mean values of maternal hemoglobin, serum iron, percent transferrin saturation, and mean corpuscular hemoglobin concentration (MCHC) were significantly lower in the low socioeconomic group than in the higher socioeconomic group. The latter group had approximately 2.7 g/100 ml hemoglobin more than the former. The mean birth weight and the mean values of hemoglobin, serum iron, percent transferrin saturation, and MCHC of newborns from the mothers of low socioeconomic status were also significantly lower.

A review of prevalence studies from *Latin America* indicates that the prevalence of anemia appears to be similar to Asia, although again there are marked differences among countries (Table 2).

In *Argentina*, a prevalence of 16% was reported from Buenos Aires for a group of 147 normal full-term infants 15 to 370 days old. In Rosario City, a prevalence of 31% was found among underweight children, 23% among overweight children, and 30% among the children with normal weights, yielding a 28% prevalence for combined data (E. B. Calvo, *personal communication*).

Survey reports in *Bolivia* indicated a high prevalence of anemia among children (0–2 years, 44%; schoolchildren, 11.2%). The causal factors identified were the environment conducive to parasitic infestation, dietary inadequacies, and faulty practices in feeding. The warm low plains and valleys are highly infested with mosquitoes. In these areas 79% of children had ascaris and 12% were infected with hookworm. The iron absorption is generally low due to the low content of animal protein and the high content of phytates and oxalates (G. Daza and Z. Vargas, *personal communication*).

Despite scarcity of reported data in *Brazil*, iron deficiency anemia is believed to be a major public health problem. Results of prevalence studies in the North, the Northeast, and the state of Sao Paulo varied between 16.1 and 89% among children. This prevalence has been attributed to inadequate iron intake among the low-income population and the high frequency of intestinal parasitism (L. G. Tone and E. D. Oliveira, *personal communication*).

In *Costa Rica*, the prevalence of iron deficiency anemia has decreased during recent years (C. de Cespedes, *personal communication*). A national dietary survey in 1978 showed a good intake of iron from animal sources. It is believed that the wider availability of safe water with the ensuing decrease in parasitism has played a vital role in the apparent improvement of iron nutritional status. Reported

TABLE 2. *Prevalence of nutritional anemia among infants and children in some selected countries in Latin America and the Caribbean*

Population	N	Prevalence (%)	Method/ parameter	Reference
Bolivia				
0–2 yr		44.3		G. Daza and Z. Vargas
School children		11.2		*(personal communication)*
Brazil		16.1–89		L. G. Tone and E. D.
				Oliveira *(personal communication)*
Chile				
6–24 mo		20–40	<11 g%	A. Stekel *(personal communication)*
Costa Rica				
0–6 yr				
rural dense		7.4		C. de Cespedes *(personal*
rural dispersed		6.2		*communication)*
urban		6.9		
Barbados		32.7	Hb < 10.5 g%	Simmons et al. (18)
0–5 yr		9.3	Hb < 11.5 g%	
5–16 yr				
Argentina				
Preschool children				
Cordoba City	59	5.0		E. B. Calvo *(personal*
Rosario City	117	28.0		*communication)*
Infants (15–370 days)		16.0	Hb and Hct	
Middle Caicos Island				
0–5 yr		67.8	Hb < 10 g%	Simmons et al. (18)
6–13 yr		100.0	Hb < 12 g%	
Jamaica				
6–12 mo		76.0	Hb < 11 g%	Simmons et al. (18)
7–15 yr		4.8	Hb < 10 g%	
Guyana				
6 mo–5 yr		41.0	Hb < 11 g%	Simmons et al. (18)
6–14 yr		57.0	Hb < 12 g%	
Cayman Islands				
0–6 yr		42.7	Hb < 11 g%	Simmons et al. (18)
St. Lucia				
2–4 yr		14.3	Hb < 11 g%	Simmons et al. (18)
5–14 yr		36.4	Hb < 12 g%	
St. Kitts-Nevi's				
6 mo–4 yr		21.6	Hb < 11 g%	Simmons et al. (18)
5–16 yr		22.3	Hb < 12 g%	
Turks and Caicos Island				
0–5 yr		39.3	Hb < 10 g%	Simmons et al. (18)
6–13 yr		86.0	Hb < 12 g%	

percentages of iron deficiency among children under 6 years of age are as follows: 6.9% for urban, 7.4% for dense rural, and 6.2% for dispersed rural populations.

In *Chile*, the prevalence of iron deficiency, particularly in infancy, has been reported to be high (19). Surveys in urban lower class and lower middle-class socioeconomic groups have shown the presence of anemia in 20 to 40% of children between 6 and 24 months of age. The causative factors given were: short duration of breast-feeding, late introduction of solid foods in the diet, rare prescription of medicinal iron for prevention of iron deficiency, and essentially the absence of any iron-fortified product available for infants.

A field trial of iron-fortified milk was conducted, starting in 1972 (6,19). Healthy term infants who had been weaned before 3 months of age received either the fortified or the unfortified (control) milk until 15 months of age. At 9 and 15 months of age, there were significant differences in hemoglobin concentration between the two groups. Anemia (Hb < 11 g %) was present in 27.7% of the control infants at 9 months and in 34.6% at 15 months of age. Corresponding figures in the fortified groups were 20.7 and 12.7% at 9 and 15 months, respectively. This study in Chile clearly demonstrates that anemia among children can be controlled by the use of milk fortified with iron and vitamin C (6,19).

In the *English-speaking Caribbean* area, the situation regarding anemia is similar to that prevailing in other developing countries of the world. It is most common among pregnant and lactating women and among preschool-age children. The three major causes of anemia are reportedly poor nutrition, parasitic infections, and hemoglobinopathies. Although the first two causes are the most important from the epidemiological point of view, all three frequently interact. The most frequent cause is iron deficiency, probably due to inadequate intake and low absorption. A deficiency of folate is also suspected in the pathogenesis of the disease. Vitamin B_{12} deficiency is rarely seen, and this has been attributed to a fairly good intake of meat. The food consumption patterns of the population have been considerably influenced by the food marketing system, which developed during the colonial era. Caribbean countries maintain a heavy dependence on foreign sources for a substantial proportion of their dietary energy and protein food supplies (20). Since the people are predominantly black, the problem of sickle cell anemia must be considered. Studies have shown that about 0.8% are homozygous and 9.0% are heterozygous for sickle cell anemia (21). Parasitic infections related to anemia include hookworm, trichuria, and schistosomiasis.

Good data are available for Barbados, Guyana (22), Jamaica, Saint Lucia, and Trinidad and Tobago. Simmons and Gurney (20) have extensively reviewed the published literature and results of surveys in 13 countries from the 17-member countries of the Caribbean Food and Nutrition Institute. Among the preschool children, the highest prevalence was reported in the Middle Caicos Islands, where 68.7% had hemoglobin levels less than 10 g/dl. The lowest prevalence was noted in Saint Lucia, where 14.3% of the children 2 to 4 years old had hemoglobin levels below 11 g/dl. Prevalence rates among preschool children in other countries using the latter criterion were 76% among 6 months to 1 year in Jamaica, 41% among 6 months to 5 years in Guyana, and 42.7% among 0 to 6 years in Cayman Islands. Among school-age children, the highest prevalence of 100% was noted in the Middle Caicos Islands, whereas in Grenada the prevalence was 65% and in Guyana, 41 and 57% in two different studies. The lowest prevalence was observed in Barbados, with a prevalence rate of 9.3%.

Perhaps the most interesting and complex nature of anemia is seen in *Africa*. As described by Fleming (23) in his extensive review of anemia in the tropics, there is no clear pattern of anemia in tropical Africa. Causes of anemia are multiple. Aside from dietary iron deficiency, other common causes are malaria, hookworm, schistosomiasis, bacterial and viral infections, folate deficiency, and sickle cell disease. A high prevalence due largely to a low intake of iron has been reported from Gambia, Ivory Coast, Ghana, Northern Nigeria, Somalia, coastal and highland Kenya, Tanzania, Zambia and Mauritius.

The pattern of nutritional anemia is also largely affected by social customs. For example, social customs dictate the nature of employment and consequently determine the population group likely to be infected by hookworm. *Schistosoma haematobium* infections have been reported among Somalis in Northeast Kenya, frequently affecting adolescent boys (24). Up to 46% of boys with less than an 8 g% hemoglobin concentration had a schistosomiasis infection.

In the *United States*, the patterns of prevalence of iron deficiency in the population have emerged from large-scale surveys such as the National Health and Nutrition Examination Survey (NHANES) I and II, and the Ten-State and the Preschool Nutrition Survey. From large-scale surveys like these, however, it is often difficult to get detailed information on the prevalence among the most vulnerable groups, infants and children, due to their limited representation in the populations sampled. Data from NHANES II indicated that iron deficiency is still a problem, particularly in the first 3 years of life, where prevalence of anemia (Hb less than 11 g%) was 7 to 14% among whites and 11 to 39% among blacks (25). After the 12th year, the hemoglobin concentration of females was between 1 and 2 g/100 ml lower than that of the males. Blacks have consistently shown lower values than whites by about 0.8 g%. Other parameters showed the same trend, suggesting a genetic factor, although this has not been entirely resolved.

SUMMARY AND CONCLUSIONS

It may be said that it is difficult to estimate the prevalence of iron deficiency among infants and children worldwide because of the lack of national data, and the variations in the methods and criteria used for diagnosis. However, despite these limitations, it can be concluded that prevalence is high, especially in developing countries.

The causative factors are similar in all developing countries. Inadequate and poor quality of diet, together with parasitism and infections, are the most common immediate causes. These, however, are very much linked to socioeconomic development, so that it is expected that the prevalence of iron deficiency will not be reduced in the long term unless direct methods of control are complemented by improvements in socioeconomic conditions. In any event, data indicate that developed countries with low prevalence of iron deficiency and anemia are most certainly those that have active ongoing programs for the control of the problem. It would do well for developing countries to do the same.

In order to get a better picture of prevalence worldwide, it is suggested that parameters of iron deficiency be categorized into those for individual diagnosis and those for community diagnosis. Where prevalence surveys are conducted, especially in conjunction with supplementation trials, distribution analysis is a very useful tool to measure the impact of the program.

ACKNOWLEDGMENTS

The authors are grateful to Miss Luzviminda Cabotaje for technical assistance and to Ms. Teresita Panelo for clerical assistance in the preparation of this manuscript.

REFERENCES

1. Finch CA. Iron nutrition: food and nutrition in health and disease. Ann NY Acad Sci 1977;300:221.
2. Baker SJ, DeMaeyer EM. Nutritional anemia: its understanding and control with special reference to the work of the World Health Organization. Am J Clin Nutr 1979;32:368.
3. Cook JD. Current definition of deficiency anemia. In: Iron nutrition revisited—infancy, childhood, adolescence. Report of the eighty-second Ross Conference on Pediatric Research. Columbus, Ohio: Ross Laboratories, 1981:25.
4. Cook JD, Finch CA. Assessing iron status of a population. Am J Clin Nutr 1979;32:2115.
5. Dallman PR. Diagnostic criteria for iron deficiency. In: Iron nutrition revisited—infancy, childhood, adolescence. Report of the eighty-second Ross Conference on Pediatric Research. Columbus, Ohio: Ross Laboratories, 1981:3.
6. Iron Deficiency in Infancy and Childhood. A report of the International Nutritional Anemia Consultative Group. New York: The Nutrition Foundation, 1979.
7. Marzan AM, Ibe MG. Formulation of standards for hemoglobin and other nutritional anemia parameters for Filipinos. Phil J Nutr 1981;34:59.
8. Soemantro AG, Soenarto, Soedigbia I. Deficiency anemias in Indonesia. In: Lee M, Hong CY, Kim SI, eds. Proceedings, fourth meeting Asian Pacific Division, International Society of Hematology. Seoul: International Society of Hematology, Asian Pacific Division, 1979:125.
9. Singla PN, Agarwal KN, Singh RM, et al. Deficiency anemias in school children: estimation of prevalence based in response to haematinic supplementation. J Trop Pediatr 1980;26.
10. Chong YH. Recent trends in population and social indicators of food and nutrition in Malaysia. Med J Malaysia 1983;(in press).
11. Marzan AM, Tantengco VO, Caviles AP, Villaneuva LE. Nutritional anemia in Filipino infants and preschoolers. Southeast Asian J Trop Med Public Health 1974;5:90.
12. Marzan AM, Tantengco VO, Rapanot N. Malnutrition and anemia in young Filipino children. Southeast Asian J Trop Med Public Health 1974;5:265.
13. Loh TT, Chang LL. Hepatic iron status in Malaysians and Singaporeans. Southeast Asian J Trop Med Public Health 1980;11:131.
14. Food and Nutrition Research Institute. First Nationwide Nutrition Survey-Philippines, 1978. Manila, Philippines: National Science and Development Board, 1981.
15. Na-Nakorn S. Deficiency anemia in Thailand. In: Lee M, Hong CY, and Kim SI, eds. Proceedings, fourth meeting Asian Pacific Division, International Society of Hematology. Seoul: International Society of Hematology, Asian Pacific Division, 1979:147.
16. Hans JS. Deficiency anemia in Korea. In: Lee M, Hong CY, Kim SI, eds. Proceedings, fourth meeting Asian Pacific Division, International Society of Hematology. Seoul: International Society of Hematology, Asian Pacific Division, 1979;139.
17. Froozani MO, Vahdani F, Montazani K, et al. Maternal and newborn iron status in a public and a private maternity hospital at delivery in Tehran. Trop Pediatr Environ Child Health 1978;24:182.
18. Simmons WK, Jutsum PJ, et al. A survey of the anemia status of preschool age children and pregnant and lactating women in Jamaica. Am J Clin Nutr 1982;35:319.
19. Dallman PR, Siimes MA, Stekel A. Iron deficiency in infancy and childhood. Am J Clin Nutr 1980;33:86.

20. Simmons WK, Gurney JM. Nutritional anemia in the English-speaking Caribbean and Surinam. Am J Clin Nutr 1982;35:327.
21. Serjeant GR. The clinical features of sickle-cell disease. Amsterdam: North Holland Publishing Co., 1974.
22. Johnson AA, Latham MC, Rae DA. The prevalence and the etiology of the nutritional anemiasis in Guyana. Am J Clin Nutr 1982;35:309.
23. Fleming AF. Iron deficiency in the tropics. Clin Haematol 1982;2:359.
24. Greenham R. Anemia and *Schistosomia haematobium* infection in the northeastern province of Kenya. Trans R Soc Trop Med Hyg 1978;72:72.
25. Lane MJ, Johnson CL. Prevalence of iron deficiency. In: Iron nutrition revisited—infancy, childhood, adolescence. Report of the eighty-second Ross Conference on Pediatric Research. Columbus, Ohio: Ross Laboratories, 1981.

DISCUSSION

Dr. Florentino: When my paper was circulated to the reviewers before this meeting, one of the major comments was that more emphasis should be put on pediatric practice, and that is precisely what I tried to do in my presentation. This is very difficult, however, because of the lack of data on infants and children in many countries, but perhaps one could get some indication of the problem by looking at the overall prevalence in various countries. There are certain other comments about specific items in the paper, for example, hemoglobinopathies should not be listed as cause of iron deficiency but simply of anemia. On the matter of absorption enhancers, meat, fish, and ascorbic acid are the ones that are most significantly affecting food iron absorption. There is still no evidence that fiber is a strong factor for diminishing iron absorption. There is a question about whether cereal-based diets would be adequate to satisfy the needs of children. From studies in the Philippines on absorption from cereal diets, we have been getting lower figures than the original estimates made before. We were talking about 5 or 10% absorption, but now we are getting figures of only 3% or even less in a rice-based diet. Based on this and on the theoretical figures of iron requirements as judged from absorption studies and iron losses, it would indeed be very difficult to satisfy the iron requirements of the infant with a cereal-based diet. The use of ascorbic acid as an enhancer presents problems in developing countries because ascorbic-acid-rich foods are not much given to infants and young children, and ascorbic acid is generally not given as a supplement in most of these countries.

Dr. Dallman: During Dr. Florentino's presentation I realized how much less ambiguous it is to talk about prevalence of iron deficiency when anemia is common. Much of the perspective of my talk was based on an industrialized country where prevalence of iron deficiency is relatively low. Under such circumstances, a small error in reference values for hemoglobin can have a major effect on the estimated prevalence of anemia. This is not such a serious problem when as many as 60% of subjects are considered anemic.

Dr. Siimes: Nevertheless, in the United States high figures of infantile iron deficiency are continuously reported. In contrast, in the Scandinavian countries with a similar standard of living as in the United States, it is extremely difficult to find an infant with iron deficiency. The difference between the Scandinavian and the American way of feeding these infants may be the use of breast milk, followed by iron-supplemented formulas and the time of introduction of cereals and solid foods that may or may not be supplemented with iron.

Dr. Stekel: I think that Dr. Siimes's comments on what happens in a highly developed society, especially in infants, are of interest. Since nutritional factors are the most important etiological factors of iron deficiency at this age, I think that prevalence in the first 2 years of life becomes a very good test of what are the feeding practices and the availability of iron in foods that are used in a community. Probably the answer to the question lies in the way infants are being fed in Scandinavia today—how early they are given fortified foods, what kind of fortification iron is used. I think this is very important to analyze.

Dr. DeMaeyer: It is a common observation that the nutritional status improves with socioeconomic development; the iron status, however, may be an exception. Higher standards of living often are accompanied by a decrease in breast-feeding and a tendency to feed young children a diet rich in milk, with the consequence that anemia becomes relatively frequent in preschool-age children. In adults, energy requirements become smaller and the energy intake decreases. Since iron intake is closely linked to the energy intake, approximately 6 mg iron/1,000 calories in a Western diet, the iron intake becomes lower and some groups of population, especially women in the reproductive age, become iron-deficient. It is therefore obvious that an improvement in the iron status of a population does not necessarily accompany socioeconomic development.

Dr. Stekel: I think that your point is very well taken. A good example is what is happening in Chile, where socioeconomic conditions have improved and specific programs of general nutrition intervention have taken place, but where no systematic program for prevention of iron deficiency exists. In the last 20 years we have seen a marked decrease in general malnutrition; severe protein-calorie malnutrition today is less than 1% and there has been a marked decrease in infant mortality rate from a figure of 120 per 1,000 live births 20 years ago to 27.2 last year. Despite these improvements in general health and nutrition, the prevalence of iron deficiency anemia in infants has remained almost exactly the same: 30 to 35% at about 1 year of age.

Dr. Hallberg: The prevalence pattern (e.g., prevalence in infants, preschool children, pregnant and nonpregnant women) may be quite different in different countries as the health service systems may have given different priorities to the problem. In Sweden in the mid-1960s, for example, there was almost no iron deficiency in infants and children, but a prevalence of 25 to 30% in women of childbearing age. Now the latter prevalence has gone down to about 7% and there is almost no iron deficiency in infants. In school children today, however, there is an increased risk for iron deficiency to develop as the diet patterns are changing. Many school children are expected to have their main meals at school just as the parents have their main meals at their work at lunch. But many children are careless about their school lunch and sometimes the nutritional value of the meal does not at all meet the requirements when analyzing what is actually served on the plates.

Dr. Guzman: Could the experts here present make some suggestions as to what should be the hemoglobin cutoff point considering the local situation.

Dr. Garby: Well, I think this touches on what was discussed yesterday, that is to agree that we have very little indication that there should be any different standards in different countries apart from the small difference of hemoglobin concentration that has been documented in some black populations in the United States. So, I don't think there is much basis for discussion whether standards should be different in developing countries. Of course, the important question that you are asking is what are the standards one should select for taking action, for intervention, and this is what is going to be very difficult to agree on and will depend on the conditions in each country.

Dr. Cook: I suggest that we continue to use WHO cutoff values for anemia because it seems to me that these are still valid.

Dr. Dallman: I agree that the WHO values are remarkably good. However, when you are dealing with a low prevalence of anemia, as in Sweden and the United States, you have to refine those values further according to age; otherwise there are large errors at the ages when the WHO criteria for anemia suddenly change by 1.0 g/dl or more. Such errors can amount to as much as 10% for prevalence of anemia at those ages.

Dr. Cook: I question what components of a nutrition-education program designed to improve iron status in a population should be emphasized. In a recent study, we were unable to demonstrate any effect on iron stores of placing a group of adult volunteer subjects on 2 g ascorbic acid daily for two years. With respect to an educational program, it is probably advisable to recommend a high intake of iron-rich and animal foods. Beyond this, I am hesitant to stress the importance of dietary bioavailability until we have more evidence that this correlates with iron status.

Dr. Dallman: In reference to Dr. Cook's findings, it seems possible that megadoses of ascorbic acid had little effect because base-line ascorbic levels were already more than adequate. It is possible that the enhancing effect of additional ascorbic acid is only striking when base-line ascorbic acid intake is relatively low.

Dr. Florentino: I would like to go back to the issue of critical prevalence in well-fed populations when the problem may be considered of public health significance. This issue is important because it might serve as a basis for recommendations for developing countries and for planning purposes. Mention was made about the figure of 2.5% of the population below the WHO standards, and I think it was Dr. Cook who suggested that this should be somewhat higher. I would be happy if we could agree on something much more definite. I would think that just getting 2.5% on the basis of statistical considerations might not be enough and, as Dr. Cook said, because of realities it might be something higher, around 4%. What does the group think?

Dr. Cook: Because WHO criteria of anemia are specified in whole numbers, I think we can assume that they do not represent the exact 2.5% cutoff level.

Dr. Stekel: I think that after seeing these figures and hearing these comments, we agree with Dr. Hallberg's comment that it is amazing how well the WHO criteria fit the very careful studies that have been done recently. I think that those criteria are excellent and should be continued to be used.

Dr. Fomon: I should like to ask Dr. Florentino about the suggestion made in his paper that vitamin B_{12} deficiency might be contributory to the anemias observed in some of the developing countries. I know that vegetarians living under highly sanitary conditions in industrialized countries may develop vitamin B_{12} deficiency, but I have been under the impression that such conditions do not exist in developing countries. I had thought that small amounts of vitamin B_{12} would be ingested inadvertently in the form of bacteria, insects, human or animal feces, or other sources, and that these small amounts of vitamin B_{12} would be sufficient to prevent development of deficiency.

Dr. Chandra: In studies that we did several years ago it was found that among infants and preschool children with anemia about 1 in 10 responded to B_{12} administration. Often, these were infants breast-fed by vegetarian mothers who may have been B_{12}-deficient themselves. This deficiency may be due to dietary factors and, even more importantly, small intestinal disorders often lumped together as tropical gastroentropathy.

Iron Nutrition in Infancy and Childhood,
edited by A. Stekel. Nestlé, Vevey/Raven Press,
New York © 1984.

Iron Nutrition in Low-Birth-Weight Infants

Martti A. Siimes

*Pediatric Hematology Division, Children's Hospital, University of Helsinki,
SF-00290 Helsinki 29, Finland*

Since the early 1920s pediatric textbooks have recognized that infants often become anemic a few months after a preterm birth. However, except for its greater severity, the anemia does not differ in any way from that of full-term infants. It can be divided into an early and a late anemia of prematurity. The early anemia represents the initial fall in concentration of hemoglobin which occurs during the first 2 months after birth. The degree of severity varies with the gestational age and the vitamin E nutrition of the premature. In contrast, the late anemia may start at any time from 2 months on, depending on the time when the premature infant's iron supply is exhausted. Over the last 60 years, increasing doses of iron have been recommended for prematures in order to compensate for the rapid growth and to prevent the late anemia. Daily doses of 10 or 20 mg/kg body weight are currently being given by many pediatricians. These doses are far above what we currently consider to be optimal for these infants.

GROWTH AND IRON NEEDS

During the last 10 years, there has been a remarkable improvement in the survival ratio of very-low-birth-weight (VLBW) infants. Table 1 compares the body composition in iron of a VLBW infant with that of a full-term infant. The latter, who grows from 3.2 kg at birth to 10 kg at 1 year of age increases his total body iron content from 210 to 365 mg. Thus, the estimated increase in total body iron is about 50%, although the body weight triples during the same time. A VLBW infant with a birth weight of 0.8 kg may increase his weight 10-fold during the first year.

TABLE 1. *Influence of growth on estimated iron needs
in infants with birth weights of 0.8, 1.6, and 3.2 kg*

| Initial birth weight (kg) | Increments in 12 months | | Ratio iron/weight (mg/kg) |
	Body weight (kg)	Body iron (mg)	
0.8	7.2	210	29
1.6	7.9	215	27
3.2	6.8	155	23

The total body iron will increase from 50 mg of iron at birth to 260 mg at 1 year of age, representing a fivefold increase in total body iron. The need for iron in very rapidly growing low-birth-weight (LBW) infants is thus larger than one would estimate by the changes in body weight. Table 1 indicates that the changes in body iron over 12 months are similar in children with birth weights of 0.8 and 1.6 kg. However, the 0.8-kg infant eats less than the 1.6-kg infant; he therefore must obtain his iron from a considerably smaller volume of food, which may not be possible without supplementation with higher doses of iron.

SERUM FERRITIN AND IRON STORES

The role of iron stores is of particular importance in LBW infants since they are relatively large at the time of birth and will be used within a short period of time. For this reason the correlation between serum ferritin concentration and iron stores will be discussed here.

The first attempt to convert a serum ferritin value into a level of storage iron was published by Walters et al. in 1973 (1). They showed that 1 ng/ml of serum ferritin is equivalent to 8 mg of storage iron in adult tissues. Subsequently, a relationship of 1 ng/ml of serum ferritin to each 10 mg of storage iron has been suggested (2). Based on these observations, one might make a rough estimation that a serum ferritin level of 10 ng/ml would correspond to 100 mg of iron stored and a level of 100 ng/ml would correspond to 1,000 mg.

The concentration of serum ferritin is relatively high at the time of birth, about 200 to 250 ng/ml, which is similar to that of a healthy adult male (about 150–200 ng/ml) (3). This seems to indicate that the serum ferritin assay might be better correlated with the concentration of stored iron per kg of body weight which is similar in newborns (about 15 mg/kg) and adult males (about 10 mg/kg), than with the absolute quantities of stored iron, about 50 mg in the newborn and 700 mg in the adult male.

The correlation between serum ferritin and storage iron, however, presents some problems. Jacob et al. have shown that serum ferritin levels fall more rapidly when iron reserves are abundant than when they are reduced (4), indicating a curvilinear response in an individual subject. It is also possible that the relationship between iron stores and serum ferritin is different in adults and in infants or that serum ferritin is not directly related to the iron stores but rather reflects the status of some labile iron pool. A fairly sudden increase in iron stores when the destruction of red blood cells exceeds production, as during the early anemia of prematurity, may perhaps increase the ratio of serum ferritin to iron stores and thus leads to an overestimation of the changes in iron stores based on serum ferritin changes.

IRON IN THE FETUS

Several developmental changes occur in the erythropoiesis of the fetus. The site of red blood cell production is primarily in the liver after about 3 months of gestational age. The bone marrow takes over gradually, starting at around 5 months of gestational age (Fig. 1). Usually in a full-term infant the bone marrow is almost exclusively responsible for erythropoiesis. In preterm newborns the liver plays a role in erythropoiesis at birth. There are also other developmental changes that occur simultaneously. The size of the red cell gradually becomes smaller during fetal life so that the red cell mean corpuscular volume (MCV) tends to be larger in prematures than in full-term infants. The concentration of hemoglobin seems to rise in the fetus during pregnancy, although the details of this development are not well known. Finally, the fetal hemoglobin is partially replaced by adult hemoglobin at term. Thus, the prematures have proportionally more hemoglobin-F than the full-term newborns.

It is well known that the fetus accumulates iron in tissue stores during pregnancy. It has been estimated that the amount of iron stored at birth is about 15 mg/kg. There seems to be a linear correlation between the body weight and quantity of total body iron (6). The concentration of serum ferritin, when estimated in cord blood, appears to be similar or lower in preterm infants at birth or in fetuses after operative abortion than in term infants (Fig. 2).

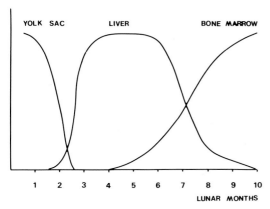

FIG. 1. The stages of hematopoiesis in the developing embryo and fetus (5).

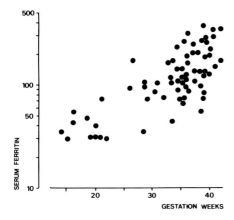

FIG. 2. Concentration of serum ferritin in cord blood serum from premature infants and fetuses aborted by laparotomy. The values are shown by gestational age.

A few fetal conditions or diseases result in low concentrations of serum ferritin at birth; these are maternal iron deficiency anemia and diabetes mellitus and occasionally conditions resulting in small-for-date newborns. In Fig. 3, storage iron has been calculated from the serum ferritin values and the respective body weights, assuming that the concentration of serum ferritin is proportional to the concentration of storage iron during this period of development. Figure 3 indicates that small-for-date infants tend to have less storage iron at birth than the controls.

We have very little information on any mechanism that regulates the accumulation of fetal iron stores. An interesting observation, that twins with separate placentas usually have similar concentrations of serum ferritin at birth (Fig. 4), may indicate that maternal iron rather than placental iron determines the accumulation of fetal iron stores. Against the placental regulation is also the finding that there is no correlation between the birth weight and the concentration of serum ferritin at birth in pairs of twins in conditions where one twin is growth retarded.

There seems to be little or no correlation between maternal hemoglobin or serum iron levels and the respective values in the newborn under normal conditions. Even in extreme cases of maternal iron deficiency anemia, the newborn can maintain a normal or only slightly decreased concentration of hemoglobin at birth (7). These observations indicate that fetal iron is well protected in practically all conditions, although the responsible mechanisms are not well understood.

HUMAN MILK FEEDING

In recent years there has been a return to the feeding of human milk to infants, after a period of several decades during which the use of proprietary formulas

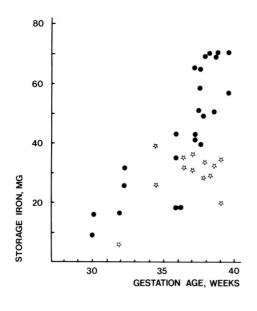

FIG. 3. Storage iron in small-for-date infants at birth. Storage iron has been calculated from the serum ferritin concentration and the body weight at birth.

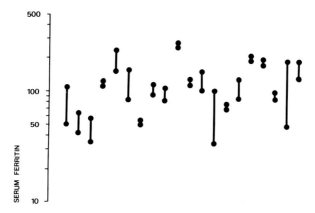

FIG. 4. Serum ferritin concentrations in 20 pairs of twins at birth. The values are presented by order of gestational age, from 19 to 39 weeks. The closed circles located next to each other indicate that the values were similar in both twins.

predominated in most industrialized countries. In Finland, the formulas never gained widespread acceptance in the feeding of premature infants; human milk has been in almost continuous use. Thus, human milk banking has been carried out on a relatively large scale. About 5,000 liters per million individuals are collected annually and used for this purpose. The iron concentration of human milk gradually decreases from a mean value of around 0.6 mg/liter soon after the birth of a full-term infant to a mean value of about 0.3 mg/liter after 6 months of lactation (8). Thus, the average banked human milk contains less iron than the milk collected immediately after delivery since it is collected mostly from mothers 2 to 3 months after delivery. Thus, the prematures receiving banked human milk ingest less iron than breast-fed full-term infants soon after birth.

In Finland, about half of the mothers who deliver VLBW infants of less than 1,500 g at birth are able to lactate enough so that the infants can be fed with their own milk. This way of feeding prematures has some advantages over banked human milk, since the milk contains more protein than the milk after a normal pregnancy. The composition also seems to be different in other respects and meets the nutritional needs of the premature infant (9). On the average, the iron content of the milk of mothers of VLBW infants is greater than the iron content of banked human milk. It should be noted, however, that the iron content of the milk secreted by some mothers is unusually low, far below the average value. There is no practical way of identifying these mothers. A premature infant would, in such a case, get much less iron from his own mother than from pooled banked human milk and be more dependent on supplementary iron. It is not clear whether the iron concentration of human milk can be influenced by maternal iron supplementation during lactation. Such supplementation might potentially be a means to improve both the infant's and mother's iron nutrition.

HUMAN MILK IRON AVAILABILITY

McMillan et al. have studied a small group of infants who were exclusively fed with human milk without any iron supplementation for periods of over a year (10). These individuals had a normal concentration of hemoglobin and serum ferritin at the end of the study. More recently, a similar study of a group of 7 infants has been published (11). It was also concluded that the infants had no signs of iron deficiency even if they received no iron supplement. Under these conditions, the availability of human milk iron must be extremely high since the concentration of iron in human milk is relatively low and decreases with the length of lactation, as discussed earlier (8). Thus both studies appear to indicate that the absorption of iron from human milk is unique and that the magnitude of the absorption should be somewhere between 50 and 100%. It is interesting that similar conclusions have also been made in studies where the extrinsic tag method for the determination of absorption of iron from human milk has been used (12).

The absorption of iron from any milk is higher in prematures than in full-term infants (13,14). Järvenpää et al. have recently observed that exclusively human-milk-fed VLBW infants (body weight lower than 1,250 g) who were getting iron supplementation from 2 months of age on had a higher concentration of hemoglobin and serum ferritin at 4 months of age than another group that was formula fed and given supplemented iron from birth on (15) (Table 2). This observation indicates that supplementary iron is better absorbed from human milk than from a formula in small LBW infants (15).

TABLE 2. *Mean (± SE) concentration of hemoglobin, serum ferritin, and free erythrocyte protoporphyrins in preterm infants (birth weight < 1,250 g) fed either human milk (n = 12 at 3 months, n = 9 at 4 months) or iron-supplemented formula (n = 32 at 3 months, n = 39 at 4 months)[a]*

	3 months	4 months
Hemoglobin (g/dl)		
Human milk	10.9 ± 0.4	12.3 ± 0.2[b]
Formula	10.2 ± 0.2	11.3 ± 0.2
Ferritin (ng/ml)		
Human milk	59 (50–69)	50 (39–65)[c]
Formula	40 (35–46)	18 (16–20)
Protoporphyrin		
Human milk	100 ± 23	64 ± 14
Formula	81 ± 6	81 ± 7

[a]The formula contained 12 mg of iron/liter. Infants fed human milk received iron supplementation (2 mg/kg/day) from 2 months of age on (15).
[b]$P < 0.02$.
[c]$P < 0.001$.

The reasons for the high bioavailability of the human milk iron are not known. Recent studies have shown that the concentration of iron in milk varies during the day and with age (8).

Lactoferrin is a major iron-binding protein in milk. The degree of its iron saturation is reported to be low. Further, some reports indicate that this protein actually decreases absorption of iron from human milk (16). Schäfer et al. have shown that a considerable part of the milk iron is bound to fat (17). Other investigators have identified part of the iron in cow's milk in the membrane of fat globules.

The variations in concentrations of iron, fat, and lactoferrin during a single nursing are shown in Fig. 5. Lactoferrin concentration decreased while concentrations of fat and iron increased in human milk with the volume of milk expressed.

Fransson and Lönnerdal have shown that a very small fraction of the iron in human milk is bound to lactoferrin, and that the latter is very unsaturated (18) (Table 3). They therefore believed that iron concentration is not correlated with lactoferrin concentration. Rather it is a reflection of the metabolic activity of the mammary gland as both protein and trace minerals progressively decline over the course of lactation. Fransson and Lönnerdal's data indicate that the iron saturation of lactoferrin is very low, at the most 4%. This is considerably lower than values reported earlier, which ranged between 10 and 40%. The low saturation may be justified by the role that lactoferrin plays in the defense against infections. It has been suggested that increasing the iron saturation of lactoferrin may result in a decrease of its bacteriostatic properties.

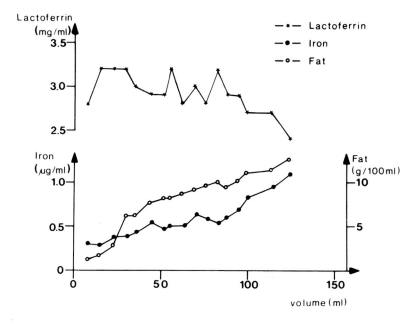

FIG. 5. Concentration of iron, fat, and lactoferrin during the course of a single nursing (18).

TABLE 3. *Iron saturation of lactoferrin*

Maximum percentage of Fe bound to lactoferrin[a]	Maximum amount of Fe bound to lactoferrin (μg/ml)[b]	Iron-binding capacity (μg/ml)[c]	Maximum saturation of lactoferrin (%)[d]
24 (16–40)	0.10 (0.04–0.23)	5.4 (2.4–14.8)	2 (1–4)

[a]100-(fat Fe)-(solids Fe)-(LMW Fe) %.
[b]Maximum % × Fe concentration (μg/ml).
[c]Concentration of lactoferrin (in moles) × 2 (each molecule binds 2 Fe) converted to μg/ml.
[d]Maximum amount of Fe bound to lactoferrin/iron-binding capacity.
Data from Fransson and Lönnerdal (18).

TABLE 4. *Percentage of iron distribution in human milk[a]*

Fat	Solids and semisolids	Low-molecular-weight compounds
30 (15–46)	9 (0–34)	36 (18–56)

[a]Data from 13–15 milk samples (18).

The unique studies of Fransson and Lönnerdal further demonstrated, by use of ultrafiltration and gel filtration techniques, that a considerable fraction of the iron in human milk is bound to low molecular weight compounds (18) (Table 4). These compounds may have very high association constants for iron, which could explain why more iron is not bound to lactoferrin. On the other hand, Lönnerdal et al. (19) have shown that citrate, which is present in a comparatively high concentration, binds a large part of the zinc in human milk, but the iron-binding compounds still have to be identified.

IRON SUPPLEMENTATION

Lundström et al. (20) have shown that there was no significant difference in hemoglobin concentration, MCV, or transferrin saturation between two groups of infants weighing at birth between 1 and 2 kg receiving no iron supplementation or 2 mg iron/kg/day between 2 weeks and 2 months of age (Figs. 6 and 7). At 2 months, however, the serum ferritin concentration was lower in the group receiving no iron supplement. This value (42 ng/ml) was still higher than the normal one for children, indicating that the unsupplemented infants were not iron deficient, even though the developmental low point in hemoglobin concentration occurs at this age. Only 7% of those who were not iron supplemented has a serum ferritin concentration below 10 ng/ml, a value which may indicate depleted iron stores and increased risk of developing iron deficiency anemia. Figures 6 and 7, however, clearly show that LBW infants cannot maintain optimal iron nutrition without iron supplementation after the age of 2 months. The hemoglobin as well as the MCV

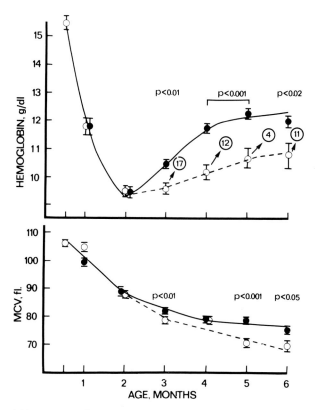

FIG. 6. Hemoglobin concentration and mean corpuscular volume (MCV) in LBW infants who received no iron supplementation *(open circles)* or 2 mg iron/kg/day from 2 weeks of age on *(closed circles)* (20). Means ± SEM are indicated. Differences between the groups became significant at 3 months of age. The number of unsupplemented infants receiving iron supplementation because of anemia is shown within circles for each age.

of red blood cells, the transferrin iron saturation, and the serum ferritin were all significantly lower in the unsupplemented infants. The difference in hemoglobin averaged 1 to 2 g/dl during a follow-up period of up to 6 months. This difference would have been greater if many of the unsupplemented infants had not received iron once the diagnosis of anemia was made.

It is difficult to indicate what is the optimal dose of iron as supplement because individual needs for iron may vary with birth weight, neonatal sickness, and blood loss. Some data indicate that infants, whose birth weight ranged between 1 and 2 kg, who were given 2 mg of iron/kg/day did not show clinical iron deficiency (20). The dose was probably adequate and was certainly not excessive for the maintenance of iron stores. However, high frequency of borderline serum ferritin values were found although no anemia was documented (20). It could be argued that a higher dose of iron such as 3 mg/kg/day would provide a more comfortable margin of safety, especially in those infants with a birth weight between 1 and 1½ kg.

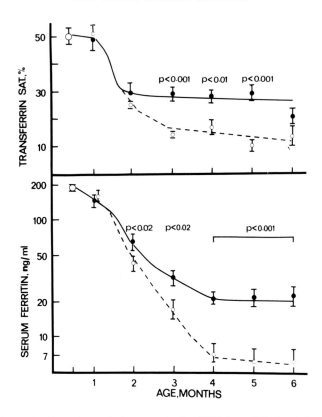

FIG. 7. Serum ferritin and transferrin saturation in LBW infants (20). Symbols as in Fig. 6.

Some recent data indicate that 4 mg of iron/kg/day administered to a group of VLBW infants with a birth weight of less than 1,000 g prevent most laboratory signs of iron deficiency (21) (Figs. 8 and 9). There was, however, a marked decline in serum ferritin despite the large dose of iron administered.

MAINTENANCE OF HEMOGLOBIN CONCENTRATION

Preterm infants experience a fall in hemoglobin concentration during the first 2 months of life that is more marked than in term infants (Table 5). It seems that the fall varies with the birth weight, even if supposedly adequate iron supplementation is provided (Fig. 10). Thus the early anemia of prematurity, which results in low hemoglobin values at 2 months of age, cannot be prevented by iron supplementation and should therefore be considered as physiological.

Lundström and Siimes (22) have shown that despite the great demands of rapid growth and the rapid increase of blood volume, the LBW infants with a birth weight above 1 kg achieve an erythrocyte count, hemoglobin concentration, and red cell indices of term infants during the first half year of life when sufficient iron is administered.

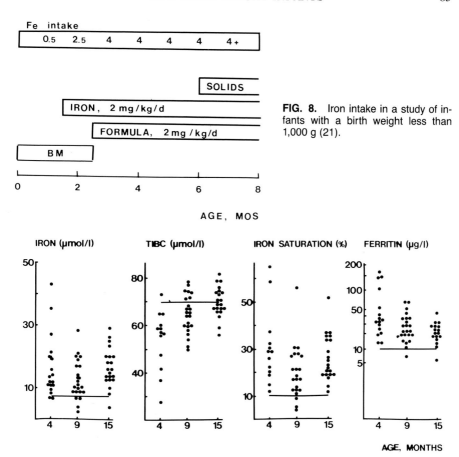

FIG. 8. Iron intake in a study of infants with a birth weight less than 1,000 g (21).

FIG. 9. Iron status of VLBW infants (less than 1,000 g) up to 15 months after birth (21). Iron was given as shown in Fig. 8. The *horizontal lines* indicate the lower or upper (in the case of total iron-binding capacity, TIBC) limits which might be considered as normal in full-term infants.

Very-low-birth-weight infants with a birth weight less than 1 kg form an exceptional group among prematures. They achieve a remarkably rapid rate of postnatal growth (Fig. 11) and present unusually high nutritional requirements. In many cases the birth weight is increased by 10-fold or more during the 15 months following birth. However, there is an unusually large individual variation in weight gain. One might anticipate that the concentration of hemoglobin might be lowest in those infants with the most rapid rate of growth, but there is no significant relationship between these values (21) (Fig. 12). Even VLBW infants are apparently able to absorb the iron needed for their high requirements. The lack of a relationship between growth rate and hemoglobin concentration not only argues against the likelihood that iron is a limiting factor in hemoglobin production under these conditions, but also makes it less likely that a deficiency of other nutrients could play a major role in limiting hemoglobin production.

TABLE 5. *Hemoglobin concentrations (g/dl) for preterm infants with serum ferritin levels ≥ 10 ng/ml (median and 95% range)*

| | Birth weight | |
Age	1,000–1,500 g	1,501–2,000 g
2 wk	16.3 (11.7–18.4)	14.8 (11.8–19.6)
1 mo	10.9 (8.7–15.2)	11.5 (8.2–15.0)
2 mo	8.8 (7.1–11.5)	9.4 (8.0–11.4)
3 mo	9.8 (8.9–11.2)	10.2 (9.3–11.8)
4 mo	11.3 (9.1–13.1)	11.3 (9.1–13.1)
5 mo	11.6 (10.2–14.3)	11.8 (10.4–13.0)
6 mo	12.0 (9.4–13.8)	11.8 (10.7–12.6)

Data from Lundström and Siimes (22).

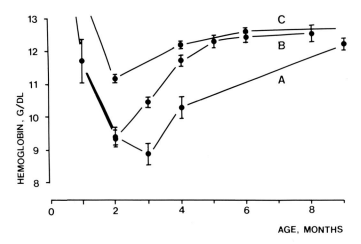

FIG. 10. Concentration of hemoglobin in iron-supplemented infants after birth. *A* = VLBW infants with a birth weight less than 1,000 g who were given iron (4 mg/kg/day); *B* = LBW infants with a birth weight of about 1,500 g who were given 2 mg iron/kg/day; *C* = full-term infants with a birth weight over 3,000 g who were given 1 mg iron/kg/day.

It is interesting that the return to normal hemoglobin concentration takes a considerably longer time in prematures with a birth weight lower than 1 kg than in larger premature infants (Fig. 10), although they were supplemented with 4 mg of iron/kg/day and there was little or no evidence of iron deficiency.

It is rare that an infant with a birth weight lower than 1 kg is treated without many laboratory studies, yet those who are compensate for such blood loss remarkably well (21). There are some infants who require no transfusion and maintain their subsequent hemoglobin concentration at levels similar to those of infants who are given transfusions (Table 6). This is another indication that regulation of iron absorption is well developed in these small infants and that provision of additional iron can effectively prevent the development of iron deficiency.

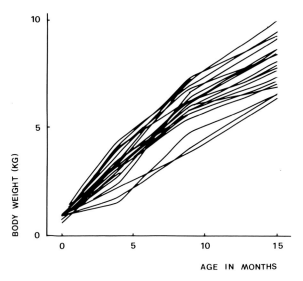

FIG. 11. Growth of VLBW infants (21).

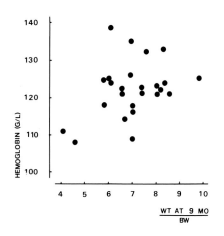

FIG. 12. Concentration of hemoglobin in VLBW infants (less than 1,000 g) (21). The concentration of hemoglobin at 9 months of age is correlated with the growth rate (body weight at 9 months/birth weight). No correlation was found.

ROLE OF VITAMIN E AND SELENIUM

One of the roles of vitamin E is the protection of biological membranes against oxidative breakdown of lipids. Premature infants are born with low serum levels of vitamin E. Feeding these infants diets rich in polyunsaturated fatty acids, particularly when the diet is supplemented with iron, can produce a hemolytic anemia if the vitamin E deficiency is not corrected (Fig. 13). Melhorn and Gross (23) have demonstrated that in VLBW infants the daily administration of 7 to 10 mg of iron/kg/day accelerates the postnatal decline in the concentration of hemoglobin. Williams et al. (24) observed increased hemolysis and lower hemoglobin levels in small premature infants fed formulas with a high polyunsaturated fatty acid content, especially when the formulas were fortified with iron. Melhorn and

TABLE 6. *Mean (± SE) hemoglobin concentration (g/dl) in 6 VLBW infants without and in 22 VLBW infants with blood transfusions during the first 2 months of life*[a]

Age in months	Without transfusion	With transfusion
Birth	18.8 ± 1.1 [6]	16.0 ± 0.7 [21]
1	11.5 ± 1.0 [5]	11.8 ± 0.4 [21]
2	9.1 ± 0.5 [6]	9.5 ± 0.4 [22]
3	9.3 ± 0.3 [4]	8.8 ± 0.4 [20]
4	10.9 + 0.3 [6]	10.1 ± 0.3 [19]
9	12.2 ± 0.1 [6]	12.2 ± 0.2 [20]
15	13.1 ± 0.4 [6]	13.0 ± 0.2 [18]

[a]The number of subjects is shown in brackets (21).

Gross have explored the relationship between gestational age and absorption of vitamin E (25). Their studies show that during the first 3 weeks of life, infants with a birth weight of less than 1,500 g and a gestational age of less than 32 weeks have decreased absorption of vitamin E. A subsequent study with a water soluble vitamin E preparation demonstrated better absorption, but the individual levels were not predictable. Greaber et al. (26) demonstrated that vitamin E adequacy, as defined by serum tocopherol levels and hydrogen peroxide hemolysis tests, can be achieved rapidly and safely by the intramuscular administration of DL-α-tocopherol. The results indicate that an intramuscular dose of vitamin E of 125 mg/kg administered over the first week of life is sufficient to maintain vitamin E adequacy during the first 6 weeks of life, even in the presence of intramuscular iron. Aside from mild erythema at the injection site, no detectable reaction could be related to vitamin E administration. In a recent article, Phelps has reviewed the potential dangers of vitamin E administration (27).

Rudolph et al. (28) have recently studied the role of selenium in LBW infants fed formulas with and without iron. Under the experimental conditions, there was no evidence of any association between selenium and early anemia of prematurity.

INTERRELATIONSHIP WITH COPPER

The metabolisms of copper and iron are linked together in many ways. The question is whether copper deficiency exists in infants after preterm delivery and, if so, whether it has any influence on iron metabolism. It has been shown that the serum concentration of copper is lower in preterm than in full-term infants during the first months after birth (29). However, it is difficult to estimate the significance of this finding. Any form of copper supplementation in formula-fed infants leads to another problem since the amount of copper ingested is primarily dependent on the copper concentration of the water that is added to the formula powder. The concentration in water varies between areas and even between houses within the same city.

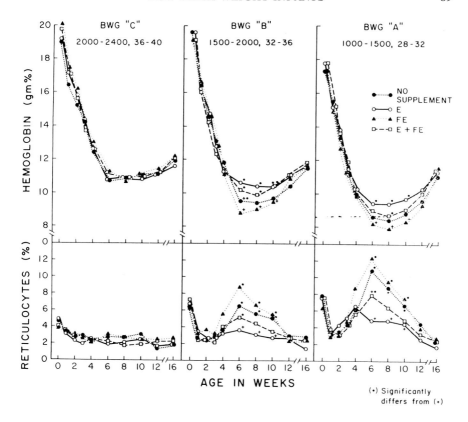

FIG. 13. Concentrations of hemoglobin in premature infants with a birth weight of 1,000–1,500 g (25). All infants were fed formula without added iron and a multiple vitamin mixture containing vitamins A, C, and D. The infants were assigned to one of the four groups as follows: *A* = no additional supplement; *B* = ferrous sulphate, 8 mg elemental iron/kg/day up to 6 weeks of age, then 8 mg/liter of formula; *C* = a-tocopherol acetate 25 IU/day between 2 and 6 weeks of age; *D* = both ferrous sulphate and a-tocopherol acetate. For the sake of clarity, first three groups are shown. The highest hemoglobin concentrations were in the vitamin-E–supplemented infants.

MOBILIZATION OF STORAGE IRON

The high physiologic concentration of hemoglobin at birth decreases to a low value at 2 months of age. This decrease in hemoglobin concentration initially results in a rise in tissue iron stores, which are subsequently used during the next 12 months to maintain a normal level of hemoglobin. In each of the developmental changes of infancy, there is a considerable individual variation, including the ability to mobilize iron from tissue stores. Thus, some infants may develop iron deficiency anemia although they have iron stores (determined by their serum ferritin values) and they have no disease, such as infection or inflammation, to explain their inability to mobilize iron stores (30). A similar situation may also occur in adults, although only after some significant blood loss. In contrast, in infants it may be physiological.

In fact, in a large series of healthy infants who were followed carefully during the first year of life, those with mild iron deficiency anemia usually had serum ferritin concentrations within the normal range (30). The relative abundance of storage iron in these cases may effectively inhibit the availability of iron from other sources, namely from intestinal absorption. Thus both sources of iron for hemoglobin synthesis, from tissue stores and from food, would be inhibited and this coincidence would subsequently increase the risk of developing iron deficiency anemia. Lundström et al. have also shown (Figs. 6 and 7) that in preterm infants anemia commonly develops prior to the time when iron stores become exhausted (20). This latter finding also indicates that the rate at which iron can be mobilized from tissues may not be fast enough in rapidly growing infants.

REFERENCES

1. Walters GO, Miller F, Worwood M. Serum ferritin concentration and iron stores in normal subjects. J Clin Pathol 1973;26:770–2.
2. Cook JD, Finch CA. Assessing iron status of a population. Am J Clin Nutr 1979;32:2115–9.
3. Siimes MA, Addiego JE, Dallman PR. Ferritin in serum: diagnosis of iron deficiency and iron overload in infants and children. Blood 1974;43:581–9.
4. Jacob RA, Sandstead HH, Klevay LM, Johnson LK. Utility of serum ferritin as a measure of iron deficiency in normal males undergoing repetitive phlebotomy. Blood 1980;56:786–9.
5. Wintrobe MM. Clinical hematology. Philadelphia: Lea and Febiger, 1961.
6. Widdowson EM, Spray CM. Chemical development in utero. Arch Dis Child 1951;26:205.
7. Dallman PR, Siimes MA, Stekel A. Iron deficiency in infancy and childhood. Am J Clin Nutr 1980;33:86–118.
8. Siimes MA, Vuori E, Kuitunen P. Breast milk iron: a declining concentration during the course of lactation. Acta Paediatr Scand 1979;68:29–31.
9. Rönnholm KER, Sipilä I, Siimes MA. Human milk protein supplementation prevent hypoproteinemia without metabolic imbalance in breast milk-fed very-low-birth-weight infants. J Pediatr 1982;101:243.
10. McMillan JA, Lansaw SA, Oski FA. Iron sufficiency in breast-fed infants and the availability of iron from human milk. Pediatrics 1976;58:686.
11. Pastel RA, Howanitz PJ, Oski FA. Iron sufficiency with prolonged exclusively breast-fed Peruvian infants. Clin Pediatr 1981;20:625–6.
12. Saarinen UM, Siimes MA, Dallman PR. Iron absorption from breast milk: high bioavailability of breast milk iron is indicated by the extrinsic tag method of iron absorption and by the concentration of serum ferritin. J. Pediatr 1977;91:36–9.
13. Bender-Götze C, Schmerlinki E, Heinrich HC. Cytochemic des Nichthämoglobineisens in Knochjenmarzellen und intestinale Eisenresorption bei vercheidenen Anämien des Kindesalters. Monatsschr. Kinderheilkd 1971;119:13.
14. Dauncey MJ, Davies CG, Shaw JCL, Urman J. The effect of iron supplements and blood transfusion on iron absorption by low birthweight infants fed pasteurized human breast milk. Pediatr Res 1978;12:899–904.
15. Järvenpää A-L, Räihä N, Gaull GE, Siimes MA. Human milk is superior to formula for iron nutrition also in preterm infants. (Submitted for publication.)
16. McMillan JA, Oski FA, Lourie G, Tomarelli RM, Lansaw SA. Iron absorption from human milk, simulated human milk, and proprietary formulas. Pediatrics 1977;60:896.
17. Schäfer KH, Breyer AM, Karte H. Das Spurenelement Eisen in Milch und Milchmisschungen. Z Kinderheilkd. 1955;76:501.
18. Fransson G-B, Lönnerdal B. Iron in human milk. J Pediatr 1980;96:380–4.
19. Lönnerdal B, Stanislowski AG, Hurley LS. Isolation and identification of a low molecular weight zinc binding ligand from human milk. Fed Proc 1979; 38:703.

20. Lundström U, Siimes MA, Dallman PR. At what age does iron supplementation become necessary in low-birth-weight infants. J Pediatr 1977;91:878–83.
21. Siimes MA, Järvenpää A-L. Prevention of anemia and iron deficiency in very low birth weight (VLBW) infants. J Pediatr 1982;101:277.
22. Lundström U, Siimes MA. Red blood cell values in low birth weight infants: ages at which values become equivalent to those of term infants. J Pediatr 1980;86:1040–2.
23. Melhorn DK, Gross S. Vitamin-E dependent anemia in the premature infants. I. Effects of large doses of medicinal iron. J Pediatr 1971;79:569.
24. Williams ML, Shott RJ, O'Neal PL, Oski FA. Role of dietary iron and fat on vitamin E deficiency anemia of infancy. N Engl J Med 1975;292:887.
25. Melhorn DK, Gross S. Vitamin-E dependent anemia in the premature infant. II. Relationships between gestational age and absorption of vitamin E. J Pediatr 1971;79:581.
26. Graeber JE, Williams ML, Oski FA. The use of intramuscular vitamin E in the premature infant. Optimum dose and iron interaction. J Pediatr 1977;90:282.
27. Phelps DL. Vitamin E and retrolental fibroplasia in 1982. Pediatrics 1982;70:420–5.
28. Rudolph N, Preis O, Bitzos EI, Reale MM, Wong SI. Hematologic and selenium status of low-birth-weight infants fed formula with and without iron. J Pediatr 1981;99:57.
29. Sann L, Rigal D, Galy G, Bienvenu F, Bourgeois J. Serum copper and zinc concentration in premature and small-for-date infants. Pediatr Res 1980;14:1040–6.
30. Saarinen UM, Siimes MA. Serum ferritin in assessment of iron nutrition in healthy infants. Acta Paediatr Scand 1978;67:745–51.

DISCUSSION

Dr. Hallberg: I have a comment about the relationship between iron stores and serum ferritin, which is used in the calculation of the changes in total body iron in infants. The relationship is based on four points: adult females, adult males, newborn infants, and infants 2 weeks old. The point used for adult males very probably overestimates the size of the iron stores. In these studies iron stores were measured by phlebotomy but no correction was made for the increased dietary iron absorption during the phlebotomy period. That gives a figure for iron stores which is about twice too high. (In 26 normal men the iron stores were 6.4 mg/kg body weight and serum ferritin 89 ng/ml.) These findings indicate that the relationship between iron stores and serum ferritin is different in adults and in infants. Another comment is that we don't know how the increased destruction of red cells after birth affects the serum ferritin level. I think that it is very difficult to interpret serum ferritin levels in nonsteady state conditions. I would therefore suggest that iron absorption calculations based on changes in serum ferritin must be looked at with great caution.

Dr. Finch: I would like to also comment on ferritin. I agree that ferritin should be equated to body weight in kilograms. We have considered that 1 µg of ferritin per liter is equivalent to about 140 µg of storage iron per kilogram body weight. It would be interesting to compare the value for ferritin in the newborn and then later, when there has been a known decrease in circulating red cell mass with an increase in iron storage and see how this correction applies. It is also of interest that ferritin levels appear to be increased when body metabolism is increased. Perhaps this would apply to the infant. Finally, I suppose one can raise the question of some tissue damage or inflammation since these conditions would give an inappropriately high ferritin concentration.

Dr. Siimes: It is well documented that there is a correlation between the concentration of serum ferritin and the level of iron stores. Dr. Hallberg started a discussion of the details of the correlation for which there are surprisingly few studies. Our drawing indicates that the correlation is better if both serum ferritin and iron stores are expressed in a specific way; the former as log values and the latter per unit of body weight. After this manipulation, the regression line is linear at all ages. Concerning the inflammation and infection, these conditions may raise the ferritin values and result in false high results, although chronic inflammations are very rare and acute infections relatively easy to recognize at this age.

Dr. Guesry: I was very interested by your comparison between human milk- and formula-fed babies because Royer in France who has published the same type of comparative study showed exactly the reverse: that babies fed with human milk from banks (and that is perhaps the difference) have a lower level of iron than babies receiving special formulas for premature babies. What was exactly the composition of the formula that your babies received?

Dr. Siimes: One difference may have been the birth weights: these were extremely low. The formula was a regular and humanized one containing the recommended amounts of vitamins and 12 mg of iron/liter.

Dr. Guesry: Did the babies who were not iron-deficient and were breast-fed up to the age of 18 months receive any iron supplement?

Dr. Siimes: The few infants recorded in the literature from the United States and Peru who were exclusively breast-fed received no iron supplementation. They developed no evidence of iron deficiency, although the number of cases was too small for conclusions. Nevertheless, I found it an interesting observation. In Finland, the pregnant mothers receive iron supplementation. It is my experience that the maternal iron supplementation during lactation does not influence the infants' iron status while they are exclusively breast-fed.

Dr. Chandra: What was the nature of the human milk fed to these babies? Was it their own mother's milk? We know that there are differences in the iron content of milk produced by mothers who deliver at preterm, compared with those who deliver at term, being almost twofold higher in the former.

Dr. Siimes: In this case it was banked milk.

Dr. Stekel: The implication of these figures is not only that they absorb the iron from breast milk but, probably more significantly so, that breast-fed infants absorb the supplementation iron better. Isn't that the implication?

Dr. Siimes: It could be there are other additional explanations, too. Possibly, chronic human milk ingestion decreases the physiological loss of iron through the intestinal tract.

Dr. Garby: You mentioned a study on iron isotope absorption from breast milk. I was wondering what is known about the isotopic exchange when you add labeled iron to breast milk.

Dr. Lönnerdal: We have been doing some studies on the distribution of an extrinsic tag in milk and compared this to the distribution of native iron. It doesn't seem that an extrinsic tag is distributed in the same manner as native iron in breast milk. The distribution of native and radioactive iron in cow's milk was more similar, but still not identical. In breast milk, an extrinsic tag almost exclusively binds to lactoferrin.

Dr. Garby: The distribution of labeled iron in the fractions must be related to the time of incubation, surely. There is no such thing as a distribution by itself; there is a distribution at a certain time.

Dr. Lönnerdal: It's true, but you can approach the problem from different angles. You can look at the starting point by incubating for an hour; the next thing you can do is to take a gastric aspirate from breast-fed infants and label it and look for the distribution. You can take tagged breast milk, incubate it at different pH, and look at the distribution again. It is not the true situation in the gastrointestinal tract, but you are approaching that situation at least. Both when we take the gastric aspirate and when we go down to pH 3 with HCl and when we are looking at it initially, a disproportionate part is definitely bound to lactoferrin. We do not see isotopic equilibrium in the breast milk.

Dr. Garby: I think you have misunderstood me. I do not want to imitate the conditions later on. One must be sure that one has incubated for sufficient time to have isotopic equilibrium. What I am saying is that, if after 1 hr of incubation at room temperature, the distribution is such and such, what is it after 2 hr, 24 hr, and so on?

Dr. Lönnerdal: This is not known as yet.

Dr. Cook: When the concept of the extrinsic tag was first presented, a number of investigators attempted to look at the distribution of radioiron incorporated biosynthetically as compared to the extrinsic tag. It was never possible to show that the distribution of the two tags in the food was similar. This does not necessarily argue against complete isotopic exchange of the extrinsic iron at some point in the gastrointestinal tract. One study that addresses the issue of isotopic exchange in milk is that of Schultz and Smith which showed that radioactive milk prepared by injecting a cow with radioiron was absorbed to the same extent as an extrinsic tag added to the milk. As far as I know, no one has prepared radioactive cow's milk since that time.

Dr. Fomon: In the study by Schulz and Smith [*Am. J. Dis. Child.* 95:109, 1958], iron absorption from cow's milk was studied in 10 subjects with the intrinsic tag and in 5 other subjects with the extrinsic tag. There was a wide range of ages (4–52 months) and, although none of the subjects was anemic, little information is available about iron nutritional status. I could not accept this study as a validation of the extrinsic tag method for determining iron absorption from cow's milk.

Dr. Cook: I agree completely. I think that this is the only observation that relates to the question.

Dr. Lönnerdal: I think we have to take account of the very specific properties of lactoferrin. First, the equilibrium of iron exchange between lactoferrin and other compounds is exceptionally slow, i.e., when you want to feed this solution it may not be fit for feeding anybody. So, coming back to Dr. Cook's comments, I think that there are a couple of factors that would speak against the fact that the conventionally assumed extrinsic-intrinsic iron exchange would happen. You have to go below pH 2 to release iron from lactoferrin. It is a very strong iron-binding protein. We are talking about a stomach of an infant where we do not even get down to that pH. The second point: lactoferrin is comparatively resistant to proteolysis. Both these points counteract the assumption that the extrinsic tag would behave as an intrinsic tag. I think in most cases that is true, but this may be an exception when it does not hold true.

Dr. Chandra: The large quantity of lactoferrin in human milk may permit the isotope label to be disproportionately tagged to it. Studies on this question must have at least two additional controls: human milk which has been depleted of lactoferrin using an immunosorbent column, and purified lactoferrin.

Dr. Dallman: From the discussion over the last 15 min, there seem to be some doubts about the reliability of the breast-milk iron absorption data. Even though there may be uncertainty about the exact values for iron absorption from breast milk, we should not lose sight of the very strong evidence that the percentage of iron absorbed from breast milk is much greater than from cow's milk or cow's milk formula.

Dr. Lönnerdal: I agree that there is a lot of support that it certainly is more available. I think we must exercise a little caution here about what is the absorption number. Dr. Siimes has indicated that in some cases you can almost calculate it to be 100%—in your case you got absorption of about 49 to 50%—maybe that was for the lactoferrin compartment which is just one part of total iron, maybe some of the other parts are better absorbed; the low molecular weight iron can have a very high availability and there is very little low molecular weight iron in the cow's milk, for example.

Dr. Siimes: I agree that the extrinsic tag method may result in underestimation rather than overestimation of iron absorption.

Dr. Guesry: I would like to come back to a suggestion made by Dr. Siimes that the difference between breast milk and formula is mainly due to protein allergy and there is now good information that the T helper cells are not mature in very-low-birth-weight infants and that there is little probability that this protein allergy would occur in a very-low-birth-weight infant.

Dr. Fomon:· That is certainly possible. It is important to keep in mind that we do not yet have data on relative amounts of blood lost from the gastrointestinal tract by breast-fed and formula-fed infants.

Dr. Siimes: I completely agree and would like to add that there are at least two mechanisms through which iron is lost: one is blood lost through the gastrointestinal tract and the other is the loss through epithelial cells, which is reported to be increased in some gastrointestinal conditions.

Dr. Stekel: Coming back to the question of the high serum ferritin levels in premature infants, some of the data that Dr. Dallman showed us indicate that infants that one would have predicted to have used all their iron stores also had high serum ferritins.

Iron Nutrition in Infancy and Childhood,
edited by A. Stekel. Nestlé, Vevey/Raven Press,
New York © 1984.

Iron and Breast Milk

Bo Lönnerdal

Department of Nutrition, University of California, Davis, California 95616, U.S.A.

The iron content of breast milk is often characterized as low. In fact, the amount of iron provided by breast milk appears to be adequate to prevent iron deficiency anemia for at least the first 6 months of life. However, if the same amount of iron is given in any food other than breast milk, this amount is inadequate and iron deficiency anemia does occur. Thus, iron in breast milk seems to be utilized by the infant to a unique extent. In addition, there is some evidence that the high degree of iron utilization in the breast-fed infant has a role in host defense mechanisms. A further understanding of the factors stimulating and limiting absorption of iron from breast milk, cow's milk, and proprietary formulas is needed in order to elucidate the mechanisms of iron absorption and metabolism as well as the role of iron on infections of the infant.

IRON CONTENT OF MILK

There appears to be a diurnal variation; morning milk contains less iron than milk in the evening (1). This led the investigators to the conclusion that the values in their initial study (2) were low due to the use of morning samples. During a single feeding, the foremilk has a lower iron concentration than the hindmilk, the range being from 0.3 to 1.0 µg/ml (3). Thus, like fat, the iron concentration of breast milk increases significantly during a single nursing. The concentration of iron in breast milk varies among women and in individual women during the lactation period, during the day, and during the nursing period. Thus, all these factors have to be considered when discussing the iron content of breast milk and the utilization of this iron. In contrast, the iron content of cow's milk or infant formulas is considered to be relatively constant compared to breast milk. Values for the total iron content of breast milk vary among laboratories where different analytical methods are used; less than optimal methods frequently yield unreasonably high values.

Recent studies usually give similar values for the iron concentration of breast milk, a range from 0.2 to 0.7 µg/ml, with colostrum values of 0.5 to 0.7 µg/ml declining to a mean value of around 0.2 to 0.4 µg/ml for mature milk (Table 1).

FACTORS AFFECTING BREAST-MILK IRON

It is not known if dietary iron or the iron status of the mother has any effect on the concentration of iron in breast milk. Some reports from India (4,5) indicate

TABLE 1. *Iron content of breast milk* (μg/ml)

Colostrum	1–3 months	4–6 months	Reference
(14 days)	0.20 ± 0.17		Picciano and Guthrie (2)
0.52–0.72	0.36–0.42	0.28–0.34	Siimes et al. (71)
	0.49–0.05	0.43–0.04	Vaughan et al. (7)
	0.41 ± 0.22		Fransson and Lönnerdal (3)
	0.20–0.69		Fransson and Lönnerdal (72)
	0.22–0.31	0.20–0.22	Dewey and Lönnerdal (13)

that groups of nursing women having a high incidence of anemia have quite a high iron content in their breast milk; the values do not appear to be lower than normal. However, analytical problems may have contributed to these values. Murray et al. (6) did not find an effect of iron status of Nigerian women on breast-milk iron content. Neither iron deficiency (Hb < 10 g/dl) nor iron overload (Hb >12.0 g/dl; transferrin saturation > 60%) was found to affect breast-milk iron concentration. It should be noted, however, that the mothers in Murray et al.'s study cannot be classified as severely anemic. Whether a severe iron deficiency anemia, which is frequently observed in many developing countries, has any effect on breast-milk iron remains to be studied. Preliminary studies indicate that the milk of severely anemic (Hb < 8 g/dl) mothers in India has an iron concentration higher than the milk of control mothers (Hb >11 g/dl) (G.-B. Fransson, M. Gebre-Medhin, and K. N. Agarwal, *personal communication*).

Other studies also fail to find an effect of dietary iron intake on milk iron content (7,8). However, the range of maternal iron intake in these studies was not large, 15 to 40 mg/day. A very high dietary intake of iron, like that in Ethiopia where intakes are as high as 300 mg/day compared to normal intakes of 10 to 15 mg/day, does not appear to affect breast-milk iron; values were similar to those of Swedish women with corresponding lactation times (G.-B. Fransson and M. Gebre-Medhin, *personal communication*). Thus, the very limited data available do not indicate a correlation between maternal dietary iron intake or iron status and breast-milk iron.

It can be noted that when using iron supplements in the form of a water-soluble chelate of iron, nitrilotriacetic acid (NTA), it has been possible to increase the concentration of iron in the milk of an experimental animal (rat) and thereby to increase tissue iron levels of the suckling pups (9). Recently, it was also shown that, when a solid diet high in iron was given to rats, a similar effect on the milk iron was obtained (10). In addition, after feeding an iron-deficient diet, milk iron concentration and pup tissue iron was significantly decreased compared to controls. However, it should be noted that the increase in iron has only been observed in one species (rat) and at very high levels of supplementation. It does not follow that a similar effect could be obtained in humans. In fact, great caution should be exercised before doing any human experiments; conceivably, an increase in milk iron could have adverse effects (11).

IRON INTAKE

The daily iron intake of the exclusively breast-fed infant can be estimated by using the above values for breast-milk iron and data for 24-hr milk intakes of breast-fed infants. Such data have been obtained for Swedish infants (12) and American infants (13) and they show reasonable similarity, although there is wide individual variation. Mean daily intake varied from 673 ml at 1 month of lactation to 896 ml at 6 months of lactation, yielding a daily iron intake of 0.21 mg/day (0.044 mg/kg/day) at 1 month of age and 0.13 mg/day (0.017 mg/kg/day) at 6 months of age (Fig. 1). The daily iron intake data are similar or somewhat lower than those found in other recent studies (8,14). Official recommendations for iron intake have been given at 0.83 mg/kg/day (United States Food and Nutrition Board). However, as will be discussed below, these values are not directly applicable to breast milk because of differences in iron bioavailability, but serve as guidelines for infants not being breast-fed (15). The iron intake of an infant receiving the same volume of iron-supplemented cow's milk formula would be 4.0 to 10.8 mg/day (0.7–1.8 mg/kg/day), the nonsupplemented cow's milk formula 0.50 to 2.4 mg/day (0.13–0.37 mg/kg/day), and the soya formula, which is commonly supplemented, approximately 2.7 to 10.8 mg/day (0.5–1.9 mg/kg/day).

RECOMMENDATIONS ON IRON SUPPLEMENTATION

It has been estimated that the infant requires 0.5 to 0.8 mg/day of iron in order to prevent iron deficiency during the first year of life. This estimate is based on the fact that the infant is born with iron endowment of 75 mg/kg body weight and that 140 to 200 mg of iron must be absorbed during the first year to ensure iron sufficiency. By giving varying levels of iron to infants, it was shown that the highest level of hemoglobin was found in infants who received 1 mg/kg/day of iron (16). The Recommended Daily Allowance (RDA) is set at 10 mg/day and the maximum

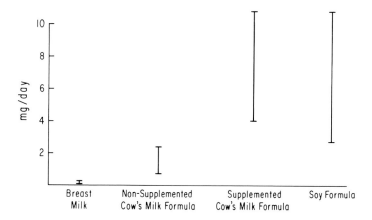

FIG. 1. Daily iron intake of infants (1–6 months).

level of supplementation recommended by the Committee on Nutrition of the American Academy of Pediatrics is 1 mg/kg/day for term infants and 2 mg/kg/day for preterm infants, up to a maximum of 15 mg/day.

In respect to infant formula, the absorption studies by Saarinen et al. (17) led to a suggested level of supplementation of 7 mg of iron as ferrous sulfate per liter. The recommendation of the American Academy of Pediatrics for iron-fortified infant formula is currently at least 6 mg of iron per liter (15). However, it should be noted that although the labeling on most iron-fortified infant formulas lists the iron content at approximately 12 mg/liter, the levels found in formulas vary considerably (18). In fact, some iron-fortified formulas contained as much as 40 to 60 mg/liter, whereas some unfortified formulas contained only 0.1 to 0.2 mg/liter. Whether the high values represent contamination caused by the production process, the container, or a mistake in the formulation is not known, but these high values (as well as the very low values) should be an area of concern.

The relationship between the mode of feeding and the incidence of iron deficiency anemia has attracted interest and is still under debate. Four breast-fed infants that had been exclusively breast-fed for 8 to 18 months had normal hematological values (19). In a subsequent larger study, exclusively breast-fed infants did not meet any criteria of iron deficiency at 6 months of age, whereas at 9 months 4% of the infants were judged as iron deficient (20). Infants fed a home-prepared formula based on cow's milk showed iron deficiency at 4 months of age; infants fed iron-supplemented formula did not show signs of iron deficiency during the first 12 months of life. Picciano and Deering (21) found similar hematological indices in infants fed breast milk and in those fed an iron-supplemented formula. In addition, Owen et al. (22) found no signs of iron deficiency in exclusively breast-fed infants at 5 months of age, although breast-fed infants had higher ferritin values when given supplemented iron. Woodruff et al. (23) found a high prevalence of low transferrin saturation in exclusively breast-fed infants at 6 months and 9 months, but according to other studies the criterion used for low transferrin might have been too stringent.

It has been argued that breast-fed infants should be supplemented with iron as ferrous sulfate at a level of 7 mg/day (24). This argument is based more on calculations of required iron supply during the first year of life than on an observed iron deficiency anemia. This recommendation has been questioned since any needs for supplemental iron would be very different in early infancy (when storage iron is still present) compared to late infancy. Furthermore, supplemented iron might bind to lactoferrin and thus inhibit the possible bacteriostatic role of this protein and increase the risk of infection (25).

The quantity of iron given is adequate to saturate lactoferrin completely and, as stated below, the lactoferrin-iron complex is very stable and stands both a lowering in pH and limited proteolysis without loss of binding capacity. It is possible, but not proven, that a bacteriostatic effect of lactoferrin may be exercised by lactoferrin in the gastrointestinal tract of the infant and that a dose of iron salt potentially could abolish this effect. It has been argued that a single dose of iron could not saturate all lactoferrin which is given in breast milk throughout the day. However, not much is known about the fate of this dose of iron. The pH in the small intestine of the breast-fed infant is comparatively high; this pH may render the iron insoluble and thus possibly cause a slower transit time and longer presence than normal in the gastrointestinal tract for potential uptake by lactoferrin. In addition, breast milk contains a high concentration of citrate, which has been shown to facilitate uptake of iron by lactoferrin. These arguments are highly speculative and only emphasize the need of further research. A significantly lower incidence of infections has been reported among breast-fed infants compared to artificially fed infants; however, it is more than likely that this finding is multifactorial and not solely due to either the iron supplementation or the lack of lactoferrin in formulas. The potential effect of iron supplementation of breast-fed infants on the incidence of infection has not yet been studied.

DISTRIBUTION OF IRON IN MILK-BINDING FACTORS

Iron in its water soluble forms, the ferrous (II) and the ferric (III) ions, is rarely found free in biological systems. These ions, of which the oxidized Fe^{3+} form is considerably more common, form complexes of varying natures, from simple complexes with anions such as phosphate and citrate to the intricate structure of metalloproteins such as transferrin and ferritin. Since the nature of these complexes has been suggested to affect the uptake of iron from milk and formulas, it is important to isolate and identify such complexes.

Milk has traditionally been regarded as composed of three major fractions: fat (lipid), casein, and whey. Conventionally, fat is removed by skimming (centrifugation) and the casein precipitated by addition of acid to a pH of 4.6. The whey is defined as the remainder from this process. In order to study the distribution of iron among, and within, the major fractions of milk, new and milder separation procedures have been introduced (26). The fat fraction can be solubilized into an outer fat globule membrane (OFGM), an inner fat globule membrane (IFGM), and a triglyceride ("core") fraction. Since acid precipitation of casein causes changes in charges of proteins and therefore redistribution of iron, ultracentrifugation has been used to sediment casein micelles. The whey can be separated by ultrafiltration into a protein fraction and a fraction containing low-molecular-weight compounds such as salts and lactose. Subsequent to this separation procedure each fraction can be further analyzed by the use of gel filtration, ion-exchange chromatography, and electrophoresis.

The results of using this separation procedure on breast milk, cow's milk, cow's milk formulas ("humanized"), and soya formulas can be seen in Fig. 2 (B. Lönnerdal and B. Sandström, *unpublished data*). (It should be noted that the whey fraction in soya formula is used to designate the fraction corresponding to the whey fraction of milk as described above.) A considerable proportion (33%) of the iron in breast milk is found in the fat fraction, whereas only 9% is found in the casein. The remainder, 58%, is consequently bound to compounds in the whey fraction.

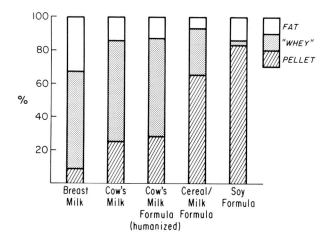

FIG. 2. Distribution of iron in milks and formulas.

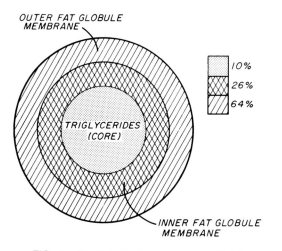

FIG. 3. Distribution of iron in human milk fat.

In contrast, casein binds a larger proportion of iron in cow's milk (24%) as well as in the soya formula. The whey-adjusted cow's milk formula consequently contains less iron bound to the casein (28%) and relatively more iron bound to the whey (59%) than in cow's milk. The fat fraction contains 14% of the iron in cow's milk, whereas only minor proportions are bound to this fraction in the formulas, most likely due to the fact that this fat is derived from a mixture of vegetable oils presumably containing no iron.

The solubilization of the breast milk fat demonstrated that iron is predominantly bound to the outer fat globule membrane (64% of the iron in fat), whereas very little iron is found in the triglyceride fraction (Fig. 3). Preliminary experiments, using gel filtration and gel electrophoresis, indicate that the major proportion of iron in the outer membrane is contained in xanthine oxidase (27). This flavine iron-molybdenum protein is known to be present in milk fat.

The iron bound to casein is believed to be electrostatically associated with negatively charged phosphoserine groups located in the casein subunits. Such a binding has been observed for iron in casein from cow's milk (26) as well as for calcium (28). This may explain the very high proportion of iron bound to casein in cow's milk. The casein content of cow's milk is 8 to 10 times higher than that of breast milk. Consequently, cow's milk formula also has a high proportion of casein-bound iron. Not much is known about the insoluble compounds binding iron in soya formulas, but possibly iron phytate can be part of this fraction.

The low molecular weight fraction, separated by ultrafiltration from the whey, contains 32% of the total amount of iron in the breast milk (55% of the whey iron). Corresponding values are 32, 21, and 2% for cow's milk, cow's milk formula, and soya formula, respectively. The nature of the low molecular weight complex(es) has not been determined, but the complex seems similar to a complex for zinc, which has been isolated and identified as zinc citrate (molecular weight 600) (29).

The whey proteins of breast milk have been separated by gel filtration and the major iron-binding protein has been identified as lactoferrin by immunoelectrophoresis (3). The peak for lactoferrin is very wide, most likely reflecting the tendency of this protein to form complexes with immunoglobulins. Transferrin is also present in breast milk; however, the concentration of this protein is very low (3) and the amount of iron bound to this protein is very small.

Lactoferrin is present in the milk of most species. The molecular weight of human lactoferrin is around 80,000 and the protein consists of one polypeptide chain. This protein has physical and chemical properties similar to those of transferrin; both proteins bind two ferric ions in the presence of bicarbonate ions. Even though both proteins bind iron strongly, transferrin releases its iron when the pH is lower than 4, whereas lactoferrin does not completely release its iron until the pH is 2 or lower (30). A remarkable property of lactoferrin is its comparatively high resistance to proteolytic degradation, especially in its iron-saturated form (31). This property has been believed to protect lactoferrin against proteolysis in the gastrointestinal tract of the infant.

Among the proteins in breast milk, lactoferrin is one of the major components. Concentrations of 1 to 2 mg/ml have been reported in mature milk (Fig. 4) (12); this constitutes around 10 to 30% of the total protein content. Higher lactoferrin concentrations have been reported in colostrum, consistent with the higher protein content of this fluid. The concentration of lactoferrin in human milk is unusually high in comparison to most species. For example, cow's milk contains only 0.01 to 0.1 mg/ml of lactoferrin, and thus any formula based on cow's milk will contain only minute amounts of lactoferrin. It is interesting to note that the concentration of lactoferrin in milk from both well-nourished and malnourished mothers in Ethiopia has been reported to be higher than in milk from well-nourished Swedish

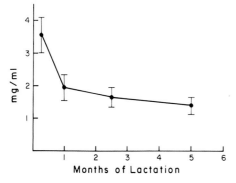

FIG. 4. Lactoferrin in human milk: Variation during lactation (12).

mothers (32). It is possible that the iron status of the mother may affect the lactoferrin concentration, although as stated above there does not seem to be an effect of iron status on breast-milk iron concentration. The common Ethiopian diet provides unusually high intakes of iron compared to most other countries. If lactoferrin synthesis can be induced by high dietary iron while milk iron concentration is unchanged, this may be a mechanism for maintaining the bacteriostatic function of unsaturated lactoferrin.

Lactoferrin has been considered as *the* iron-binding protein in milk, yet, as stated above, there are other compounds in milk that bind iron. In fact, only 20 to 30% of the iron in breast milk is bound to lactoferrin, the remainder being distributed between fat globule membrane proteins, casein, and low molecular weight ligands. Thus, the degree of iron saturation of lactoferrin is exceptionally low, only 3 to 5% of its total capacity; this may prove to be important in its function. Earlier reports have given a higher degree of iron saturation for lactoferrin, between 10 to 30%. However, this is not possible, a fact which can be shown by calculating the total iron-binding capacity of lactoferrin, which is around 2.1 μg/ml. If the iron concentration of mature breast milk is 0.4 μg/ml and 25% of this iron is bound to lactoferrin, only 0.1 μg of the total capacity of 2.1 μg/ml can be occupied, which equals 4.8%.

The biological function of lactoferrin is not yet fully understood. There are data supporting a bacteriostatic role for lactoferrin in breast milk. Since the initial report by Bullen et al. (25) showed that lactoferrin can inhibit the growth of *Escherichia coli*, several studies have demonstrated that the growth of bacteria such as *Candida albicans, Streptococcus mutans, Vibrio cholerae, Pseudomonas aeroginosa*, and *pyocyaneus* can be inhibited by lactoferrin *in vitro* (33). The bacteriostatic function of lactoferrin in milk is decreased by the addition of excess iron. This implies that unsaturated lactoferrin inhibits bacterial growth, and that it does so by its strong iron-sequestering capacity. With an exceptionally strong association constant for iron ($K_{ass} = 10^{30}$), lactoferrin can successfully compete with bacterial siderophores and thus inhibit proliferation and growth of bacteria. Although some *in vivo* studies support the results obtained *in vitro*, no studies have been done in human infants.

Some *in vitro* studies also show that lactoferrin may act in concert with secretory IgA, a specific type of antibody present in milk (34).

The fact that iron in human milk is very well absorbed by the infant has led to the suggestion that lactoferrin may promote the absorption of iron. The data available from experimental animals and humans are conflicting and will be discussed in detail in the next section. An interesting hypothesis has recently been proposed by Brock (35) in which the function of lactoferrrin changes with age, and thus the degree of physiological maturation of the infant. In the newborn, iron absorption is poorly controlled, but high levels of lactoferrin in the milk and low gastrointestinal proteolytic activity tend to prevent iron from becoming available for absorption. As the infant grows older, the need for exogenous iron increases, milk lactoferrin levels decrease, and proteolytic activity increases, resulting in progressively more iron being released from lactoferrin and subsequently absorbed. Although intellectually challenging, the various facets of this hypothesis remain to be proven experimentally. The effect of lactoferrin on iron absorption will be discussed below.

BIOAVAILABILITY OF IRON

A difference in iron nutrition between breast-fed and artificially fed infants has been implicated for a long time. In 1928 MacKay (36) found that the hematological status of infants that had been exclusively breast-fed for the first 7 months was better than that of infants fed cow's milk or formula. Although a lower incidence of anemia was observed or estimated in breast-fed infants compared to cow's milk or formula-fed infants, it was not until 1954 that it was explained by the very high proportion (45–75%) of iron that is absorbed from breast milk (37,38). However, Feuillen's study (37) was very limited ($N = 2$) and the tedious balance technique was used. Introduction of the use of radioisotopes allowed more sensitive measurements to be performed in infants, children, and adults. Schultz and Smith (39) showed, by using both extrinsic (adding the isotope *in vitro* to milk) and intrinsic (giving the isotope to the cow to have it incorporated into the synthesized milk) labeling, that about 10% of the iron in cow's milk is absorbed. Cow's milk actually inhibits the absorption of ferrous iron from a test dose while it has no effect on iron absorption from heme (40). The same authors also pointed out that the percentage of iron absorption decreases with the amount of iron provided. Therefore, only a small fraction (4%) of iron is absorbed from formula supplemented to a level of 12 mg/ml (41).

The first experiments to assess bioavailability of iron from breast milk by using radioisotopes were done by McMillan et al. (19) and Saarinen et al. (17). These two groups used different experimental designs but reached very similar conclusions. In the studies of McMillan et al. (19,42), adults were used and the incorporation of radioiron into red blood cells from extrinsically labeled human milk was measured after 2 weeks. A red blood cell incorporation of 20.8% was observed. The corresponding value for cow's milk was 13.6%. The authors reason that red blood cell iron incorporation corresponds to 80% of the total body iron uptake and thus 25% would have been absorbed. Making the assumption that iron absorption in infants is twice that of adults, the estimated level of absorption of breast-milk iron in infants is 50%, and that of cow's milk 34%. Saarinen et al. (17) and Saarinen and Siimes (43) also used an extrinsic tag but measured whole body retention after 2 weeks in infants fed human milk, cow's milk, and cow's milk formula. These investigators found an iron absorption of 49% from breast milk, 10% from cow's milk, and 7 to 9% from supplemented formula.

The contrast in the results obtained for iron absorption from cow's milk between these two studies may be explained by a difference in digestive capacity between the adult and the infant. Although iron absorption in the infant may be twice that of the adult for a test dose of iron or an easily digested food, this may not be true for iron given in cow's milk. Cow's milk is very high in casein, almost 10 times higher than human milk, and it is known that casein in the stomach of an infant can form hard curds that can pass through the gastrointestinal tract without complete digestion. While there is very limited data on the human infant, we have recently observed in fasted suckling rats that 4 hr after a tube feeding of breast milk or cow's milk the stomach of pups fed breast milk was virtually empty whereas that of pups given cow's milk were full of white hard curd (44). Thus, cow's milk may be well digested in the adult but only to a lesser extent in the infant, making the assumed factor of two incorrect. It is possible that the value for iron absorption from cow's milk obtained by McMillan et al. (19), 17%, should not be doubled but rather corrected downward for less absorption of iron in infants fed cow's milk. Therefore, a value closer to 10% obtained by Saarinen et al. (17) may be derived.

The finding of a high bioavailability of iron from breast milk led to the hypothesis that a factor(s) present in this milk promotes iron absorption. The high concentration of the iron-binding protein lactoferrin in breast milk and a significantly lower concentration in cow's milk stimulated several studies on the role of lactoferrin in iron absorption. However, the results appear to be conflicting. McMillan et al. (42) demonstrated a decreased uptake of iron from a "simulated" human milk when iron-saturated lactoferrin was added. However, the iron content of the formula containing lactoferrin was three times higher than that of the formula without this protein, which may have affected the results considerably. Also, it is not described how the iron was added to lactoferrin and how much time was allowed to lapse between the addition of the iron and the consumption of the formula. By using everted duodenal sacks from rats and guinea pigs, DeLaey et al. (45) showed *in vitro* that human apo-lactoferrin (lactoferrin free from iron) inhibited mucosal transfer as well as serosal uptake of iron. Lactoferrin saturated with iron was not found to have any effect. In addition, when animals were given antibodies to lactoferrin, iron uptake increased significantly. DeVet and van Gool (46) found a negative correlation between the amount of duodenal lactoferrin and iron absorption in human adults. Both these groups suggested that lactoferrin may protect the intestinal mucosa from absorbing excessive amounts of iron by binding the iron in the intestine and thus making it unavailable to the infant. Iron uptake by lactoferrin can, despite its very high association constant, be very slow and will be dependent on factors such as pH, presence of bicarbonate, and chelators. It has been shown that saturation of lactoferrin with iron as an inorganic salt (ferrous sulfate) is not complete at 24 hr. Thus, if iron saturation of lactoferrin is not analyzed, it is possible that iron is present in an inorganic form and may in fact become complexed by other compounds. That this may have occurred is also indicated by the exceedingly high iron to lactoferrin ratio in the lactoferrin preparation that was added to the formula, namely 200:1 instead of the stoichiometric 2:1 ratio. Therefore, a role for lactoferrin in iron absorption in human infants cannot be ruled out by the experiments of McMillan et al. (42).

In a series of studies, the bioavailability of lactoferrin-iron has been assessed in experimental animals. Absorption of iron bound to lactoferrin was similar to that from ferrous sulfate in weanling rats fed a purified diet (47). Using the suckling pig and a radioactive isotope of iron, uptake of iron into red blood cells and plasma was significantly faster from a milk formula supplemented with lactoferrin-iron than from the same formula with iron sulfate (48). Whole body retention after 7 days, however, was similar for both groups. Similarly, iron retention was the same for iron-adequate and iron-deficient weanling mice fed a milk diet. Apo-lactoferrin added to the iron-supplemented milk yielded values for tissue iron and hematological values similar to milk without lactoferrin, speaking against an inhibiting role for lactoferrin in iron absorption (49). It should be mentioned that in the above studies bovine lactoferrin was used. There are some data indicating that there may be a difference between heterologous and homologous lactoferrin (50). Thus, this possible species effect should be investigated even though the chemical properties of lactoferrin from different species appear to be very similar.

An enhancing role for lactoferrin (or another breast-milk component) in iron absorption from breast milk may be indicated from the study by Saarinen et al. (17). A tracer dose of radioiron appeared to be better absorbed when it was given with a meal of breast milk than when it was given alone to a fasted breast-fed infant, although the value for iron absorption in the fasted breast-fed infant was higher than for fasted infants fed cow's milk. Others have suggested that iron absorption is "tuned" by homeostatic control to a level corresponding to the previous diet. Alternatively, as discussed previously, digestion of breast milk is considerably faster and the stomach in breast-fed infants is more likely to be empty than when cow's milk is fed. In the case of cow's milk feeding, a factor inhibiting iron absorption still may be present in the stomach when the tracer dose is given. In the infants fed cow's milk, serum ferritin levels were lower than in the infants fed breast milk; this would lead one to expect a higher iron absorption in association with lower iron stores. The fact that this was not observed would support the existence of a hypothetical factor in cow's milk inhibiting iron absorption in infants.

A developmental change in iron transport may be hypothesized for the breast-fed infants: as iron stores are depleted, more iron is absorbed and if the iron status of the body is still "suboptimal," an even higher "gear" of homeostatic control may be exerted by the mucosal transfer system so that a developmental gradient of iron absorption is created. While this reasoning is speculative, it would be interesting to study iron absorption at various ages. In contrast, Götze et al. (51) found increasing iron absorption with increasing age of the infant. It appears from the studies by Dauncey et al. (52) and Lundström and Siimes (53) that the premature infant has mechanisms controlling iron absorption that are quite different than the term infant. Consequently, it is evident that the preterm infant has other iron requirements and thus possibly a different efficiency of absorption of iron than term infants.

Lundström and Siimes (53) estimated that increase in total body iron in preterm infants (as inferred from hemoglobin and serum ferritin concentrations at 3 to 4 months of age) was similar in infants fed breast milk and a humanized (whey-adjusted) cow's milk formula not supplemented with iron, whereas that of infants fed a home-prepared cow's milk formula was considerably lower. This apparent contrast to term infants is hypothesized to be due to a difference in intestinal control of iron absorption in these infants allowing them to absorb similar amounts of iron, or to a lack of inhibition of iron absorption from any kind of milk in preterm infants. The lower iron gain of infants fed cow's milk is believed to be due to increased intestinal loss of blood.

A necessary prerequisite for validating radioisotope iron absorption studies done with extrinsically labeled foods is that the results are similar to those that would be obtained with an intrinsic label, i.e., that isotope exchange is virtually complete. It was shown by Schultz and Smith (39) that extrinsically and intrinsically labeled cow's milk iron was absorbed to the same extent. However, the intrinsic and extrinsic tags were studied in different subjects, which makes the results difficult to compare. Corresponding findings in adults were reported for a broader range of foods by Björn-Rasmussen et al. (54). Although the above studies indicate that isotope exchange occurs under many circumstances, it cannot be assumed *a priori* that this will be the case for breast milk. Recent data show that a tracer dose of radioiron will bind virtually exclusively to lactoferrin in human milk, whereas in cow's milk the tracer will be distributed among the various fractions in a manner similar to that observed for native ("cold") iron (55). Furthermore, it was shown that even after incubation of labeled breast milk with gastric juice aspirated from an infant, or lowering the pH to 3, lactoferrin was still binding the radioiron almost exclusively. Thus, it may be that isotope exchange is incomplete in the infant when a ligand with an unusually high binding constant for iron is present in an unsaturated form. If this is the case, it may be concluded that the previous studies on iron absorption using an extrinsic tag have been conducted on the lactoferrin-bound fraction of the iron in breast milk, i.e., approximately 30% of the total iron. The absorption of iron from other complexes may therefore not have been studied and may be different. Naturally, there is a possibility that redistribution of iron occurs in the gastrointestinal tract, so that iron bound to weaker ligands will be released and subsequently incorporated into lactoferrin. In the case that that would happen to the extent that virtually all iron in breast milk became bound to lactoferrin, the results obtained previously may be representative for the total pool of breast milk iron. Further studies are needed to elucidate the extent of isotope exchange and digestion of lactoferrin.

Another approach to estimate bioavailability of iron from various milk regimens has been suggested by Saarinen and Siimes (56). This method is based on estimating the increment in total body iron, expressed as the sum of hemoglobin iron and body storage iron, during specific times for which the intake of iron is known. However, although a reasonable estimate of the hemoglobin iron pool can be obtained, storage iron is admittedly more difficult to assess. These investigators used serum ferritin as a measure and attempted to correlate the logarithm of serum ferritin with storage iron (expressed as mg/kg body weight) based on values from adult males and females as well as newborn and young infants. The monthly increment in total body iron was found to be 20 mg for breast-fed infants, 6.5 mg for infants fed a home-prepared cow's milk formula, and 33.5 mg for infants fed a humanized cow's milk formula supplemented with iron (11 mg/liter). When these authors assumed a milk or formula intake of 1,000 ml/day at 2 to 4 months of age and an iron content of 0.7 mg/liter in cow's milk and 1.0 mg/liter in breast milk, the comparative values as percentage retained of total intake were estimated at 70% for breast-milk iron, 30% for cow's-milk iron, and 10% for the formula iron. The authors point out that monthly increments of total body iron were quite different after the age of 4 months when solid foods were introduced. Breast-fed infants did not gain any iron and formula-fed infants gained less than one-third of the iron gained in the previous months. In contrast, infants fed cow's milk increased their total body iron more than earlier and considerably more than the breast-fed group.

Thus, the differences between the groups were of the same relative magnitude as those found by radioisotope studies. As pointed out by Saarinen and Siimes (56), these are not retention values and are not absolute figures because physiological loss of iron was ignored. In breast-fed infants this loss must be insignificant, whereas it is possible that occult blood loss was occurring in the infants fed cow's milk.

The values obtained by the indirect method were considerably higher than those obtained by radioisotope studies. This may be explained by the fact that the infants in the isotope study were 6 months of age, whereas the infants in the total body iron increment study were 4 months of age. It was also speculated that a continuous supplementation with ascorbic acid may have increased the iron absorption values in the study using the indirect method.

Garry et al. (57) have recently used the approach of Saarinen and Siimes to estimate iron absorption from breast milk and formula with and without iron supplementation. In their study a correction was made for estimated daily loss of iron from skin, urine, and intestinal mucosa. From birth to 3 months of age, the increment of total body iron, for breast-fed infants (B) was 49 mg, whereas that of breast-fed infants supplemented with iron (B+) was 59 mg. Corresponding values for nonfortified formula (F) were 24 mg and for fortified formula (F+) 28 mg. Between 3 and 6 months the increments for the same four groups were -3 mg (B), 26 mg (B+), 7 mg (F), and 23 mg (F+). The percentage of iron intake absorbed during the first three months of life was calculated to be 81, 10, 97, and 6%, respectively, and for the period 3 to 6 months, 10, 4, 22, and 3%, respectively. The data by Garry et al. (57) also suggest a high bioavailability of breast-milk iron, at least for the first 3 months of life. These investigators suggest that the iron content of human milk is insufficient between the ages of 3 to 6 months; the negative iron balance observed by the other investigators when solid food is given to breast-fed infants is not the cause in this study because the infants were exclusively breast-fed up to at least 5 months of age; however, body storage iron may shortly become depleted if exclusive breast-feeding is continued.

The method used in the studies by Saarinen and Siimes (56) and Garry et al. (57) has been questioned by Fomon (58). Using a more appropriate value for iron concentration of breast milk, 0.4 mg/ml, rather than the 1.0 µg/ml used by the previous investigators, he concludes that more than 100% of the iron in breast milk was absorbed. This appears to be correct, especially since the daily milk volume ingested by breast-fed infants is closer to 800 ml than 1,000 ml (as used in the calculated intake). It is pointed out by Fomon that the assumption that plasma concentration of ferritin bears the same relation to body storage iron in the infant as in the adult may be invalid. The approach of Saarinen and Siimes (56) must therefore be revised somewhat to yield more reasonable results. If one takes the two values from infants for serum ferritin and storage iron and makes this admittedly limited material into a linear function, a monthly total body increment of 5 mg instead of 20 mg may be obtained for breast-fed infants. With a daily intake of 800 ml of breast milk having an iron concentration of 0.4 µg/ml, 9.6 mg of iron will be fed monthly to a breast-fed infant. Thus, an absorptive value of 52% may be derived, very similar to that from radioisotope studies (49%). Therefore, with further information regarding the correlation between serum ferritin and storage iron in infancy, this approach may prove to be a valuable method.

ADDITIONAL FACTORS AFFECTING THE BIOAVAILABILITY OF IRON

In milk, as well as in other foods, there is a variety of factors enhancing or limiting the absorption of iron. Even with knowledge of the effects of the individual components, it is impossible to make predictions about the net result on iron absorption of all the components together. As shown previously, human studies clearly show a superior bioavailability of iron from breast milk as compared to cow's milk. Although a few factors (lactoferrin, casein) have been mentioned as examples, there are several differences between human milk, cow's milk and formulas that may be responsible for the differences observed.

The carbohydrate source has been shown to affect iron absorption (59). Lactose has a more stimulating effect than starch, which may be partially responsible for the lower bioavailability of iron from starch-based soya formula (60). Although both human and cow's milk contain lactose, breast milk contains 7 to 8% compared to 5% in cow's milk. It is not known whether such a difference will affect iron absorption. The fat content and source have also been shown to affect iron bioavailability (59); however, considerably less is known about this area. It may be the fat content directly affecting iron absorption but it also may be the concomitant changes in carbohydrate and/or protein content. A low protein formula (15 g/liter) has been shown to enhance iron absorption compared to a high protein formula (24 g/liter) at the same level of iron supplementation (61). It is possible that a high content of casein will limit iron absorption by binding iron tightly. Thus, there could be a negative effect of a protein such as casein in cow's milk and formula, while possibly a protein like lactoferrin could enhance iron absorption in breast-fed infants; therefore, it is not necessarily the total protein content affecting iron absorption, but rather the composition of the protein.

There are several low molecular weight compounds affecting iron absorption from milks and formulas. Ascorbic acid is a known promoter of iron absorption, whereas phosphate is known to form insoluble iron complexes, thus limiting absorption. The phosphate content of cow's milk is considerably higher than that of human milk, and most formulas are also higher in phosphate (62). In addition, other cations such as calcium, zinc, and manganese may interact with the absorption of iron. A high zinc-to-iron ratio has been shown to decrease iron absorption in rats (63). It is not known whether the commonly used zinc supplementation of formulas affects iron absorption. Likewise, it is not known if the manganese supplementation used in some formulas will affect iron absorption. However, it has been shown that iron supplementation at a modest level (6 mg/liter) significantly decreases manganese absorption in experimental animals (49), demonstrating an interaction between these two elements. The higher calcium content of cow's milk and formulas compared to human milk may also affect iron bioavailability, either directly or indirectly, by potentially competing for the same promoters of absorption, such as lactose. A low content of copper in milk can precipitate a copper deficiency, which in severe cases can lead to anemia (64). However, this anemia is not caused by an effect on iron absorption but rather by a decrease in iron mobilization from the liver and the reticuloendothelial system caused by a reduction in the activity of ferroxidase, a copper-dependent enzyme. It is apparent that excess or deficiency of other elements will affect the iron status, even though our knowledge in this area is very limited.

Giving a solid diet (strained pears) in addition to a meal of breast milk has been shown to decrease iron absorption in adults (65). In addition, Saarinen and Siimes (56) showed a marked drop in monthly total body iron increments shortly after solid foods (vegetables, fruits) were introduced. This decrease was noticed in both breast-fed and formula-fed infants. Evidently, the effects of mixed diets on iron absorption should be investigated further.

The fecal flora of breast-fed infants is quite different from that of artificially fed infants. Whereas breast-fed infants are primarily colonized with *Lactobacilli*, formula-fed infants have mostly coliform bacteria (62). The *Lactobacilli* produces a lower intestinal pH (approximately 5) than the *E. coli* (approximately 7), thus facilitating iron absorption. It is known that iron absorption is increased with lower pH. In addition, cow's milk has a higher buffering capacity compared to human milk. Thus, the stomach content will be relatively more acidic in breast-fed infants than in infants fed cow's milk, again favoring iron absorption from breast milk. Another factor that should be considered is the effect of hormones on the gastrointestinal physiology. It has recently been shown that human milk, but not cow's milk, is high in concentration of a peptide similar to epidermal growth factor (EGF) (66). This peptide hormone has been shown to decrease gut acid secretion and also to stimulate growth and proliferation of intestinal mucosal cells, which may be envisioned to enhance iron absorption. Prostaglandins may also affect acid balance as well as intestinal mucosal transfer.

IRON, BREAST MILK, AND HOST RESISTANCE

The effect of iron status on host resistance has attracted considerable attention. As pointed out recently, several of these studies have been retrospective, and infection was not directly confirmed or characterized; therefore, criticism with regard to the control groups can be raised (67). In the past, iron deficiency was believed to increase the incidence of infection; however, there currently are studies with results to the contrary. Some studies show either no effect of iron deficiency or a lower incidence of infection with iron deficiency. A defect in the cell-mediated immune response has been documented in iron deficiency, but the overall effect of iron deficiency on host defense mechanisms in infants remains to be studied in carefully controlled prospective studies. In contrast, iron overload or iron supplementation in humans has also been implicated to have an effect on the incidence of infection. High doses of iron are postulated to result in a high degree of saturation of transferrin. Serum *in vitro* has been shown to inhibit growth of some bacteria; this effect can be abolished by the addition of iron. This presumed function of unsaturated transferrin and its inhibition is thus similar to what has been previously described for lactoferrin. Some support for the theory of a harmful effect of iron supplementation has been gained by the study of Murray et al. (6) in which the iron supplementation of iron deficient subjects appeared to be related to a reactivation of malaria.

The relationship between iron status, mode of feeding, and incidence of infection is even more uncertain (68). As mentioned previously, a low incidence of infection in infants has been ascribed to breast-feeding; it has been hypothesized that lactoferrin may, at least in part, be responsible for this protective effect. The low concentration of iron in breast milk and the rapid uptake of iron by mucosal cells, together with an unsaturated (still functional) lactoferrrin in high concentration, would be prerequisite for such an effect. Although the two former prerequisites have been established, the latter prerequisite, high concentrations of unsaturated lactoferrin in the gastrointestinal tract, needs confirmation. Other antibacterial and antiviral factors in breast milk such as secretory IgA, lysozyme, and mono-laurylate should also be considered in connection to lactoferrin and investigated. It has been shown that the bacteriostatic property of breast milk can be inhibited or destroyed by the addition of iron or by boiling; however, this does not prove that lactoferrin saturation was directly affected nor that the effect of lactoferrin was destroyed by boiling (34). Until the questions about lactoferrin bacteriostatic function *in vivo* have been resolved, it seems reasonable to avoid iron supplementation of breast-fed infants since, as stated before, iron status of exclusively breast-fed infants appears to be adequate (15,68).

In the case of formula-feeding, it is evident that iron supplementation should be used in order to prevent iron deficiency anemia. Since lactoferrin is present in very low concentrations or absent in formulas, the supplemental iron would have little effect on any possible bacteriostatic mechanisms provided by lactoferrin in the intestine. It has been shown *in vitro* that varying the iron content of formula from 0 to 12 g/liter did not affect the formula's ability to sustain bacterial growth of *E. coli* (69). In addition, it has been argued that the increased amount of iron absorbed from supplemented formula will have little effect on transferrin saturation in serum, thus making it unlikely that there would be a systemic effect (68). However, it is not necessary that supplemented iron that is needed would counteract a potential beneficial effect of minimized iron accessability to bacteria. It has been suggested that iron bound to lactoferrin may be a valuable form of iron supplementation (48,70). Although lactoferrin is a minor component of bovine whey, it is quite possible to purify or concentrate this protein in large quantities from this source. Whey is a major by-product of cheese manufacturing; the huge quantities produced are considered more as a waste problem than a source of nutrients, primarily because of its low protein and high lactose content. It is possible that partially saturated lactoferrin can be used as a supplement, providing both a source of iron and as a protection against infection. Although iron from lactoferrin appears to be highly available, further research is clearly needed to show if this hypothesis of using lactoferrin in infant formulas is viable.

CONCLUDING REMARKS

It is evident that iron in breast milk has a very high bioavailability and that term breast-fed infants do not need iron supplements for the first 6 months of life. The mechanisms responsible for this high bioavailability are not known; however, at least part of the difference in bioavailability between human milk, cow's milk, and formulas may be explained by the difference in content of factors enhancing binding and iron absorption. Further studies on the role of lactoferrin in breast milk will give information about the role of this protein in iron absorption and host defense mechanisms. Other factors to be considered with regard to iron bioavailability are growth factors, intestinal pH, and microflora. With increased knowledge about factors promoting iron absorption in breast-fed infants, it may be possible to design formulas with improved iron bioavailability to be used when mothers cannot successfully nurse their infants.

REFERENCES

1. Picciano MF. Mineral content of human milk during a single nursing. Nutr Rep Int 1978;18: 5–10.
2. Picciano MF, Guthrie HA. Copper, iron, and zinc contents of mature human milk. Am J Clin Nutr 1976;29:242–54.
3. Fransson G-B, Lönnerdal B. Iron in human milk. J Pediatr 1980;96:380–4.
4. Karmarkar MG, Ramakrishnan CV. Studies on human lactation. Relation between the dietary intake of lactating women and the chemical composition of milk with regard to principal and certain inorganic constituents. Acta Pediatr 1960;49:599–604.
5. Khurana V, Agarwal KN, Gupta S. Iron content of breast milk. Indian Pediatr 1970;7:659–61.
6. Murray MJ, Murray AB, Murray NJ, Murray MB. The effect of iron status of Nigerian mothers on that of infants at birth and 6 months, and on the concentration of Fe in breast milk. Br J Nutr 1978;39:627–30.
7. Vaughan LA, Weber CW, Kemberling SR. Longitudinal changes in the mineral content of human milk. Am J Clin Nutr 1979;32:2301–6.
8. Vuori E. Intake of copper, iron, manganese and zinc by healthy, exclusively breast-fed infants during the first 3 months of life. Br J Nutr 1979;42:407–11.
9. Keen CL, Lönnerdal B, Sloan MV, Hurley LS. Effect of dietary iron, copper, and zinc chelates of nitrilotriacetic acid (NTA) on trace metal concentrations in rat milk and maternal and pup tissues. J Nutr 1980;110:897–906.
10. Anaokar SG, Garry PJ. Effects of maternal iron nutrition during lactation on milk iron and rat neonatal iron status. Am J Clin Nutr 1981;34:1505–12.
11. Keen CL, Lönnerdal B, Hurley LS. Increased milk iron by dietary supplementation—entirely beneficial? (Letter) Am J Clin Nutr 1982;35:627–8.
12. Lönnerdal B, Forsum E, Hambraeus L. A longitudinal study of the protein, nitrogen and lactose contents of human milk from Swedish well-nourished mothers. Am J Clin Nutr 1976;29:1127–33.
13. Dewey K, Lönnerdal B. Milk and nutrient intake of breast-fed infants from one to six months: relation to growth and fatness. J Pediatr Gastroenterol Nutr 1983;2:497–506.
14. Picciano MF, Calkin EJ, Garrick JR, Deering RH. Milk and mineral intakes of breast-fed infants. Acta Paediatr Scand 1981;70:189–94.
15. Committee on Nutrition. Iron supplementation for infants. Pediatrics 1976;58:765–8.
16. Sturgeon P. Studies of iron requirements in infants and children. Pediatrics 1954;13:107–25.
17. Saarinen UM, Siimes MA, Dallman PR. Iron absorption in infants: high bioavailability of breast milk iron as indicated by the extrinsic tag method of iron absorption and by the concentration of serum ferritin. J Pediatr 1977;91:36–9.
18. Lönnerdal B, Keen CL, Ohtake M, Tamura T. Iron, zinc, copper and manganese in infant formulas. Am J Dis Child 1983;137:433–7.
19. McMillan JA, Landaw SA, Oski FA. Iron sufficiency in breast-fed infants and the availability of iron from human milk. Pediatrics 1976;58:686–91.
20. Saarinen UM. Need for iron supplementation in infants on prolonged breast-feeding. J Pediatr 1978;93:177–80.
21. Picciano MF, Deering RH. The influence of feeding regimens on iron status during infancy. Am J Clin Nutr 1980;33:746–53.
22. Owen GM, Garry PJ, Hooper EM, Gilbert BA, Pathak D. Iron nutriture of infants exclusively breast-fed the first five months. Pediatr Res 1981;99:237–40.
23. Woodruff CW, Latham C, McDavid S. Iron nutrition in the breast-fed infant. J Pediatr 1977;90: 36–8.
24. Fomon SJ, Strauss RG. Nutrient deficiencies in breast-fed infants. N Engl J Med 1978;299: 355–7.
25. Bullen JJ, Rogers HJ, Leigh L. Iron-binding proteins in milk and resistance to Escherichia coli infection in infants. Br Med J 1972;1:69–75.
26. Hegenauer J, Saltman P, Ludwig D, Ripley L, Ley A. Iron-supplemented cow milk. Identification and spectral properties of iron bound to casein micelles. J Agric Food Chem 1979;27:1294–301.
27. Fransson G-B, Lönnerdal B. Trace elements in human milk fat. Am J Clin Nutr 1984; *(in press).*
28. Greenberg R, Groves ML, Peterson RF. Amino terminal sequence and location of phosphate groups of the major human casein. J. Dairy Sci 1976;59:1016.

29. Lönnerdal B, Stanislowski AG, Hurley LS. Isolation of a low molecular weight zinc binding ligand from human milk. J Inorg Biochem 1980;12:71–8.
30. Masson P. La Lactoferrine. Bruxelles, Belgium: Editions Arscia, 1970:232.
31. Brock JH, Arzabe F, Lampreave F, Pineiro A. The effect of trypsin on bovine transferrin and lactoferrin. Biochim Biophys Acta 1976;446:214–25.
32. Lönnerdal B, Forsum E, Gebre-Medhin M, Hambraeus L. Breast milk composition in Ethiopian and Swedish mothers. II. Lactose, nitrogen, and protein contents. Am J Clin Nutr 1976;29:1134–41.
33. Arnold RR, Cole MF, McGhee JR. A bactericidal effect for human milk lactoferrin. Science 1977;197:263–5.
34. Spik G, Cheron A, Montreuil J, Dolby JM. Bacteriostasis of a milk-sensitive strain of *Escherichia coli* by immunoglobulins and iron-binding proteins in association. Immunology 1978;35:663–71.
35. Brock JH. Lactoferrin in human milk: its role in iron absorption and protection against enteric infection in the newborn infant. Arch Dis Child 1980;55:417–21.
36. MacKay HMM. Anemia in infancy: its prevalence and prevention. Arch Dis Child 1928;3:1175.
37. Feuillen YM. Iron metabolism in infants. II. Absorption of dietary iron. Acta Paediatr 1954;43:138–44.
38. Feuillen YM, Plumier M. Iron metabolism in infants. I. The intake of iron in breast feeding and artificial feeding (milk and milk foods). Acta Paediatr 1952;41:138–44.
39. Schultz J, Smith NJ. A quantitative study of the absorption of food iron in infants and children. J Dis Child 1958;95:109–19.
40. Heinrich HC, Gabbe EE, Whang DH, Bender-Götze Ch, Schäfer KH. Ferrous and hemoglobin $^{-59}$Fe absorption from supplemented cow milk in infants with normal and depleted iron stores. Z Kinderheilk 1975;120:251–8.
41. Rios E, Hunter RE, Cook JD, Smith NJ, Finch CA. The absorption of iron as supplements in infant cereal and infant formulas. Pediatrics 1975;55:686–93.
42. McMillan JA, Oski FA, Lourie G, Tomarelli RM, Landaw SA. Iron absorption from human milk, simulated human milk, and proprietary formulas. Pediatrics 1977;60:896–900.
43. Saarinen UM, Siimes MA. Iron absorption from infant milk formula and the optimal level of iron supplementation. Acta Paediatr Scand 1977;66:719–22.
44. Sandström B, Keen CL, Lönnerdal B. An experimental animal model for studies of zinc bioavailability from milk and infant formulas using extrinsic labelling. Am J Clin Nutr 1983;38:420–8.
45. DeLaey P, Masson PL, Heremans JF. The role of lactoferrin in iron absorption. Protides Biol Fluids 1968;16:627–32.
46. deVet BJCM, van Gool J. Lactoferrin and iron absorption in the small intestine. Acta Med Scand 1974;196:393–402.
47. Fransson G-B, Hambraeus L, Lönnerdal B. Availability of iron from lactoferrin to weanling rats. Nutr Rep Int 1983; *(in press)*.
48. Fransson G-B, Keen CL, Lönnerdal B. Supplementation of milk with iron bound to lactoferrin using weanling mice. I. Effects on hematology and tissue iron. J Pediatr Gastroenterol Nutr 1983;2:693–700.
49. Fransson G-B, Keen CL, Lönnerdal B. Iron supplementation of milk through iron-lactoferrin: effect on tissue iron and manganese. Fed Proc 1982;41:778.
50. Cox TM, Mazurier J, Spik G, Montreuil J, Peters TJ. Iron binding proteins and influx of iron across the duodenal brush border. Biochem Biophys Acta 1979;588:120–8.
51. Götze C, Schafer KH, Heinrich HC, Bartels H. Eisenstoffwechselstudien an Fruhgeborenen und gesunden Reifgeborenen wahrend des ersten Lebensjahres mit dem Ganzkorperzahler und anderen Methoden. Mschr Kinderheilk 1970;118:210–3.
52. Dauncey MJ, Davies CG, Shaw JC, Urman J. The effect of iron supplements and blood transfusion on iron absorption by low birthweight infants fed pasteurized human breast milk. Pediatr Res 1978;12:899–904.
53. Lundström U, Siimes MA. Iron gain in low-birthweight infants: role of milk feeding. Early Hum Dev 1978;2:277–81.
54. Björn-Rasmussen E, Hallberg L, Walker RB. Food iron absorption in man. II. Isotopic exchange of iron between labeled foods and between a food and an iron salt. Am J Clin Nutr 1973;26:1311–9.

55. Fransson G-B, Lönnerdal B. Distribution of added ^{59}Fe among different fractions of human and cow's milk. Nutr Res (SW) 1983;3:108–9.
56. Saarinen UM, Siimes MA. Iron absorption from breast milk, cow's milk, and iron-supplemented formula: an opportunistic use of changes in total body iron determined by hemoglobin, ferritin, and body weight in 132 infants. Pediatr Res 1979;13:143–7.
57. Garry PJ, Owen GM, Hooper EM, Gilbert BA. Iron absorption from human milk and formula with and without iron supplementation. Pediatr Res 1981;15:822–8.
58. Fomon SJ. Absorption of iron calculated from estimated changes in total body iron (Letter). Pediatr Res. 1982;16:161–2.
59. Amine EK, Hegsted DM. Effect of dietary carbohydrates and fats on inorganic iron absorption. J Agric Food Chem 1975;23:204–8.
60. Cook JD, Morck TA, Lynch SR. The inhibitory effect of soy products on nonheme iron absorption in man. Am J Clin Nutr 1981;34:2622–9.
61. Gross S. The relationship between milk protein and iron content on hematologic values in infancy. J Pediatr 1968;73:521–30.
62. Fomon SJ. Infant nutrition. Philadelphia: WB Saunders, 1974:575.
63. Lönnerdal B, Davidson L, Keen CL. Effect of varying dietary iron and zinc levels on tissue concentrations in the rat. In: Health effects and interactions of essential and toxic elements. Nutr Res (suppl) 1984; *(in press)*.
64. Cordano A. Copper deficiency in clinical medicine. In: Hambridge KM, Nicholds Jr BL, eds. Zinc and copper in clinical medicine. New York: SP Medical and Scientific Books, 1978;119.
65. Oski FA, Landaw SA. Inhibition of iron absorption from human milk by baby food. Am J Dis Child 1980;134:459–60.
66. Carpenter G. Epidermal growth factor is a major growth-promoting agent in human milk. Science 1980;210:198–9.
67. Beisel WR. Single nutrients and immunity. Am J Clin Nutr 1982;35:417–68.
68. Committee on Nutrition. Relationship between iron status and incidence of infection in infancy. Pediatrics 1978;62:246–50.
69. Baltimore RS, Vecchitto JS, Pearson HA. Growth of Escherichia coli and concentration of iron in an infant feeding formula. Pediatrics 1978;62:1072–3.
70. Fransson G-B, Thoren-Tolling K, Jones B, Hambraeus L, Lönnerdal B. Absorption of lactoferrin-iron in suckling pigs. Nutr Res 1983;3:373–84.
71. Siimes MA, Vuori E, Kuitunen P. Breast milk iron: a declining concentration during the course of lactation. Acta Paediatr Scand 1979;68:29–31.
72. Fransson G-B, Lönnerdal B. Distribution of trace elements and minerals in human and cow's milk. Pediatr Res 1983;17:912–915.

DISCUSSION

Dr. Stekel: May I ask you for a first comment: how would you summarize your view of the way that iron is absorbed from breast milk? Why is it absorbed as well as we think it is?

Dr. Lönnerdal: I think that you have to take it as an educated guess. I think that the lactoferrin iron is highly available. I think it will be taken up by the infant—to what extent I don't know—but I certainly do not believe in an inhibitory effect of lactoferrin on iron absorption. I think that the low molecular weight iron, if being in the low molecular weight form or by that time taken up by lactoferrin, also represents an available pool of iron. It is possible that the flavin part of the xanthine oxidase molecule in the fat also could be available. So, I think that we have potentially three promoters of iron absorption in the breast milk, whereas we have a relative lack of inhibitors of iron absorption. We have very little casein; the casein that is there is very easily digested. I think it is very interesting that if you do intubation studies in suckling rat pups and give human milk, formula, and cow's milk, and open the pups after various time periods, it is amazing how fast and well the human milk is cleared compared with the cow's milk and the formulas, in which you see a cheesy rubbery clot both in the stomach and in the upper part of the intestine. I think this would be the case for human milk: relative abundance of promoters and the relative lack of inhibitors of iron absorption, such as calcium, phosphate, and casein.

Dr. Fomon: If lactoferrin iron is available, do you speculate that it became available through digestion of the lactoferrin molecule? If so, the molecule would presumably not reach the colon where it is believed to interfere with bacterial growth.

Dr. Lönnerdal: I think that the lactoferrin molecule would be undegraded to a large extent. I think that there are receptor sites in the small intestine, which facilitate the uptake of iron because of a very strong binding constant. The receptor site possibly could take care of that. The abundance of intact, or at least immunologically intact, lactoferrin in the feces would support that. I have quantitative determination of lactoferrin per g feces. We made an extract and ran immunoelectrophoresis, but I don't have the amount of feces produced by the infant. So I don't have any balance figures, but I was amazed that on doing a fairly diluted extract from the feces and just doing immunoelectrophoresis there was a high concentration of lactoferrin.

Dr. Fomon: What is your final conclusion about the percentage of human milk iron in lactoferrin?

Dr. Lönnerdal: Twenty-five percent.

Dr. Dallman: I have two related questions. First, is there any evidence that the lactoferrin might be binding other metals. The other question is whether you have tried any experiments under conditions that simulate digestion to see if there are any shifts in the iron distribution as the milk is subjected to pH changes and other conditions that correspond to the stomach and upper duodenum.

Dr. Lönnerdal: For the first question, I think that lactoferrin is present in a very unsaturated form. We recently found that virtually all the manganese in human milk is bound to lactoferrin, but there is so little manganese. About 2 to 5% of the binding capacity of lactoferrin is utilized by iron. We don't find any zinc bound to lactoferrin and we don't find any copper. Even if you can force copper or zinc on lactoferrin *in vitro*, we don't find anything there *in vivo*. Concerning the second question, we don't have any results yet, but we are at present digesting milk, both *in vivo* and *in vitro*, to study what is happening with the distribution among the compartments.

Dr. Hallberg: Is there really a need for iron in the full-term infant during the first 6 months? Has nature designed the composition of the breast milk in such a way that it should be a good source of iron—or is it possible that the very small amount of iron in the breast milk has other biological functions not related to the iron status of the baby?

Dr. Lönnerdal: We are not sure what the physiological importance of some of these sources of iron in the breast milk is, but I still think that the low quantity of iron that the infant gets from breast milk is important if you look at the data of Dr. Siimes. If an infant is given a nonfortified cow's milk formula, for example, instead of breast milk, you see signs of iron deficiency anemia quite early, even at 4 months.

Dr. Cook: Lactoferrin is a fairly strong iron chelate. I wonder then why iron saturation of lactoferrin is so low in milk and why only 10 to 20% of the iron in milk is bound to that protein.

Dr. Lönnerdal: I think that the iron within the flavin compartment of xanthineoxidase is not easily exchangeable with the lactoferrin; even if the lactoferrin has such a strong binding constant it does not get through to it. With regard to the low molecular weight iron, we also have to consider that binding is the product of the binding constant and the concentration of the ligand. Take, for example, citrate: you have a concentration of 1 mM in the breast milk, which is a high concentration if you compare it to the molar concentration of lactoferrin. You always have to calculate the equilibrium between those compartments and that may be the reason why you will see part of iron bound to citrate.

Dr. Cook: Another explanation may be the pH effect. Perhaps there is a major shift in lactoferrin binding after ingestion of the milk at a lower pH. Perhaps a much higher proportion of iron is taken up by lactoferrin at the lower pH of the gastric content.

Dr. Lönnerdal: That is quite possible because the binding of, for example, citrate iron will rapidly decrease with pH, much more than for lactoferrin.

Dr. Garby: Is lactoferrin from one species the same as lactoferrin from another species?

Dr. Lönnerdal: They are very similar, that is, they crossreact immunologically, but they seem to have slightly different physiological activity. There are very few comparative studies that have been done and they seem to show that the homologous form for the species will be more efficient than the heterologous form and, of course, in these studies that I refer to, we used bovine lactoferrin because we used such large quantities. When we do these studies in the human we will use human lactoferrin and we will compare it with bovine lactoferrin.

Dr. Fomon: If in the gastrointestinal tract there are receptors that remove iron from the lactoferrin, it would seem important to know the quantitative aspects of this process. One might imagine that the addition of iron to human milk would result in greater saturation of the lactoferrin and, therefore, a larger amount of iron to feed to the receptors.

Dr. Lönnerdal: It is a possibility.

Dr. Cook: Another possibility might be that there is a specific receptor for lactoferrin or that the iron-lactoferrin complex actually enters the cell. Dr. Huebers has suggested that the transferrin may facilitate iron absorption by its secretion into the gastrointestinal lumen and its reentry with iron into the mucosal cell. Perhaps lactoferrin also enters the mucosal cell and is a species-specific phenomenon in that bovine lactoferrin would not enter the human mucosal cell. I wonder if you care to speculate on that, Dr. Finch?

Dr. Finch: We have done some studies involving lactoferrin but our work is so limited that I hesitate to comment. We did bind iron to lactoferrin derived from human milk and fed this to adults. Absorption of iron was markedly reduced as compared to the absorption of an iron salt. Other studies have involved gut loops in rats. There we have used human lactoferrin which may negate physiological interpretation. However, in this instance also, there was a marked reduction in absorption. Thus, we have been unable to demonstrate any positive role of lactoferrin in iron absorption.

Dr. Siimes: My comment relates to Dr. Lönnerdal's concern about the deficiencies of other minerals. There are very few data up to now that have any real clinical significance in this regard, but my concern relates to the excessive intake of other minerals in the presence of marginal iron intake, especially since there are no recommendations even for industrially made formulas.

Dr. Fomon: What is your speculation about the percentage of the iron in the whey-protein fraction associated with proteins other than lactoferrin?

Dr. Lönnerdal: I would say that a very small proportion of iron could be bound to other proteins than lactoferrin: it is virtually exclusively lactoferrin.

Dr. Stekel: It has been traditionally believed that the iron concentration in breast milk has little to do with the iron nutrition of the mother. Do you think that what you would have to do would be to raise the levels of serum iron as the mother is secreting milk and that this is what you are really changing with your oral iron supplementation?

Dr. Lönnerdal: I think it is very difficult to speculate, especially in the light of the most recent reports mentioned in the paper, in which it was found in India in severely anemic mothers that both lactoferrin and iron was higher than in the milk of nonanemic mothers. One could formulate a lot of nice hypotheses, but we don't have much evidence.

Dr. Hallberg: I would like to come back again to my first question, because I am not quite satisfied. What good data do we actually have about the total amount of iron in the body at 6 months in relation to the total amount of iron at birth; how much extra iron needs to be absorbed during that period of time to cover the growth and to cover the losses? How much extra iron do we need; what do we know about it?

Dr. Fomon: The best data on iron content at birth are those of Southgate, Hey, and Widdowson *(unpublished data)* from whole-body analyses of stillborn infants or of infants who died soon after birth. The iron content of an infant with a birth weight of 3.0 kg is about 227 mg (85 mg iron/kg of fat-free body mass) and that of an infant with a birth weight of 3.5 kg is about 268 mg (90 mg iron/kg). I am reasonably confident about data on iron content at birth. At 6 months of age, there are no satisfactory data, but I think it is possible to make a reasonable estimate by a factorial approach. Most of the iron will be in the circulating red cell mass and this quantity can be estimated on the basis of available data. Next, an estimate of muscle mass can be made and, from this, an estimate of iron in the form of myoglobin. Finally, an estimate of storage iron must be made and this is the most difficult. However, in the 6-month-old infant, storage iron will account for a small percentage of total body iron so that a relatively large percentage error in estimating quantity of storage iron will result in only a small error in the estimate of total body iron. It is not very good, but it is the best we can do at present.

Dr. Stekel: I would like to show some calculations. According to these calculations a relatively small increase in total body iron would be expected between birth and 6 months of age on the average, and maybe even the little amount of iron that can be absorbed from breast milk would be enough.

Dr. Hallberg: How much iron is in store at that time?

Dr. Dallman: We may not know very much about iron in terms of total body composition data, but we do have information on serum ferritin in infants that allow some inferences about storage iron. In term infants, iron stores become marginal at about 4 to 6 months of age, especially with cow's milk formulas that are unfortified with iron.

Dr. Siimes: In my mind, this is fairly clear. However, in some individuals there is quite a large need of iron even during the first 6 months, in particular if they are exclusively on breast milk because the concentration of iron in breast milk is very variable. The infant cannot determine the concentration. Secondly, the infant's individual hemoglobin mass at birth and at 6 months of age is quite variable. Thirdly, the growth rate (iron need) varies.

Dr. Stekel: Studies that compare iron nutrition status of breast-fed infants and infants that are fed unfortified cow's milk show very clearly that at 6 months of age there are differences between the groups as measured by various laboratory parameters. This could be due to the increased iron absorption from breast milk, to smaller iron losses, or to the facilitating effect of breast milk on iron availability from the rest of the food that the infant is taking. I think this discussion has been very interesting, but we should make clear that this group is not really doubting that breast-milk-fed infants during the first 6 months of age have an advantage in iron nutrition over artificially fed infants not receiving fortified foods.

Dr. Hallberg: I would also like to ask Dr. Lönnerdal about the different composition of milks in different species. Does that have anything to do with differences in iron nutrition or is it mainly explained by differences in requirements for energy, proteins, and so on for different rates of growth? Do you think that nature's design of milks has taken into account a good iron nutrition? Can we learn anything about the importance of the iron in milk from studies on other species?

Dr. Lönnerdal: I think that I can agree to the extent that the overall composition of milk is more important in reflecting the requirements for growth; I don't think the primary concern is iron.

Iron Nutrition in Infancy and Childhood,
edited by A. Stekel. Nestlé, Vevey/Raven Press,
New York © 1984.

Availability of Iron from Infant Foods

*J. D. Cook and **T. H. Bothwell

*Division of Hematology, Department of Medicine, University of Kansas Medical Center,
Kansas City, Kansas 66103, U.S.A.; and **Department of Medicine, University of the
Witwatersrand Medical School, Johannesburg 2001, South Africa*

The full-term infant receives a generous and relatively fixed iron supply from the mother. As a result, iron absorption in the early postnatal period is lower than at any later time in childhood; the amount and availability of dietary iron are therefore less important before 2 months of age. The infant then enters a period during which body growth rapidly outstrips the maternal supply of iron, and by 4 to 6 months of age the iron status of the infant becomes almost totally dependent on dietary iron supply.

Iron balance in the infant is characterized not only by this sudden change in iron requirement but by an equally dramatic alteration in the nature of the dietary iron consumed. It is convenient to review dietary iron availability during infancy in relation to three overlapping periods (Fig. 1). Initially, when the infant's iron needs are lowest, dietary iron is derived largely from milk or milk products. Weaning or transitional foods, mainly processed cereals, are then introduced. In addition, in poor socioeconomic segments of the populations of developing countries there are often programs to enhance caloric and protein intake at this age using so-called infant food supplements. It is during this period in infancy that iron needs are not only the highest but the prospect for meeting these needs by manipulating dietary intake is also greatest. During the latter part of infancy there is an increasing dependence on solid foods, so that by 1 year of age the diet approaches that of other members of the household.

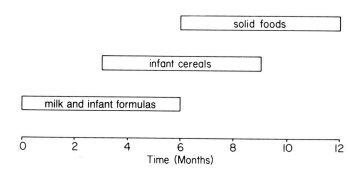

FIG. 1. Dietary iron patterns during infancy.

119

Studies of food iron availability in infants and children have been conducted for several decades. However, it is only in recent years that the methodology has advanced to the point of furnishing reliable quantitative information. Although a detailed review of this technology will not be attempted here, interpretation of recent studies of food iron absorption does require a thorough understanding of certain basic methodologic concepts.

MEASUREMENTS OF FOOD IRON ABSORPTION

It is possible to make certain inferences about food iron availability by placing infants on differing dietary regimens and comparing their iron status at a later time. However, the body's ability to modulate assimilation according to iron needs is so effective that such therapeutic trials provide only a crude and indirect measure of iron availability. Chemical iron balance studies have also been used to assess iron absorption in infancy, but this approach has proven to be too imprecise to measure the limited iron exchange in infants. Consequently, reliable information on food iron absorption has required the use of radioisotopic methods. The technical aspects of radioiron absorption measurements have been reviewed recently (1). The key features include the techniques for determining retention of administered radioiron, for eliminating the effect of differences in iron status of the participants in the study, and, perhaps most importantly, for isotopic labeling of the test meal.

Radioiron Absorption Measurements

Except for a few early studies in which the retention of administered radioiron was determined by measuring excreted fecal radioactivity, radioiron absorption has usually been determined in infant studies from the radioactivity incorporated into circulating blood 10 to 14 days following administration of the test dose. Although some uncertainty is introduced by the prediction of circulating blood volume from body weight and by the assumption of a fixed red cell incorporation of absorbed radioiron, these errors are negligible in relation to the marked variation in iron absorption between subjects. In adults, an excellent correlation has been obtained between measurements based on red cell incorporation and direct determinations of whole body radioactivity with a specially designed total body counter (2), which indicates that the method for measuring absorbed radioiron is not a critical methodologic consideration.

A major methodologic problem in iron absorption studies is the enormous variability in the percentage absorption. This variation is comprised of day-to-day differences within the same subject and of biological differences between subjects (3). In certain infant studies, day-to-day variability has been reduced to some extent by administering test doses over several days rather than using only a single test meal. However, the largest and most troublesome component of variability is that due to differences in the iron status of the subjects. In studies designed to assess iron bioavailability rather than biological response, the optimal approach is to administer two or more test meals to the same individual to permit comparisons of absorption from different meals in the same subject. By employing two radioisotopes (^{55}Fe and ^{59}Fe) and performing sequential studies, it is possible to perform as many as four separate iron absorption tests in each subject. This approach eliminates those errors introduced by predicting the size of the blood volume and by assuming a constant red cell incorporation. More importantly, it allows iron assimilation to be examined over a wide spectrum of iron status in subjects with levels of percentage absorption ranging from 1 to over 50%.

Because of the natural concern about administering radioisotopes to infants and children, multiple measurements in this age group have usually been limited to two. In evaluating studies of iron bioavailability it is very important to take into account this particular aspect of study design. If test meals have been administered to separate groups of infants, two- to threefold differences in absorption can easily be obscured by subject-to-subject variability. In contrast, paired measurements in the same subject can usually detect absorption differences of 20 to 30%.

Corrections for Iron Status (Reference Dose)

Although using multiple tests in the same subject is an effective way of comparing iron bioavailability from any pair of test meals, it is very desirable to be able to compare data obtained in different studies and in different subjects. Since the percentage absorption is profoundly influenced by iron status, and iron status invariably differs from study to study, it is necessary to adjust absorption data for such differences. The use of a reference dose for this purpose has been a major technical advance in iron absorption studies. The method involves administering a standard dose of inorganic radioiron to all subjects as one of the test meals. By general agreement among investigators, a dose of 3 mg iron as $FeSO_4$ containing a 2:1 molar ratio of ascorbic acid to iron is now used. By expressing absorption from a given test meal as a ratio of the reference dose, a measurement is obtained which is largely independent of the iron status of the subject (4).

The use of a reference dose makes it possible not only to compare the results in different studies but also to estimate the relative absorption of iron from different foodstuffs in subjects with widely differing iron stores. Current data suggest that an iron-replete male absorbs 15 to 20% of the reference dose as compared with 50 to 60% in a subject with advanced iron deficiency. It has been suggested that all food iron absorption data be adjusted to a reference value of 40%, which is taken to represent the absorption figure for individuals with depleted iron stores but without frank iron deficiency anemia. Reference dose measurements in iron-deficient infants have indicated that 60% is more appropriate in this age group (5).

One important question relating to reference dose corrections is whether absorption measurements of iron-replete individuals can be used with confidence to estimate absorption in individuals with severe iron deficiency. This is especially relevant to infants and children because of the concern about administering isotopes to younger age groups. Therefore, studies of iron availability from infant foods are often performed in adult subjects and the results are extrapolated to iron-deficient infants who have a different caloric intake. Although additional validation of reference dose corrections would be desirable, at present there is no concrete evidence that the approach is not methodologically sound (6).

Isotopic Labeling

Biosynthetic Labeling

The most critical aspect of food iron availability in relation to isotopic studies is the method by which the label is introduced into the test meal. The technique of biosynthetically labeling was first introduced in the early 1950s by Moore and Dubach (7), who tagged vegetable foods with a so-called intrinsic label by growing them in hydroponic media containing radioiron. Animal food (including fish, poultry, and dairy products) was prepared in a similar manner by injecting radioiron into the animals several weeks or months prior to obtaining the food. Because of the marked food interactions which occur when several foods are included in the same meal, an intrinsic tag provides useful information only if the test meal consists of a single food item. Probably the one dietary situation in which synthetic labeling is still relevant is in the newborn infant whose dietary intake consists solely of milk. Nevertheless, although biosynthetic labeling is cumbersome and time-consuming, it remains the standard by which the accuracy of other methods for measuring food iron absorption is assessed (1,6).

Extrinsic Tag Labeling

Since the introduction in the early 1970s of extrinsic radioiron tagging, numerous disadvantages of biosynthetic labeling have been circumvented (8–10). Extrinsic tagging is based on the observation that when one adds a small quantity of inorganic radioiron (0.1 mg was used in early studies) to a food that has been biosynthetically tagged with an alternate radioiron form, absorption of the two labels is virtually identical (9,11,12). This has held true when tested with a large variety of foods (wheat, maize, sorghum, soybean, and black bean), when the dose of the extrinsic tag varies from between 1 to 2 μg and 5 to 10 mg, and when iron availability of the test meal is either markedly decreased by adding desferrioxamine or sharply enhanced by adding ascorbic acid (6,9,12–15). Although extrinsic radioiron tagging has been explained on the basis of complete isotopic exchange of the intrinsic and extrinsic labels within the gastrointestinal lumen, absorption of the radioiron tags is also identical in patients with complete achlorhydria (1). Thus, the low pH of gastric contents, which would favor iron solubility and isotopic exchange, is not a prerequisite.

Extensive experience with extrinsic tagging has identified some important technical considerations. The extrinsic tag must be thoroughly mixed with the food before administration because inappropriately high absorption occurs if the tag is simply consumed in a drink after the bulk of the meal has been eaten (1). When the test meal contains several food items, the extrinsic tag should be mixed with the bulkiest item or distributed on the food items in rough proportion to iron content (6). It is not necessary to introduce the label before cooking the food; $FeCl_3$ and $FeSO_4$ (dose of iron 1–100 μg) are equally suitable as extrinsic labels.

Although the use of an extrinsic tag for measuring absorption of nonheme iron has been adequately validated, certain exceptions have been noted. In one such study, absorption of the extrinsic tag remained higher than that of the intrinsic tag when rice was fed as a whole grain but not when it was first thoroughly ground (14). Apparently the extrinsic tag did not completely permeate the polished rice grain (16). Layrisse et al. (17) demonstrated that iron absorption from the storage iron compounds ferritin and hemosiderin cannot be measured by an extrinsic label. There is also evidence that insoluble iron salts such as sodium iron pyrophosphate and ferric orthophosphate are also less well absorbed than an extrinsic tag (18). Thus it is clear that absorption of all forms of iron added to or contained in a meal are not measured by this technique and some forms of extraneous food iron, such as that resulting from soil contamination or food processing, undergo little if any exchange with an extrinsic radioiron tag (16,18).

While the discussion of extrinsic tagging has focused thus far on nonheme iron, it is noteworthy that the absorption of heme iron, the second major pool of dietary iron, can by the same principle be similarly measured (8,19). Radioactive iron is injected into rabbits and the animals are subsequently phlebotomized to obtain labeled hemoglobin. A small quantity of this hemoglobin is then extracted and added to the test meal in order to obtain a measure of the total absorption of the heme iron contained in the meal. However, during infancy the absorption of heme iron is of lesser importance because of the small amounts that are ingested.

Fortification Iron

One of the pitfalls in using an extrinsic tag is to assume that any form or amount of radioiron added to a meal will adequately measure absorption from the nonheme pool. As noted previously, both $FeCl_3$ and $FeSO_4$ can be used for extrinsic tagging in doses ranging from one to several hundred micrograms of iron. Even at much higher quantities of the extrinsic tag, absorption of the intrinsic and extrinsic labels remains equivalent if the latter is in a relatively soluble form. This is not true, however, for all the forms of fortification iron that are currently used and it is therefore essential that the bioavailability of such preparations be assessed prior to their introduction. In such studies it is important that the labeled iron compound be prepared under the same conditions as those for large scale commercial preparation and they should then be added to a meal that has been extrinsically labeled in the standard way using another radioisotope of iron. If absorption of the tags is identical, availability of the fortification iron can be measured in subsequent studies by extrinsic tagging. Studies of this type have shown that some forms of fortification iron, such as $FeSO_4$ or reduced iron of small particle size, undergo complete exchange with the dietary pool, whereas other forms, such as orthophosphate and sodium iron pyrophosphate, do not (20).

Another assumption to be avoided when using an extrinsic tag is that the amount of iron added as the label is unimportant. Even if complete isotopic exchange can be established between the fortification iron and the dietary nonheme iron, larger amounts of added iron can be expected to alter the percentage absorption from the dietary nonheme pool. Although the relative effects of different dosages of added iron have not been determined, it should not be assumed that this iron is a true extrinsic tag when it exceeds 10% of the native iron content of the meal.

SALIENT FEATURES OF FOOD IRON ABSORPTION

Heme and Nonheme Pools of Dietary Iron

The importance of extrinsic tagging extends far beyond the technical convenience of avoiding the need to prepare biosynthetically labeled foods. A critically important outcome of studies using the extrinsic tag is the realization that all forms of nonheme iron in a meal, regardless of the source, form a single common pool within the gastrointestinal lumen. This was initially established by adding an extrinsic tag to a homogenized meal containing several food items, one of which was a small quantity of biosynthetically tagged maize. Absorption of the two radioiron forms was virtually identical (9). It has been shown that when two biosynthetically tagged foods (which have markedly different absorptions when fed separately) are given in the same meal, percentage absorption becomes identical. For example, in one study absorption of labeled eggs and bread averaged 1 to 2% and 30%, respectively, when fed separately, but when fed together nearly identical mean absorptions of 5.0% were observed (14). The ability to measure total absorption of nonheme iron from a complex meal has become the cornerstone of our approach to studying food iron availability.

In recent studies emphasis has been placed on the availability of nonheme iron because this constitutes the major fraction of dietary iron. However, there is a second compartment consisting of heme iron which enters the mucosal cells as an intact porphyrin complex and is therefore affected little if any by the nature of the meal (1). There is a striking difference in the availability of iron from the heme and nonheme iron pools. In a study by Bjorn-Rasmussen et al. (8), meals containing proportional amounts of all foods consumed in a typical 6-week diet were labeled with double extrinsic tags of heme and nonheme iron and given to 32 young men. The daily intake of iron from this diet was 17.4 mg, of which 1 mg was heme. The absorption of heme and nonheme iron averaged 37 and 5.3%, respectively, corresponding to daily absorptions of 0.37 and 0.88 mg (Fig. 2). Thus, in this meat-eating population, heme iron provided nearly one-third of the daily iron requirement even though it represented less than one-tenth of the dietary iron.

Biochemical Determinants of Food Iron Availability

The objective of current studies on iron absorption is not simply to determine iron availability from different foods but to catalog and quantitate the potency of

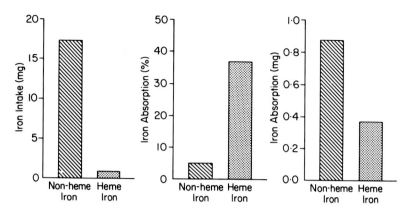

FIG. 2. Absorption in 10 subjects of nonheme and heme from a diet in which almost all the iron was present as nonheme iron (8).

various biochemical determinants in the diet which either facilitate or impair absorption from the common pool. The assumption by earlier workers that iron assimilation can be explained simply on the basis of valency and solubility is now recognized as an oversimplification and there is increasing awareness of the complex nature of the iron-binding reactions that occur in the gastrointestinal tract. The effect of a given ligand depends on its concentration, its chelating efficiency which is often sharply pH dependent, and the types and concentrations of competing ligands in the meal. Although it may eventually be possible to design *in vitro* models which can predict iron assimilation from a given meal, at present it is necessary to measure iron absorption in human subjects under different dietary conditions to obtain meaningful data.

Enhancers of Iron Absorption

The quantity of animal tissue in a given meal is probably the single most important determinant of iron availability. Except for milk intake, it is the only dietary factor that has been found to correlate with iron status in population studies (1,21). The beneficial effect of meat is partly explained by the high content of heme iron. For example, the percentage absorption of nonheme iron from a meal containing only meat is 20 to 30% as compared to 2 to 3% in vegetable foods or dairy products (8,10). Meat fulfills a second role: its addition to a meal enhances the absorption of nonheme iron by a factor of 2 to 3 (22). Despite continued study, the biochemical factor responsible for the facilitating effect of animal tissue is still unknown. Martinez-Torres et al. (23) have suggested that cysteine is the factor but this has not yet been confirmed. Others have assumed that the enhancing effect of iron absorption is related to the protein fraction of the meat; if so, however, it must be the type of protein rather than protein per se. In studies of the effect of macronutrients, protein but neither fat nor carbohydrate was found to inhibit iron absorption

(22). It is possible that the stimulating effect of meat relates to the rate or products of protein digestion.

The enhancing effect of ascorbic acid on nonheme iron absorption is profound whether it is contained naturally in the food or is added as the synthetic vitamin (1,15,18,24–26). The facilitating effect of vitamin C relates not so much to the valency state of iron but more to its ability to form a soluble complex with iron at a low gastric pH. This complex then promotes iron absorption by preventing the formation of the insoluble hydroxides at the higher pH of the small intestine. However, it is not easy to predict the importance of naturally occurring ascorbic acid on food iron absorption because much of the vitamin may be rendered inactive during preparation of the food. For example, ascorbic acid is destroyed by baking (15). The relative roles of other organic acids in potentiating iron absorption have not been defined. There is, however, preliminary evidence that lactic acid (27) and citric and malic acids do exert some effect (28). It is noteworthy that all the vegetables associated with higher iron bioavailability contain citric, malic, and ascorbic acids in various combinations (28). The vegetables include potato, beetroot, pumpkin, tomato, broccoli, cauliflower, cabbage, and turnip.

Inhibitors of Iron Absorption

The importance of dietary inhibitors first became apparent when a dramatic inhibiting effect of tea on iron absorption was demonstrated (29). It was shown that a single cup of tea reduced the absorption of $FeCl_3$ from 22 to 6% and of nonheme dietary iron from 11 to 2.5% (Fig. 3). This inhibition, which also occurs to a lesser extent with coffee, results from the formation of insoluble iron tannates. Tannins are widely distributed in vegetable foods and may be partly responsible for the overall low bioavailability of iron in many such foods (28).

Another important inhibitor of iron absorption is bran, which impairs iron absorption in a dose-dependent fashion (30,31). It is widely assumed that the effect is due to phytate. This has been inferred from studies in which the effect of adding large amounts of sodium phytate to a meal has been measured but it is not certain whether naturally occurring phytate also impairs iron absorption. For example, wheat and oat bran appear to be equally inhibitory despite widely differing phytate contents (32). In addition, destruction of the phytate content of whole bran by

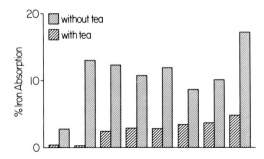

FIG. 3. The inibitory effect of tea on the absorption of the nonheme iron in a meal containing rice, potato, and onion soup, and 100 mg ascorbic acid (29).

enzymatic hydrolysis did not diminish its inhibiting effect in a recently reported study (33). Moreover, monoferric phytate, the major form of iron in bran, has relatively high bioavailability as determined by studies in both animals and humans (34). The inhibitory effect of bran may also be due to its fiber content or possibly to a component contained in a soluble extract of bran.

The propensity of iron to form highly insoluble complexes with phosphates has led to the assumption that they are important inhibitors of iron absorption (32). Certainly, egg yolk contains a phosphoprotein that seems to explain its very low bioavailability. However, in a more recent study the addition of either a soluble calcium salt or soluble phosphate salt had little effect on iron absorption, whereas marked inhibition was observed when these were added simultaneously. Apparently, absorption was inhibited by the adsorption of iron onto an insoluble complex of calcium phosphate (35).

Another potent inhibitor of food iron absorption is EDTA, which is widely used as a food preservative. The effect of EDTA on iron absorption depends on its molar ratio to iron. When only small amounts are added to a meal, nonheme iron absorption is actually enhanced (36,37). This observation has led to the suggestion that sodium iron EDTA may be useful for iron fortification. However, when EDTA is added in a molar ratio greater than 2:1, absorption of nonheme iron is progressively impaired (38). There is reason to believe that such quantities of EDTA may exist in a broad range of prepared foods.

Many workers have suggested that fiber is an important inhibitory substance but this is based largely on indirect studies of *in vitro* iron binding (39). There is little direct evidence that fiber inhibits the absorption of nonheme iron in humans and, in fact, we have observed no effect whatsoever of certain purified fibers such as pectin and cellulose. Moreover, in a recent study, isocaloric meals were matched in terms of their major biochemical determinants but differed markedly in their content of naturally occurring fiber. Iron absorption from the low fiber meal was significantly higher but the relatively modest twofold difference between the extremes in fiber content suggests that fiber does not represent a major inhibitory factor in the diet.

Fortification Iron

There is evidence that a number of compounds that were used in the past as iron fortificants are poorly absorbed. These include large particle reduced iron, ferric orthophosphate, and ferric pyrophosphate (18,20,40). The relative bioavailability of such compounds in relation to a well-absorbed form of iron such as ferrous sulfate has been assessed in a number of ways. These include *in vivo* animal models using rats or chicks (41) and several *in vitro* studies aimed at testing the relative solubility of different iron compounds and of dietary iron in conditions similar to those operating in the upper gastrointestinal tract (42,43). However, before any fortificant is added to a diet, its bioavailability should be directly measured in humans by administering test meals that are representative of the diets consumed by the population concerned (44,45).

Currently the most commonly used fortification compounds are ferrous sulfate and various iron powders, including reduced iron, electrolytic iron, and carbonyl iron. Former problems relating to the absorbability of iron powders have been largely overcome by reduction of their particle size and surface area, and it has been shown that the reactive surface area and the dissolution rate in hydrochloric acid are good predictors of absorbability (46). The particular compound chosen depends not only on its bioavailability but also on its compatibility with the chosen vehicle and with other constituents in the diet. Thus high-density iron powders may be difficult to distribute evenly in powdered foods, whereas metallic iron may be removed by the magnets employed in food processing to detect metallic contaminants. On the other hand, more reactive compounds such as ferrous sulfate may be associated with undesirable changes in the color, odor, and flavor of the food (45).

IRON ABSORPTION FROM INFANT FORMULAS

Infant Formulas

Iron absorption from milk is of critical importance during infancy since this food often represents the only source of dietary iron during the first few months of life (47). In discussing this subject it is important to distinguish between human and cow's milk—the iron in breast milk is much more bioavailable than that in cow's milk (48–50). Since iron absorption from breast milk is the subject of another report, the major emphasis here will be on cow's milk. In this connection, it is essential to distinguish between the fortified and unfortified products, as the percentage absorption is affected significantly by the iron content. There is no clear evidence that commercial processing has a significant effect on iron availability. Therefore, no distinction will be made between fresh cow's milk, pasteurized milk, condensed milk, evaporated milk, or reconstituted powder. Moreover, since carbohydrate and fat have relatively little effect on iron absorption, milk and milk-based formulas will be considered equivalent. Attention must be paid, however, to the presence of nutritional additives and supplements such as ascorbic acid since they can be expected to affect the amount of iron absorbed.

Cow's Milk

A frequent question that is asked in relation to infant formulas is whether milk in general is a good or poor source of dietary iron. There is no clear-cut answer to this question because it involves comparison with other foods and there is no agreement at present on what constitutes a reference food with respect to iron availability. In addition, it is not clear whether comparisons between test meals should be made on the basis of equal calories, equal bulk, equal protein, or equal iron content. Despite these conceptual problems, there are several observations in the literature that have a bearing on the question.

One of the few studies in infants and children in which iron absorption from milk as a single food item was compared with other foods was that reported a number of years ago by Smith and Schulz (51). Using biosynthetically tagged foods, they observed that iron absorption from cow's milk averaged 9.1% in 10 children under the age of 5 as compared with 8.3% from eggs in 49 children. These findings imply low availability of iron in milk since the phosphoprotein of egg has been shown in adults to be a strong inhibitor of iron absorption (1). Iron absorption from liver and cereals was found to be similar to eggs and milk. However, there are two defects in this particular study that make interpretation difficult. First, no details of the iron status of the subjects were provided. Second, iron absorption was measured by fecal radioiron balance, which was subsequently shown to be a relatively inaccurate method.

The most stringent way to evaluate iron absorption from milk is to administer it with iron and compare the absorption to a similar iron dose given with water. When Schulz and Smith (52) fed 30 mg iron as ferrous sulfate with 180 cc milk instead of water, the average absorption dropped from 15 to 5%. Surprisingly, the same reduction was observed when the iron was given with 100 cc orange juice containing 42 mg of added ascorbic acid. It therefore seemed as if milk was no more inhibitory than orange juice in terms of fortification iron. Similar findings were reported by Davis and Bolin (53) who gave 5 mg iron as ferric ammonium citrate with either 300 ml full-cream powdered milk or with water and then measured iron absorption by whole body counting. The use of milk as a vehicle for the iron resulted in a moderate decrease in absorption from 23 to 10%. In a more recent study carried out by Heinrich et al. (54) in infants, the absorption of 5 mg iron as $FeSO_4$ in water fell from 18 to 4% when given with 50 ml cow's milk.

While these studies suggest that milk does not have a major inhibitory effect on iron absorption, the iron it contains is distinctly less available than some other types of animal protein. This point was underlined by the findings in one study in which the effects of various sources of animal protein were assessed by substituting them in protein equivalent amounts in complete meals (22). When milk was substituted for beef in a typical American meal, absorption fell from 5.1 to 2.6%, but no difference was observed when milk replaced egg albumen as the protein source in a meal containing semipurified ingredients. In addition, it was found that iron absorption from several dairy products, including milk, cheese, egg, and ovalbumen, was similar and distinctly lower than from animal tissue such as beef, pork, lamb, liver, chicken, and fish.

From a pediatric standpoint, it is pertinent to ask whether the iron in milk products is less or more bioavailable than the iron in foods which are used as substitutes for milk during infancy. The evidence suggests that iron absorption from milk is relatively high. For example, Ashworth and March (5) noted that when maize was added to a formula consisting of dried skim milk and sugar, absorption of the fortification iron which was present as $FeSO_4$ fell significantly from 9.5 to 6.3% in 16 iron-deficient children (reference absorption 59.6%). More recently, Oski and Landaw (55) studied the effect of strained pears on the absorption of iron from milk. In 5 iron-replete adult males, the mean percentage absorption from

100 ml human milk fell significantly from 24 to 5.7% when it was given with one jar (128 g) of this common baby food. This result might be partly explained by an increase in the amount of iron, neutral detergent fiber, volume of the meal, and perhaps EDTA. Nevertheless, these various studies suggest that while milk does not promote iron absorption, it has a significantly less inhibitory effect than infant cereals or solid food.

Human Milk

One of the most intriguing observations in relation to food iron absorption that has been made in recent years is the exceptionally high bioavailability of iron in human milk as compared with that in cow's milk (Fig. 4). In one study, McMillan et al. (49) fed 3 oz of extrinsically tagged milk to 10 adult subjects and observed a mean absorption of 13.6% (1.7–34.2%) from cow's milk containing 40 to 60 μg iron as compared to 20.8% (2.2–50.2%) from pooled human milk with the same iron content ($p < 0.02$). Extrapolating these findings to infants, the authors estimated mean absorptions of approximately 35 and 50% from formulas and breast milk, respectively. These estimates were confirmed in a later study by Saarinen et al. (56), who observed a very high mean absorption of 48.8% when a tracer dose of radioiron ($FeSO_4$) was given during breast-feeding to 11 infants 6 to 7 months old. When a tracer dose of iron was fed in the fasting state to breast-fed infants, the mean absorption was 38.1%, significantly higher ($p < 0.05$) than the 19.5% obtained with infants who were on a cow's milk diet. This technique may not have fully labeled the iron in breast milk but the differences suggest that breast milk may in some way modify conditions in the upper gastrointestinal tract so that they favor iron absorption. Whatever the explanation, it seems clear that the bioavailability of iron is greater when infants are being breast-fed.

Possible biochemical reasons for higher absorption from breast milk as compared to infant's formula have not been identified. Cow's milk contains a much higher concentration of phosphate, which is known to inhibit iron absorption under certain

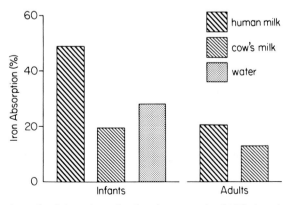

FIG. 4. Comparison of radioiron absorption from human and unfortified cow's milk. Results are shown for studies in normal 6-month-old infants (56) and normal adults (49).

conditions (35). The ascorbic acid content of breast milk is substantially higher than that of cow's milk and the enhancing effect of ascorbate is well known (1). McMillan et al. (49) recently attempted to identify the factor responsible for the high iron assimilation from human milk. They found that iron absorption from human milk in adult subjects averaged 15.4% as compared with 9.0% from simulated human milk. Although absorption from the human milk was higher than that from the simulated food, the difference was not statistically significant. The addition of lactoferrin, which is present in high concentrations in human milk, to the simulated preparation depressed absorption to 4.78%. This finding indicates that it is not lactoferrin that accounts for the high bioavailability of iron in human milk and the authors speculated that a higher content of cysteine or perhaps adenine nucleotides may be of importance.

Soya-Based Formulas

It is currently estimated that soya-based formulas account for 10 to 20% of infant formula sales in the United States. Recent studies of the effect of soya on nonheme food iron from complex meals are reviewed in the following section. It is of interest here that no obvious differences have been observed between the bioavailability of iron present in milk and soya-based infant formulas. Rios et al. (57) measured radioiron absorption by whole-body counting in 4- to 7-month-old infants using three infant formulas that had been fortified with 12 mg $FeSO_4$/liter. The mean absorption in groups of 13 to 15 infants averaged 3.9 and 3.4% from two milk-based formulas as compared to a mean of 5.4% from the soya-based formula; the small difference was not statistically significant. The study indicates that iron availability from infant formulas is the same with cow's milk as the base as it is with soya, at least when the product is in liquid form, has a low pH, and is fortified with both iron and ascorbic acid.

Processed Cereal and Legume-Based Food

Cereals

The three major cereal grains, rice, wheat, and maize, are produced in roughly equal amounts on a worldwide basis (32). Rice is particularly important because it is the major food of over half the world's population. Since cereal grains are the major constituents of weaning foods, it is useful to consider first the bioavailability of iron from these foods. Much of the following information is derived from a recent extensive review of this subject (32).

The results of several selected studies in which the absorption of iron from cooked cereals was measured are summarized in Fig. 5. Although some of the meals contained other food items, no results are included from studies in which the meal contained food known to enhance or inhibit nonheme iron absorption. The native iron content of the test meals varied in different reports from 0.5 to 10 mg. All data were adjusted to a reference absorption of 40%. The review included

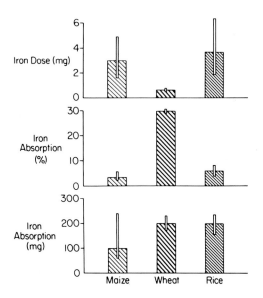

FIG. 5. Iron absorption from cereal foods. Results are summarized for published studies containing 10 or more subjects given a meal consisting only of cooked rice, wheat, or maize. All percentage absorption values have been corrected to a mean reference dose of 40%. All means are weighted means. *Vertical bars* represent range of reported means (32).

eight studies with maize (189 subjects), three studies with wheat (48 subjects), and two studies with rice (149 subjects). Weighted averages were calculated for the iron content of the meal, the percentage absorption, and the absolute absorption (μg iron). A major problem that bedevils this type of analysis is the difference in iron content of the test meals. For example, the quantities of iron averaged 3.0 and 4.7 mg, respectively, in the maize and rice meals as compared with only 0.6 mg in meals containing wheat flour of high extraction. Since the percentage absorption is influenced by the iron content of the meal, a valid comparison of the relative bioavailability of iron in different cereals is not possible. It was, nevertheless, apparent that there were striking differences in the bioavailability of iron in these different cereals. Absorption from maize and rice averaged 6.3 and 3.5%, respectively, as compared with a value of nearly 30% for wheat flour of 70% extraction. When converted to the amounts of absorbed iron, the figure from the maize-based meals averaged about 100 μg iron as compared with 200 μg from both wheat and rice. It is therefore apparent that although the iron contained in wheat is highly available, its value as a source of dietary iron is lessened because of its low iron content.

An additional comparison of the absorption of iron from wheat, rice, and maize was performed recently (32). In an initial study, absorption from rolls containing approximately 1.5 mg iron averaged 11.8% when prepared with wheat flour and 3.0% when prepared with rice flour. This fourfold difference in the percentage absorption was highly significant statistically. Similar findings were obtained when rolls were prepared with starch extracted from either wheat, rice, or maize. When meals containing 1 to 2 mg iron were given, the absorption ratios for rice:wheat averaged 0.37 and for maize:wheat 0.59. Although the absorption ratios noted with starch were somewhat different from those obtained with flour, it is apparent that the iron in white wheat is better assimilated than is the iron in rice or maize.

Sorghum is also used in infant cereals in certain developing countries although its total consumption is much less than that of the other major cereals. While there are only limited data on the bioavailability of iron in sorghum, the evidence that has been collected suggests that it is low. In one recent report, iron absorption from meals containing red sorghum, white sorghum, and maize averaged 3.6, 2.8, and 4.4%, respectively (32). In a recent study by Derman et al. (27), the geometric mean absorption of a maize and sorghum gruel was less than 2%. Fermentation of the gruel was found to enhance iron absorption, an effect that may have been due to several factors including a lower pH, a reduced content of solids, and the formation of lactic acid and alcohol. In further unpublished studies by the same workers, the geometric mean absorption of iron from whole grain sorghum porridge varied between 1.7 and 2.4% in different experiments (reference absorptions 34 and 41%, respectively).

Legumes

The bioavailability of iron in soya products is especially relevant to iron nutrition in infants. Soya-based infant formulas are used extensively to avoid suspected or proven allergies to milk, and soya is also a major constituent of infant protein supplements. The composition of soybean differs markedly from cereals in that more than half of the bean consists of protein and fat (40 and 20%, respectively). Soybeans are used in the preparation of a wide range of products, which are classified into three groups on the basis of their protein content. Soya flour and grits have a protein content of 40 to 50%, soya concentrates about 70%, and soya isolates between 90 and 95% (32). Another important difference between cereals and legumes is the high native iron content in the legumes. In a survey based on more than 30 samples of soya flour, the mean iron content was 8.6 mg iron/100 g product, while the iron content of 4 soya concentrates and 18 soya isolates averaged 11.9 and 15.0 mg/100 g, respectively.

The results of early studies using intrinsically labeled foods suggested that iron availability from whole soybean is relatively good. However, striking differences in availability were observed despite the fact that the soybean that was tested in the different studies had been biosynthetically tagged in the same institution (Table 1). Similar percentage absorptions of 11.0 and 12.3%, respectively, were observed by Layrisse et al. (10) and by Sayers et al. (15) from meals containing approximately 4 mg native soybean iron. On the other hand, a mean absorption of only 1.5% was observed by Bjorn-Rasmussen et al. (14), who fed a smaller meal. Low figures for iron absorption were also observed by Ashworth and March (5), even though their studies were conducted in children, many of whom had severe iron deficiency. It has been assumed that the marked differences in results that were noted were related to a number of factors, including the particular batch of soybean, the state of maturity at the time of harvest, differences in the method of preparing the food,

TABLE 1. *Absorption of iron from intrinsically labeled soybean*

References	No. of subjects	Iron content (mg)	Geometric mean absorption (%)
Layrisse et al. (10)	17	4.0	11.0
Sayers et al. (15)	10	4.6	12.3
Bjorn-Rasmussen et al. (14)	15	2.5	1.5
	10[a]	0.5	2.6
Ashworth and March (5)	16[a]	0.5	6.7

[a]Children.

and perhaps also variations in the iron status of the test subjects. Incidentally, excellent agreement was observed in these studies between the absorption of the intrinsic and extrinsic radioiron tags.

Findings in more recent studies suggest that soya impairs the absorption of nonheme iron (58). In one recent study conducted in normal male volunteers, protein equivalent amounts of egg albumen, casein, and isolated soya protein were substituted in a meal containing semipurified ingredients (59). Absorption from meals containing egg albumen and casein averaged 2.5 and 2.7%, respectively, as compared to a mean figure of 0.5% with isolated soya protein. It should be noted that these meals were designed as an experimental model for assessing biochemical determinants of iron absorption and it would be hazardous to extrapolate the findings directly to iron absorption from a normal diet. Moreover, because of the low iron content of egg albumen and casein, it was necessary to add large amounts of $FeCl_3$ to the meals containing these protein sources in order to offset the high native iron content of the soya-based meal. In another study, full-fat soya flour, textured soya protein, and isolated soya protein were substituted in the same semipurified meal and were compared to a control meal containing egg albumen (60). The mean absorption of iron of 5.5% for the control meal fell significantly to 1.0, 1.9, and 0.4%, respectively, with the three soya products. This striking inhibition in percentage absorption by soya protein could not be explained by the method for preparing the meal. Iron absorption with isolated protein was the same whether the food was uncooked or baked, and absorption from meals containing whole soybean was the same whether the food was boiled or baked prior to serving.

Prepared Infant Cereals

There have been a limited number of studies in which iron availability from prepared infant formulas has been measured. It should be noted that in almost all cases the foods were fortified with relatively large amounts of iron. The percentage absorptions recorded in these studies do not therefore necessarily reflect an inhibitory effect of cereal foods on iron availability but rather the interaction between fortification iron and its cereal-based vehicle. It should also be noted that the fortification iron was actually tagged in only a few of these studies and in most reports it has been tacitly assumed that the added extrinsic tag underwent complete isotopic exchange with the iron fortificant.

The first isotopic study of absorption from infant cereals was performed by Schulz and Smith (52), who reported a mean absorption of 9.1% from mixed infant cereals that had been fortified with sodium iron pyrophosphate. These findings are in striking contrast to absorption values of 1 to 2% that have been observed in later studies (32). Although the exact reason for the disparity is not known, there are two possible explanations. First, the labeled iron pyrophosphate used by Smith and Schulz (51) differed in several respects from the compound presently used for fortifying infant cereals. Second, they measured iron absorption by radioiron balance, which has often contributed to falsely high values due to incomplete collection of fecal samples.

In a more complete study of the same type, iron absorption was measured in infants from a mixed grain cereal of oat flour, soft wheat flour, and barley malt flour (57). A 10-g portion of dry cereal containing 5 mg iron was mixed with the formula and fed on five successive days to 25 normal infants ranging in age from 4 to 7 months. Special care was taken in this study to prepare labeled forms of iron comparable to those actually used commercially. This was done by adhering to specifications laid down for the production of enrichment and fortification forms of iron for cereal manufacture. Particle size and solubility characteristics were rigidly controlled and were similar to those used for industrial fortification. The iron compounds that were studied included iron orthophosphate and sodium iron pyrophosphate, both of which were used extensively for cereal fortification at the time of the investigation. Two additional forms, reduced iron of small particle size (95% of the particles between 5 and 10 μm) and $FeSO_4$, were also studied. While $FeSO_4$ is not suitable for commercial use because of its tendency to cause rancidity in cereals after prolonged storage, it is highly soluble and therefore serves as a useful reference compound. Iron absorption from ferric orthophosphate and iron pyrophosphate was uniformly low, with a composite mean of only 0.9%. Comparable figures for $FeSO_4$ and reduced iron were 2.7 and 4.0%, respectively.

These results are very similar to those obtained when adult subjects were fed rolls fortified with the same forms of iron (20). In the adult study it was also noted that the absorption of ferrous sulfate and reduced iron could be measured with an extrinsic tag, whereas the less available forms of iron did not undergo complete isotopic exchange. As a result of these studies, there has been a reduction in the use of less soluble forms of iron for the fortification of infant cereals. Elemental iron powders of small particle size are now extensively used in the United States to fortify proprietary dry cereals. Electrolytic iron, which has not been studied isotopically, is the predominant form (45). It should be noted that it has never been established whether the absorption of different types of elemental iron powders such as electrolytic iron, hydrogen-reduced iron, and carbonyl iron is the same.

Infant Food Supplements

An important subgroup of processed infant cereals are the so-called blended foods, which are distributed to developing countries as infant protein supplements under the U.S. Food for Peace Program (32). While these foods are provided mainly for weaning infants, their use is also advocated in children, pregnant women, and lactating mothers. The most popular food of this type is corn-soya-milk (CSM), which is made up of 59% maize meal, 17.5% soya flour, 15% nonfat dry milk, and 5.5% soybean oil. In addition, a mineral premix is added, which provides, among other vitamins and minerals, 18 mg iron as ferrous fumarate and 40 mg ascorbic acid per 100 g dry food. Provided there is no degradation of the ascorbic acid, the CSM provides a molar ratio of ascorbic acid:iron of about 0.7. An intake of CSM at the recommended level of 100 g/day for a 1-year-old infant should meet the recommended dietary intake of iron for this age group.

The only study in which the absorption of iron from CSM has been measured in children was the one performed by Ashworth and March (5), who studied absorption from an extrinsically labeled test meal containing 30 g CSM, 15 g sugar, and 4.5 mg iron as ferrous fumarate. In 14 clinically healthy Jamaican children, absorption averaged 6.0% (reference absorption 63.5%), which was considered adequate by the authors. More recently, iron availability from several protein supplements was studied in iron-replete adult males (33). The foods included CSM, corn-soya blend, wheat-soya blend, wheat protein concentrate, and whey-soya drink. The protein contributions from each source are listed in Table 2. Iron absorption from the three products was compared to a reference dose of ferrous iron in two groups containing 13 and 14 volunteers. Corn-soya-milk absorption was measured in both groups as an additional study control. When the results were adjusted to a reference absorption of 60% (the mean reference absorption was 27 and 13% in the two groups), iron absorption from the five supplements ranged between 1.7 and 4.1% (Fig. 6), which is in close agreement with the results by Ashworth and March (5). After correcting to geometric means by assigning values of 0.1% to 2 subjects with zero absorption, mean absorption with CSM in the infant study was 3.1% as compared to 2.6 and 3.1% in the adult study. One limitation common to both reports is the fact that the ferrous fumarate used for fortification was not isotopically labeled and it was necessary to assume that its absorption could be measured by extrinsic tagging. However, if isotopic exchange

TABLE 2. *Percentage of total protein contributed by the different major ingredients*

	Soya	Cornmeal	Milk	Wheat	Whey	Total %
Corn-soya-milk	45	27	28			100
Corn-soya blend	63	37				100
Wheat-soya blend	55			45		100
Wheat-protein-concentrate blend	61			39		100
Whey-soya drink	74				26	100

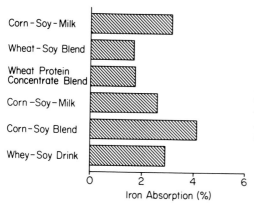

Corn – Soy – Milk
Wheat – Soy Blend
Wheat Protein Concentrate Blend
Corn – Soy – Milk
Corn – Soy Blend
Whey – Soy Drink

Iron Absorption (%)

FIG. 6. Iron absorption from infant food supplements. The data derived from studies in two groups of iron replete adult males, which accounts for the fact that there are two observations with corn-soya-milk. Absorption values have been adjusted to a reference absorption of 60% (33).

had in fact been incomplete, iron absorption from these foods would have been even lower.

These recent findings suggest that although relatively large amounts of iron are added to infant food supplements, they may still fall short of iron requirements. For example, the recommended iron intake for a 1-year-old infant is 15 mg/day, which assumes a 10% absorption of dietary iron. The study by Morck et al. (33) indicates that the iron-deficient child may only absorb between 0.3 and 0.7 mg iron from 100 g of supplement, the amount recommended by WHO/UNICEF, which would not meet the daily iron requirements of 0.7 to 1.0 mg. This disparity is probably of little importance in industrialized countries where the diet contains several iron sources, but it may be a matter for concern in developing countries where fulfillment of iron requirements may be heavily dependent on blended cereals.

Ascorbic Acid Supplementation

The ability of ascorbic acid to enhance the absorption of nonheme iron has been discussed previously. In view of the low bioavailability of iron added to infant formulas and cereals, one alternative to the addition of more iron to the diet is to fortify with iron plus ascorbic acid. This approach, which is common with proprietary formulas in developed countries, has proven effective in Chile, where 80% of the infants are now fed an iron-fortified milk powder (48). In pilot studies, iron absorption averaged only 3 to 4% in iron-deficient infants who were fed 100 g low-fat (12%) milk powder containing 15 mg iron as $FeSO_4$. In a field trial in which milk was supplied until the age of 15 months, 12% of infants receiving the iron-fortified milk had anemia, as compared with 34.6% in the control group. Although the difference was statistically significant, anemia was still present in the group receiving iron-fortified formula. In a further pilot study it was possible to show that the addition of 100 to 200 mg ascorbic acid to 15 mg iron increased absorption by a factor of 2 to 3 and, in a second field trial using milk fortified with both iron and ascorbic acid, anemia at 15 months was reduced to less than 2%. While this series of studies provides clear evidence of the efficacy of ascorbic acid in promoting absorption of fortification iron, the cost effectiveness of the approach still needs to be established in a national intervention program.

Further convincing evidence of the efficacy of ascorbic acid fortification was obtained recently by Derman et al. (24) from studies in iron-deficient adult subjects. Absorption was measured from an iron-enriched infant milk formula, a protein supplement, and three cereals differing mainly in the type of iron fortification (Fig. 7). The results with cereal-based foods were of particular interest. Thirty grams of cereal containing 5 to 9 mg iron were fed with or without 20 to 50 mg ascorbic acid, which was added immediately prior to serving. A highly significant enhancement in iron absorption with ascorbic acid was noted in all studies regardless of the iron fortification compound (ferric ammonium citrate, $FeSO_4$, or iron pyrophosphate). The relative increase in iron absorption from cereals ranged from 1.4 to 12.9% with corresponding molar ratios of ascorbate to iron of 1.1 to 3.2. These results indicate that a molar ratio of about 1.5 can cause a two- to threefold increase in iron absorption and suggest that the molar ratio of ascorbic acid to iron should be placed well above the value of 0.7 currently used for infant protein supplements. It has recently been calculated that if a molar ratio of 1.5 were used, it would increase the cost of ascorbic acid per ton from $5.85 to $8.27, which would affect the total cost of the food less than 2% per ton (32).

An important question with regard to the use of ascorbic acid is the length of time the vitamin remains active after its addition to various infant foods. This may be a particular problem in developing countries where foods are exposed to higher

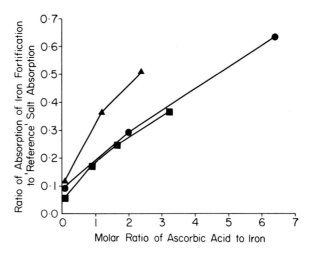

FIG. 7. The improvement in the absorption of iron fortificants due to increasing the ratio of ascorbic acid to iron. The ratio of the amount of iron absorbed from the fortified foodstuff to the amount absorbed from a standard dose of ferrous ascorbate was used as a measure of iron absorption, since the ratio corrects results for individual variations in nutritional status (24). *Circles,* infant milk formula; *triangles,* infant cereal B; *squares,* infant cereal C.

and more humid temperatures. Studies under controlled laboratory conditions suggest that degradation of the vitamin may be fairly rapid and, on this basis, Bookwalter et al. (61) recently suggested the use of a more stable ethyl cellulose-coated ascorbic acid preparation. The proposal has now been accepted and will be used for the formulation of CSM and wheat-soya blend (32). The additional cost of the stabilized preparation is negligible and it may well have a wide application. However, there is clearly a need for more studies to determine the efficacy of coated ascorbic acid under prevailing conditions of preparation, distribution, and consumption of infant cereals.

Solid Foods

Solid foods are progressively introduced during the second 6 months of life so that the diet of children over the age of 1 year approaches that consumed by the rest of the household. While attention in the past has been directed to the iron content of different foods, it is now apparent that the percentage absorbed from different foods varies over a very wide range (1). Iron is well absorbed from meat and foods containing ascorbic acid and is poorly absorbed from cereals and legumes. In passing, it should be emphasized that not all animal foodstuffs enhance iron absorption. The iron in dairy products is much less available than that in meat (22). The relevance of individual foodstuffs lies not only in the relative bioavailability of the iron contained within them but also in their overall effects on the absorption of iron from a mixed meal. For example, meat and ascorbic acid enhance the absorption of iron from the entire meal. With data currently available it is possible to construct a model that provides an estimate of the availability of iron in different diets. These estimates are based on the amount of heme and nonheme in the meal and on the content of both animal tissue (meat, poultry, or fish) and ascorbic acid. On the basis of these variables, meals are then classified as being of low, medium, or high iron bioavailability (Fig. 8). A meal of low bioavailability contains less

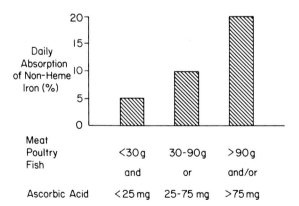

FIG. 8. The percentage absorption of nonheme iron by individuals with no body iron stores from three different types of diet (62).

than 30 g animal tissue and less than 25 mg ascorbic acid. A meal of medium bioavailability contains 30 to 90 g meat, poultry, or fish or 25 to 75 mg ascorbic acid. A meal is considered to be of high bioavailability if the figures for either of these components are greater than this. The model is obviously an oversimplification since it ignores the possible enhancing effects of dietary constituents such as organic acids, and also the many inhibitors that can be present in mixed diets. Nevertheless, it provides a more rational basis for determining the adequacy of dietary iron intake than do traditional calculations that are based solely on total iron content of the diet. In addition, it suggests strategies by which iron nutrition in later infancy might be improved. For example, the addition of orange juice to a meal is sufficient to double the amount of iron absorbed from the entire meal (63).

SUMMARY AND CONCLUSIONS

Much of our current knowledge concerning iron nutrition is based on radioisotopic studies. It has been established that heme iron in food is well absorbed regardless of the composition of the diet. Nonheme food iron is generally less bioavailable. During digestion most of the nonheme iron enters a common intraluminal pool so that its bioavailability is determined by the relative concentrations of the various enhancing and inhibiting ligands present in the meal. The dietary factors that actively promote nonheme iron absorption include certain animal tissues including meat, poultry, and fish, and a number of organic acids, the most important of which is ascorbic acid. Milk and cheese are relatively "neutral" in terms of their effects on iron absorption since they exert neither a strong enhancing nor inhibiting effect. Cereals and legumes are poor sources of bioavailable iron, presumably due to the presence within them of variable amounts of tannins, phytates, and bran. However, the inhibitory effects of these can be overcome, in part at least, if cereals and legumes are fed together with adequate amounts of animal tissue or ascorbic acid.

These various points have special relevance to iron nutrition in infancy because milk and cereals represent staple foodstuffs at critical stages of development. There are three overlapping periods in infancy. During the early part of infancy when the infant's needs are lowest, dietary iron is largely derived from milk and milk products. Weaning or transitional foods, which are mostly processed cereals, supplement and then gradually replace milk in the diet during a period when requirements are high. Solid foods, including meat, fruit, and vegetables, are introduced in the latter part of infancy and the diet progressively approaches that of the rest of the family.

Although the reasons are not clear, there is good evidence that the iron in breast milk is significantly better absorbed than is the iron in cow's milk. However, fortified cow's milk is an adequate source of iron in that it does not exert a significant inhibitory effect on iron absorption. Although the overall absorption rate from infant cereals is low, the relatively large amounts of fortification iron they currently contain should be able to meet the needs for dietary iron of healthy infants. In circumstances where iron requirements are greater, it is possible to increase iron bioavailability in cereals by raising the level of ascorbic acid fortification. Concern about the low bioavailability of the iron in soya-containing protein supplements, which are widely used as weaning foods in developing countries, has led to the recommendation that the molar ratio of ascorbic acid to iron fortification be increased from 0.7 to 1.5 and that the more stable preparation ethyl cellulose-coated ascorbic acid be used.

REFERENCES

1. Bothwell TH, Charlton RW, Cook JD, Finch CA. Iron metabolism in man. Oxford: Blackwell Scientific, 1979:7–42, 256–2.
2. Larsen L, Milman N. Normal iron absorption determined by means of whole body counting and red cell incorporation of ^{59}Fe. Acta Med Scand 1975; 198:271–4.
3. Cook JD, Layrisse M, Finch CA. The measurement of iron absorption. Blood 1969; 33:421–9.
4. Magnusson B, Bjorn-Rasmussen E, Rossander L, Hallberg L. Iron absorption in relation to iron status. Model proposed to express results of food iron absorption measurements. Scand J Haematol 1981;27:201–8.
5. Ashworth A, March Y. Iron fortification of dried skim milk and maize-soy-bean-milk mixture (CSM): availability of iron in Jamaican infants. Br J Nutr 1973;30:577–84.
6. Hallberg L. Bioavailability of dietary iron in man. Annu Rev Nutr 1981; 1:123–47.
7. Moore CV, Dubach R. Observations on the absorption of iron from foods tagged with radioiron. Trans Assoc Am Physicians 1951;64:245–56.
8. Bjorn-Rasmussen E, Hallberg L, Isaksson B, Arvidsson B. Food iron absorption in man. Application of the two-pool extrinsic tag method to measure heme and nonheme iron absorption from the whole diet. J Clin Invest 1974;53:247–55.
9. Cook JD, Layrisse M, Martinez-Torres C, Walker R, Monsen E, Finch CA. Food iron absorption measured by an extrinsic tag. J Clin Invest 1972;51:805–15.
10. Layrisse M, Cook JD, Martinez C, Roche M, Kuhn IN, Walker RB, Finch CA. Food iron absorption: a comparison of vegetable and animal foods. Blood 1969; 33:430–43.
11. Hallberg L, Bjorn-Rasmussen E. Determination of iron absorption form whole diet. A new two-pool model using two radioiron isotopes given as haem and nonhaem iron. Scand J Haematol 1972;9:193–7.
12. Layrisse M, Martinez-Torres C, Cook JD, Walker R, Finch CA. Iron fortification of food: its measurement by the extrinsic tag method. Blood 1973;41:333–52.
13. Bjorn-Rasmussen E. Food iron absorption in man. III. Effect of iron salt, ascorbic acid and desferrioxamine on the isotopic exchange between native food iron and an extrinsic inorganic iron tracer. Scand J Haematol 1973;11:391–7.
14. Bjorn-Rasmussen E, Hallberg L, Walker RB. Food iron absorption in man. I. Isotopic exchange of iron between labeled foods and between a food as an iron salt. Am J Clin Nutr 1973;26:1311–9.
15. Sayers MH, Lynch SR, Jacobs P, Charlton RW, Bothwell TH, Walker RB, Mayet F. The effects of ascorbic acid supplementation on the absorption of iron in maize, wheat and soya. Br J Haematol 1973;24:209–18.
16. Hallberg L, Bjorn-Rasmussen E, Garby L, Pleehachinda R, Suwanik R. Iron absorption from South-east Asian diets and the effect of iron fortification. Am J Clin Nutr 1978;32:1403–8.
17. Layrisse M, Martinez-Torres C, Renzi M, Leets I. Ferritin iron absorption in man. Blood 1975;45:689–98.
18. Derman D, Sayers M, Lynch SR, Charlton RW, Bothwell TH, Mayet F. Iron absorption from a cereal-based meal containing cane sugar fortified with ascorbic acid. Br J Nutr 1977;38:261–9.
19. Layrisse M, Martinez-Torres C, Gonzales M. Measurement of the total daily dietary iron absorption by the extrinsic tag method. Am J Clin Nutr 1974;27:152–62.
20. Cook JD, Minnich V, Moore VC, Rasmussen A, Bradley WB, Finch CA. Absorption of fortification iron in bread. Am J Clin Nutr 1973;26:861–72.
21. Takkunen H. Iron deficiency in the Finnish adult population: an epidemiological survey from 1967-1972 inclusive. Scand J Haematol 1976;(Suppl 25):1–91.

22. Cook JD, Monsen ER. Food iron absorption. III. Comparison of the effect of animal proteins on nonheme iron absorption. Am J Clin Nutr 1976;29:859–67.

23. Martinez-Torres C, Romano E, Layrisse M. Effect of cysteine on iron absorption in man. Am J Clin Nutr 1981;34:322–7.

24. Derman DP, Bothwell TH, MacPhail AP, Torrance JD, Bezwoda WR, Charlton RW, Mayet F. Importance of ascorbic acid in the absorption of iron from infant foods. Scand J Haematol 1980;25:193–201.

25. Lynch SR, Cook JD. Interaction of vitamin C and iron. Ann NY Acad Sci 1980;355:32–43.

26. Sayers MH, Lynch SR, Charlton RW, Bothwell TH, Walker R, Mayet F. Iron absorption from rice meals cooked with fortified salt containing ferrous sulphate and ascorbic acid. Br J Nutr 1974;31:367–75.

27. Derman DP, Bothwell TH, Torrance JD, Bezwoda WR, MacPhail AP, Kew MC, Sayers MH, Disler PB, Charlton RW. Iron absorption from maize (Zea mays) and sorghum (sorghum vulgare) beer. Br J Nutr 1980;43:271–9.

28. Gillooly M, Bothwell TH, Torrance JD, MacPhail AP, Derman DP, Bezwoda WR, Mills W, Charlton RW, Mayet F. The effects of organic acids, phytates, and polyphenols on the absorption of iron from vegetables. Br J Nutr 1983;49:331–42.

29. Disler PB, Lynch SR, Charlton RW, Torrance JD, Bothwell TH. The effect of tea on iron absorption. Gut 1975;16:193–200.

30. Bjorn-Rasmussen E. Iron absorption from wheat bread. Influence of various amounts of bran. Nutr Metab 1974;16:101–10.

31. Simpson KM, Morris ER, Cook JD. The inhibitory effect of bran on iron absorption in man. Am J Clin Nutr 1981;34:1469–78.

32. International Nutritional Anemia Consultative Group. Iron absorption from cereals and legumes. A report of the International Nutritional Anemia Consultative Group. New York: The Nutrition Foundation, 1982:1–41.

33. Morck TA, Lynch SR, Skikne BS, Cook JD. Iron availability from infant food supplements. Am J Clin Nutr 1981;34:2630–4.

34. Lipschitz DA, Simpson KM, Cook JD, Morris ER. Absorption of monoferric phytate by dogs. J Nutr 1979;109:1154–60.

35. Monsen ER, Cook JD. Food iron absorption in human subjects. IV. The effects of calcium and phosphate salts on the absorption of nonheme iron. Am J Clin Nutr 1976;29:1142–8.

36. Layrisse M, Martinez-Torres C. Fe(III)-EDTA complex as iron fortification. Am J Clin Nutr 1977;30:1166–74.

37. MacPhail AP, Bothwell TH, Torrance JD, Derman DP, Bezwoda WR, Charlton RW. Factors affecting the absorption of iron from Fe(III)-EDTA. Br J Nutr 1981;45:215–77.

38. Cook JD, Monsen ER. Food iron absorption in man. II. The effect of EDTA on absorption of dietary nonheme iron. Am J Clin Nutr 1976;29:614–20.

39. Reinhold JG, Garcia JS, Garzon P. Binding of iron by fiber of wheat and maize. Am J Clin Nutr 1981;34:1384–91.

40. Elwood PA. Radio-active studies of the absorption by human subjects of various iron preparations from bread. In: Iron in flour. Ministry of Health Reports on Public Health and Medicine. Subject No. 117. London: Her Majesty's Stationery Office, 1968:1–50.

41. Pla GW, Harrison BN, Fritz JC. Comparison of chicks and rats as test animals for studying bioavailability of iron, with special reference to use of reduced iron in enriched bread. J Assoc Off Anal Chem 1973;56:1369–73.

42. Lock S, Bender AE. Measurement of chemically available iron in foods by incubation with human gastric juice in vitro. Br J Nutr 1980;43:413–20.

43. Miller DD, Schricker BR, Rasmussen RR, van Campen D. An in vitro method for estimation of iron availability from meals. Am J Clin Nutr 1981;34:2248–56.

44. Bothwell TH, Charlton RW. Iron deficiency in women: a report prepared for the International Nutritional Anemia Consultative Group. New York: The Nutrition Foundation, 1981:1–68.

45. International Nutritional Anemia Consultative Group. Guidelines for the eradication of iron deficiency anemia. A report of the International Nutritional Anemia Consultative Group. New York: The Nutrition Foundation. 1977:1–29.

46. Bjorn-Rasmussen E, Hallberg L, Rossander L. Absorption of fortification iron. Br J Nutr 1977;37:375–88.

47. Saarinen UM, Siimes MA. Iron absorption from infant milk formula and the optimal level of iron supplementation. Acta Pediatr Scand 1977;66:719–22.
48. Dallman PR, Siimes MA, Stekel A. Iron deficiency in infancy and childhood. Am J Clin Nutr 1980;33:86–118.
49. McMillan JA, Landaw SA, Oski FA. Iron sufficiency in breast fed infants and availability of iron from human milk. Pediatrics 1976;58:686–91.
50. McMillan JA, Oski F, Lourie G, Tomarelli RM, Landaw SA. Iron absorption from human milk, simulated human milk, and proprietary formulas. Pediatrics 1977;60:896–900.
51. Smith NJ, Schulz J. The absorption of iron in infants and children. In: Wallerstein RO, Mettier SR, eds. Iron in clinical medicine. Berkeley: University of California Press, 1958:65–73.
52. Schulz J, Smith NJ. A quantitative study of the absorption of iron salts in infants and children. J Dis Child 1958;95:120–5.
53. Davis AE, Bolin TD. Iron fortification of milk powder. Med J Aust 1976;1:359–60.
54. Heinrich HC, Gabbe EE, Whang DH, Gotze Ch, Schafer KH. Ferrous and hemoglobin-^{59}Fe absorption from supplemented cow milk in infants with normal and depleted iron stores. Z Kinderheilkd 1975;120:251–8.
55. Oski F, Landaw SA. Inhibition of iron absorption from human milk by baby food. Am J Dis Child 1980;134:459–60.
56. Saarinen UM, Siimes MA, Dallman PR. Iron absorption in infants: high bioavailability of breast milk iron as indicated by the extrinsic method for iron absorption and by the concentration of serum ferritin. J Pediatr 1977;91:30–9.
57. Rios E, Hunter RE, Cook JD, Smith NJ, Finch CA. The absorption of iron as supplements in infant cereals and infant formulas. Pediatrics 1975;55:686–93.
58. Morck TA, Cook JD. Factors affecting the bioavailability of dietary iron. Cereal Foods World 1981;26:667–72.
59. Cook JD, Morck TA, Lynch SR. The inhibitory effect of soy products on nonheme iron absorption in man. Am J Clin Nutr 1981;34:2622–9.
60. Morck TA, Lynch SR, Cook JD. Reduction of the soy-induced inhibition of nonheme iron absorption. Am J Clin Nutr 1982;36:219–23.
61. Bookwalter GN, Botrast RJ, Kwolek WF, Gumbmann MR. Nutritional stability of corn-soy-milk blends after dry heating to destroy Salmonellae. J Food Sci 1980;45:975–80.
62. Monsen ER, Hallberg L, Layrisse M, Hegsted DM, Cook JD, Mertz W, Finch CA. Estimation of available dietary iron. Am J Clin Nutr 1978;32:134–41.
63. Rossander L, Hallberg L, Bjorn-Rasmussen E. Absorption of iron from breakfast meals. Am J Clin Nutr 1979;32:2484–9.

DISCUSSION

Dr. Hurrell: Could you give some details of the *in vitro* system that you have just discussed.

Dr. Cook: This is a system that involves adding extrinsic radioiron to a homogenized meal, incubating at pH less than 2 in the presence of pepsin, readjusting the pH to about 5, and finally determining the proportion of radioiron remaining in the supernatant after centrifugation. There are actually several *in vitro* methods of this type described in the recent literature and I believe they all give fairly similar results.

Dr. Chandra: Two questions: firstly, what was the impact of the content of other minerals and trace elements within different foods on availability of iron?

Dr. Cook: This is an important question and I have no information whatsoever about it.

Dr. Chandra: Secondly, have you considered the amount of different cereals eaten in an average meal as being a determinant of the total amount of iron absorbed?

Dr. Cook: This hasn't been taken into account in the data that I showed to you.

Dr. Chandra: You showed the results as percentage absorption of iron rather than the total amount of iron taken in an average meal.

Dr. Cook: We have not taken into account the amount of iron that would be ingested in the average meal. All these studies were done with isolated food sources, such as wheat alone or rice alone, rather than with a complete meal.

Dr. Stekel: Regarding the effect of milk on iron absorption, I think this is just a matter of opinion and we could be discussing forever what it is; my opinion is that cow's milk is a relatively poor iron source. One reason for this opinion is that, when one compares it with human milk, cow's milk iron has a much lower absorption. A second consideration, which is of very practical importance, is what is the absorption of iron from different foods in relation to their caloric content. I think that in this respect Dr. Hallberg's concept of bioavailable nutrient density is a very useful one because it relates the bioavailability of your nutrient, in this case iron, to the total caloric intake. Infants may be fed only cow's milk for long periods of time which will fulfill their total caloric needs but not their iron needs, thus I would consider cow's milk a poor iron source. Also, the effect of milk on nonheme iron absorption is marked. Studies in our laboratory indicate that ferrous sulphate in 6- to 18-month-old infants is absorbed about 35 to 40% when given in water, but is absorbed only about 3 to 4% when given with milk. I would consider this a marked inhibitory effect.

Dr. Cook: The effect you describe seems more pronounced than that reported in other published studies. In the studies which I reviewed in our manuscript, the difference in absorption between water and milk was on the order of two- to threefold, not as dramatic as in the studies you describe.

Dr. Hallberg: In our experience the effect of milk on nonheme iron absorption depends on the experimental conditions used. In a meal composed only of wheat bread we observed a reduction of the iron absorption when serving milk instead of water. However, with a hamburger meal the nonheme iron absorption was the same when the drink was water or milk.

Dr. Cook: There is an inhibitory effect on iron absorption of adding almost any food to water.

Dr. Florentino: Would you comment on the relative effects of dietary ascorbic acid compared to supplementary ascorbic acid.

Dr. Cook: I know of no data to indicate any difference in the enhancing effect of dietary ascorbic acid as opposed to ascorbic acid supplement, assuming that the ascorbic acid in the food source has not been destroyed by heating or during preparation of the food.

Dr. Hallberg: Our studies indicate that the absorption-promoting effect of ascorbic acid is the same when the same amount is given in pure chemical form or, for example, as orange juice, as a mixed vegetable salad, as cabbage, as broccoli, or as papaya.

Dr. Fomon: Could we have some discussion of availability of contamination iron? In most instances in developing countries, the iron intake of a breast-fed infant will be appreciably greater from dirt than from human milk.

Dr. Hallberg: Iron in dirt is partially bioavailable for humans. We have not made any extensive studies but the results we have so far indicate that in a few samples of clay, iron has a relative bioavailability of around 30 to 40%. In a few other soil samples that we have studied, the bioavailability is much lower; the iron in the abyssinian red soil found on teff had a relative bioavailability of about 2%. Iron in some other red soils was not available at all. Considering the high iron content in many soils, however, the intake of soil iron must be considered in human nutrition, especially in the diets in developing countries where the intake of soil iron can be quite considerable.

Dr. Cook: The inhibitory effect of soya on iron absorption is presumably of little importance in relation to soya formulas because of the large amounts of iron that are commonly added. There is nothing in the literature to suggest a difference in the effect of fortification iron added to soya formulas as opposed to a milk-based formula. We have studied the question of soya in relation to an infant food such as corn-soya milk containing corn, soya, and maize. When we deleted each of these components serially, we found no effect when the maize or milk was deleted but about a twofold increase absorption when soya was eliminated. I don't consider this a dramatic effect and would suggest that the inhibitory effect of soya is of little consequence in regard to iron-fortified formulas.

Dr. Stekel: Are there any data on the iron status of infants who have been fed soya formulas?

Dr. Fomon: Sales of soya protein isolate formulas account for about 20% of total sales of infant formulas in the United States. However, some of the soya formulas are consumed by children beyond infancy or by adults and the best estimate is that about 15% of formula-fed infants receive soya protein isolate formulas. These formulas are fortified with 1.8 mg iron/100 kcal and include, in addition, substantial amounts of native iron. Iron nutritional status of infants fed such formulas appears to be adequate, but there has been no specific, well-designed, large-scale study.

Dr. Hallberg: It should be remembered that when soya flour is added to a meal there may be a significant increase in the iron content of the meal as soya flour products have a high iron content. In a recent study we compared the effect of adding soya flour to a simple Latin American-type meal composed of black beans, maize, and rice with the addition of the same amount of protein as meat and the same amount of iron as ferrous sulphate. We reached about the same level of amount of iron absorbed. The addition of soya protein to a simple diet to improve the protein nutrition will thus also improve the iron nutrition.

Dr. Guirriec: Textured vegetable protein is being promoted as a meat substitute; I should like to know what is its iron availability?

Dr. Hallberg: The effect of soya protein on nonheme iron absorption depends on the basis of comparison. When soya is added as a meat extender (to make a bigger hamburger), the amount of iron absorbed is increased as there is a considerable increase in the amount of iron ingested due to the high iron content of soya protein products. The percentage of iron absorbed, however, is somewhat decreased for unknown reasons. When soya is used as a substitute for meat, thus replacing a certain part of the meat, there is a decrease in the total amount of iron absorbed, due to a reduction in the heme iron content of the hamburger and a reduction of the enhancing effect of meat on nonheme iron absorption. This has been explained in greater details in the INACG report "The effect of cereals and legumes on iron availability," 1982 [see the chapter by Hurrell, ref. 41, this volume].

Iron Nutrition in Infancy and Childhood,
edited by A. Stekel. Nestlé, Vevey/Raven Press,
New York © 1984.

Bioavailability of Different Iron Compounds Used to Fortify Formulas and Cereals: Technological Problems

Richard F. Hurrell

Nestlé Products Technical Assistance Co. Ltd., CH-1814 La Tour-de-Peilz, Switzerland

BIOLOGICAL AVAILABILITY OF IRON COMPOUNDS USED TO FORTIFY INFANT FOODS

Bioavailability of a single iron source is difficult to predict. It can vary considerably due to the enhancing or inhibitory effects of other food components on iron absorption and, especially for the less-available sources, it is strongly influenced by the physical characteristics of the iron compound itself. It is sometimes difficult for the food manufacturer or food scientist to interpret the many apparent contradictions in the literature, further complicated by the different methodologies used by different research groups and the difficulties in extrapolating from rats to humans.

Table 1 shows an advisory list of iron sources that may be used in foods for infants and young children (1). It includes the most frequent uses of these salts and an estimate of their relative bioavailability when compared to ferrous sulphate in both rats and humans. In rat studies, iron compounds have been compared to ferrous sulphate by evaluating the regeneration of hemoglobin in iron-depleted rats. In human studies, differences in iron absorption in iron-replete healthy men have been measured using radioactive isotopes. It should be remembered that the studies of Brise and Hallberg (6), which were used to calculate most of the reported values, were made by giving fasting subjects iron sources containing 30 mg elemental iron. The relative properties of different iron compounds may change when given with food. Nevertheless, it is readily noticeable from the information available that both rat and human assays give the same ranking to the bioavailability of the different salts and that, in general, iron sources added to infant formulas are more highly available than those commonly added to infant cereals.

Iron Sources Added to Formula

Ferrous sulphate is by far the most commonly added iron source to both liquid and powder formulas although ferrous ammonium citrate, ferrous citrate, ferrous gluconate, and ferrous lactate may also be added. For liquid soya-based formulas, ferric citrate and ferric gluconate are suggested by Codex (1). The relative bio-

TABLE 1. *Codex advisory list (1) of iron sources that may be used for infants and young children: their common use and average bioavailability*

Source	Common use	Average bioavailability relative to ferrous sulphate	
		Rat[a]	Human[b]
Ferrous carbonate stabilized		4	—
Ferrous citrate	Liquid formula	76	74
Ferrous fumarate		95	101
Ferrous gluconate		97	89
Ferrous lactate	Liquid formula	—	104
Ferrous succinate		—	123
Ferrous sulphate	Liquid and powder formula	100	100
Ferric ammonium citrate	Liquid formula	107	—
Ferric citrate	Liquid soya formula	73	31
Ferric gluconate	Liquid soya formula	—	—
Sodium iron pyrophosphate		14	5[d]
Elemental iron			
H-reduced	Cereals		
Electrolytic	Cereals	8–76	13–90[e]
Carbonyl	Cereals		
Ferric pyrophosphate	Cereals	45	—
Ferric orthophosphate[c]	Cereals	7–32	31[d]
Ferric oxide saccharated[c]	Cereals	—	—

[a]Hemoglobin repletion test from Fritz et al. (2) and Fritz and Pla (3).
[b]Absorption measured using radioiron isotopes (6).
[c]Not on Codex list but commonly used.
[d]Absorption from bread rolls measured using radioiron isotopes (5).
[e]Absorption measured using radioiron isotopes (4).

availability of all these salts is relatively high, at least when fed alone, with the exception of ferric citrate, which is 31% as well absorbed as ferrous sulphate (6), and ferric gluconate, for which there are no published data.

Ferrous sulphate can be obtained in two forms, the heptahydrate and the mono-hydrate, known as dried ferrous sulphate. The reagent-grade heptahydrate $(FeSO_4 \cdot 7H_2O)$ has become the standard for comparison in almost all iron availa-bility studies performed today. Its absorption by humans, however, was found to vary from less than 1 to over 50% of the initial dose (6), depending on the subject and not including other interferences due to diet composition or level of added compound. Most ferrous sulphate used in foods is the purified and dried by-product of sulphuric acid cleaning baths used in steel production (7). Despite reports by Lee and Clydesdale (7) that dried ferrous sulphate is the more commonly used form and that the heptahydrate is often unsuitable because it is difficult to grind finely and because its loosely bound water migrates into dry foods, the heptahydrate is commonly added to both powder and liquid formula.

Rios et al. (8) measured the absorption of radioactively labeled ferrous sulphate added to milk-based and soya-based formulas. The formulas contained 12 to 17 mg of added Fe per liter and were fed to 42 apparently healthy infants between 4 and 7 months old. Mean iron absorptions of 3.9% (range 0.7–23.1%) for the milk-based formula and 5.4% (range 1.0–21.9%) for the soya-based formula were recorded. It was concluded that the iron supplement in these products could essentially meet the iron needs of healthy infants (0.5 mg Fe/day at 4–6 months).

There is much less information concerning the other salts. Ferrous fumarate appears to be highly available in both humans and rats and has been used to fortify corn-soya-milk preparations used by USDA in overseas food assistance programs (7). Ferrous gluconate and ferrous lactate are also highly available and appear to maintain their high availability in thermally processed milk and soya-based infant formulas fed to anemic rats (9,10). The use of ferric ammonium citrate, which is produced as a brown or green-colored powder, is minor. When fed to anemic rats, it was equally as well used as ferrous sulphate. Bothwell et al. (11) recommend the use of ferric ammonium citrate in infant foods and they describe its bioavailability in humans as good.

The absorption of iron from fortified infant formulas has been found by several authors (8,12,13) to be in the range of 3 to 10% of the administered dose. This has been reported to be very low when compared to the 49 to 70% absorption of breast-milk iron administered to infants (13,14) or the 15 to 20% of breast-milk iron fed to adults (12,15). Saarinen and Siimes (13) measured iron absorption by changes in the calculated total body iron of infants fed breast milk, cow's milk, or an iron-supplemented infant formula containing 11 mg Fe/liter in the form of ferrous gluconate. They estimated iron absorption from breast milk to be 70% of the administered dose as compared to 30% for cow's milk iron and 10% for supplemented iron in infant formulas. McMillan et al. (12) measured absorption of iron from breast milk and iron-supplemented formulas in adults using the extrinsic tag technique. They reported a 15% absorption from breast milk as compared to 3% from infant formulas. The comparison of the percentage absorption, however, is misleading since breast milk contained 0.66 mg/liter of iron compared to 12.5 mg/liter for the iron-fortified formula. It is well known that as the amount of iron fed as a soluble salt is increased, the percentage absorption decreases (16), although the absolute amount absorbed increases. In fact, when they fed a formula containing almost the same level of iron as in breast milk (0.7 mg/liter), they reported the percentage absorbed as 9%, slightly more than half that of breast-milk iron. In absolute terms, however, there was almost four times as much iron absorbed from the fortified formula as from breast milk.

Iron absorption from breast milk appears to be considerably more efficient than that from cow's milk or infant formulas. The reason for this high bioavailability is unknown (17). It does not appear to be due to lactoferrin (12,18), but could possibly be due to chelating agents keeping the iron soluble during digestion. Ascorbic acid, cysteine, inosine, and taurine are generally higher in human milk than in cow's milk or formulas and have been suggested by McMillan et al. (12) as possible enhancers of absorption. Cow's milk is also higher in phosphate, which is known to decrease absorption.

The influence of milk components on iron availability is not clear. Milk has been found to decrease iron absorption from meals with a low iron bioavailability (17). Abernathy et al. (19) reported that iron absorption was significantly increased in 7- to 9-year-old girls by removal of milk from the diet. However, in a recent study of a hamburger meal, no decrease in iron absorption was seen when water was exchanged for milk (20). In rat studies, Ranhotra et al. (21), using the hemoglobin repletion test, also found that milk and milk components did not adversely affect the bioavailability of added iron, although Amine and Hegsted (22) reported that the ferrous sulphate added to infant formulas was around 30% less well utilized than ferrous sulphate alone.

Iron Sources Added to Cereals

With cereals the food manufacturer is caught in a difficult situation. Those iron compounds that exhibit the best availability reduce product quality and shelf-life. The use of the less offensive iron sources may satisfy label claims and regulations, but there is a question concerning their bioavailability. The sources that are commonly used are elemental iron, ferric pyrophosphate, and ferric orthophosphate. Saccharated ferric oxide is occasionally used. Sodium iron pyrophosphate is no longer commonly used for fortifying infant cereal. All these sources have shown a mediocre to low relative bioavailability in both rat and human assays when compared to ferrous sulphate. The bioavailability of elemental iron and orthophosphate varies greatly, depending on the physical characteristics of the product.

Elemental Iron

This is perhaps the most well-researched iron source because of its common use in infant cereal fortification in the United States and its potential use in flour enrichment. As can be seen from Table 1, there are considerable variations in the relative bioavailability of elemental iron powders. There are three basic types of elemental iron, depending on the method of manufacture: (a) reduction under hydrogen or carbon monoxide, (b) electrolytic deposition, and (c) the carbonyl process (7). Reduced iron is produced by reduction of ground iron oxide by either hydrogen or carbon monoxide. Electrolytic iron is produced by electrolytic deposition of ingot ore onto stainless steel cathode sheets. Carbonyl iron is produced by heating scrap metal with pressurized carbon monoxide to yield iron pentacarbonyl, which is then decomposed to yield iron powder. This iron powder is further reduced under hydrogen, yielding carbonyl iron, which is extremely fine (spherical particles, mean particle size about 3 μm). Reduced iron is about half the price of electrolytic or carbonyl iron but double the price of ferrous sulphate (11).

There has been considerable research into the variation of bioavailability of elemental iron with particle size, solubility in dilute acid, and reactive surface area (4,23–28). It would appear that for each iron type, bioavailability is increased with an increased solubility and a smaller particle size. Solubility in dilute HCl seems to be the best *in vitro* method of predicting bioavailability and this is governed more by reactive surface area than by particle size (4).

Shah et al. (28) measured the relative biological value (RBV) of eight commercial iron powders in anemic rats. The properties of four of these powders are shown in Table 2 where RBV is compared with solubility in 0.2% HCl at 37°C and particle size. The particle size distributions by number of the different types are shown in Fig. 1. These show a similar pattern to the particle size distribution values by weight given by Cocodrilli et al. (23) and Lee and Clydesdale (7) for different

TABLE 2. *Physical characteristics and relative biological value (RBV) of four commercial iron powders fed to anemic rats*

Iron source	Mean particle size (μm)	% Solubility (0.2% HCl, 37°C, 90 min)	RBV
Carbonyl	4	98	61
Electrolytic	8	91	32
H-reduced	21	57	18
CO-reduced	28	49	12

Adapted from Shah et al. (28).

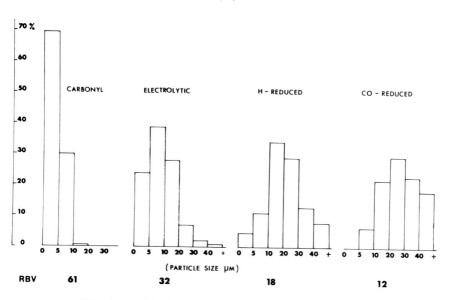

FIG. 1. Particle size distribution of different iron sources (28).

commercial powders. Shah et al. (28) found that carbonyl iron had the smallest particle size, the highest solubility, and the highest bioavailability (RBV = 61). They found in general that RBV increased with increasing solubility and smaller particle size and they ranked the iron powders in the order of carbonyl, electrolytic, H-reduced, and CO-reduced, the latter having an RBV of only 12 and a mean particle size of 28 μm.

A similar relationship between particle size and RBV was shown by Fritz (29) (Table 3). He separated the different sized particles and found that, for each iron type, the finer the particle size the greater the relative bioavailability in rats. The same sized particles produced electrolytically, however, gave almost twice the RBV as those produced by CO reduction. Pennell et al. (26) similarly found in rats and in humans that electrolytic iron particles of 7 to 10 μm and 20 to 30 μm had about 1.5 and 2 times, respectively, the RBV of the same sized particles of reduced iron. According to Lee and Clydesdale (7), the electrolytic procedure produces unique fern-like crystals with a larger surface area than the irregular porous-reduced iron crystal, which presumably makes it more soluble and thus more available.

Rather surprisingly, however, Björn-Rasmussen et al. (4) showed commercial electrolytic iron, presumably from European suppliers, to have a low reactive surface area. The few samples they investigated, however, had no resemblance in terms of particle size distribution to the electrolytic iron described by American authors. Mean particle sizes were 3, 5, 35, and 42 μm. Using specially produced H-reduced powders, these workers showed that bioavailability in humans (13–90% of ferrous sulphate) also correlated well with *in vitro* solubility in dilute HCl and reactive surface area.

TABLE 3. *Influence of particle size on bioavailability of reduced iron*

Production method	Particle size (μm)	RBV[a]
Electrolytic 1	7–10	64
	27–40	38
Electrolytic 2	0–10	76
	10–20	75
	20–40	48
	>40	45
H reduction	10–20	54
	<40	34
CO reduction	7–10	36
	14–19	21
	27–40	13
Carbonyl	<4	69
	4–8	64

[a]Hemoglobin repletion tests with rats; RBV of ferrous sulphate = 100.
Adapted from Fritz (29).

Clearly there is a wide variation in commercially available iron powders. It should be possible, however, for the manufacturer to screen different samples for solubility, particle size, and reactive surface area. Carbonyl iron would appear to be most highly available; however, it appears that, like other highly soluble iron sources, it also causes rapid organoleptic deterioration of the product. Another problem is that finely powdered iron is pyrophoric, burning to incandescence when exposed to air (7). In cereal test systems, we have found that electrolytic iron (Glidden A-131) similar to that reported by Shah et al. (28) has caused no organoleptic problems.

Shah et al. (28) have recommended specifications for the quality of elemental iron powders used by food manufacturers: (a) the iron content of the powder should be not less than 96%; (b) 95% of the particles should be less than 40 μm; and (c) at least 90% by weight of the powder should be soluble in 0.2% HCl after 90 min at 37°C. For their solubility test, they simulated gastric digestion. They took 100 mg iron powder in 250 ml 0.2% HCl (pH about 1.2) at 37°C and shook for 90 min on an orbital shaker. Other workers have used very different methods of measuring solubility (4,23,27). These methods differ in the quantity of powder taken, the concentration and volume of HCl, the temperature and time of shaking, and the method of shaking. Although all methods may rank the solubility of iron sources in a similar way, some standardization is required before a meaningful comparison with bioavailability can be made.

Ferric Orthophosphate

The material used in foods is light in color and is hydrated with two or four molecules of water. Like elemental iron, its bioavailability appears to vary considerably from batch to batch. Fritz et al. (2) evaluated four samples in the hemoglobin repletion test with rats and reported RBVs from 7 to 32 (Table 1). Harrison et al. (30) similarly found that the RBVs of five commercial samples of ferric orthophosphate varied from 6 to 46 (Table 4) and they also demonstrated that it was strongly influenced by particle size and solubility in 0.1 N HCl. Shah et al. (31) found the RBVs of ferric orthophosphate added to cereals varied from 33 to 60.

TABLE 4. *Physical characteristics and relative biological value of five commercial samples of ferric orthophosphate*

Particle size (μm)	% Solubility (0.1 N HCl, 3 hr)	RBV (Ferrous sulphate = 100)
15	11.6	6
12	11.6	7
<1	41.9	33
<1	45.5	33
<1	63.4	46

Modified from Harrison et al. (30).

Hallberg (17) reported that the bioavailability of ferric orthophosphate in humans also varied considerably between different commercial preparations.

Ferric Pyrophosphate

This white powder, although widely used in Europe to fortify infant cereals, is less utilized in the United States and consequently has been less well investigated. It may be added as the ferric pyrophosphate alone; as a coprecipitate of ferric pyrophosphate and ferric citrate, containing about half citrate by weight; or as a coprecipitate of ferric pyrophosphate (1 mole) and ammonium citrate (2 moles). It has been called a mediocre source of available iron and had an RBV of 45 in the studies of Fritz et al. (2). We could not find an RBV on the coprecipitates, although Pla et al. (27) have reported an RBV of 96 for stabilized ferric pyrophosphate, which they described as ferric pyrophosphate solubilized with sodium citrate.

Sodium Iron Pyrophosphate

This salt has shown a somewhat variable but always low relative availability in both rats (RBV 2–22) and humans, and it would seem unwise to use it for infant food fortification. Shah et al. (31) found the RBV of sodium iron pyrophosphate added to cereals to vary from 14 to 40.

Saccharated Ferric Oxide

This compound comes as an amorphous brownish red powder containing from 3 to 10% iron. It is very soluble in water and an aqueous solution has been used in intravenous injection to treat anemic patients (32). It is made from ferrous chloride, sodium carbonate, sucrose, and sodium hydroxide. It has no fixed formula but it is reported to be a mixture of ferric oxide and saccharose. It is used only to a limited extent and there is little information on its bioavailability, although because it is highly soluble it should theoretically have a fairly good availability. When this compound was fed to anemic rats, we obtained an RBV of 90.

Bioavailability for Infants

Rios et al. (8) added radiolabeled sodium iron pyrophosphate, ferric orthophosphate, hydrogen-reduced elemental iron, and ferrous sulphate at the level of 50 mg Fe/100 g to mixed grain infant cereals. Iron absorption was measured in infants 4 to 6 months of age. Rios et al. (8) showed that sodium iron pyrophosphate and ferric orthophosphate were poorly absorbed (<1.0%), and that reduced iron and ferrous sulphate were 4.0% and 2.7% absorbed, respectively. The sodium iron pyrophosphate and the ferric orthophosphate were of similar particle size and solubility as would be used in industrial fortification. These authors concluded that these materials were not dependable sources of iron to meet the nutritional needs of infants. The absorption of sodium iron pyrophosphate and ferric orthophosphate relative to ferrous sulphate was 37 and 26%, respectively, and was similar to that predicted by rat assays. Reduced iron, on the other hand, had 148% the absorption of ferrous sulphate. This was a hydrogen-reduced product of a very small particle size containing 95% of the particles in the 5- to 10-μm range. This is similar to carbonyl iron but much smaller than other sources of elemental iron currently available. Electrolytic iron A-131 from Glidden (Durkee Industrial Foods) has 40% by weight of the particles less than 10 μm; an electrolytic iron used by Shah et al. (28) had 63% of the particles by number less than 10 μm. It is evidently possible, therefore, to have an elemental iron source of the same bioavailability as ferrous sulphate. This has been confirmed by Cook et al. (5) and Björn-Rasmussen et al. (4); however, these powders are apparently unsuitable for addition to cereal products because they lead to the same discoloration and reduced shelf-life as reported for the soluble iron salts (5). This remains to be confirmed.

Cook et al. (5) baked the same iron sources as used by Rios et al. (8) into dinner rolls and measured their bioavailability in humans as compared to ferrous sulphate. The results of the two studies were similar. Cook et al. (5) found mean absorption ratios relative to ferrous sulphate of 5% for sodium iron pyrophosphate (mean absorption 0.3%), 31% for ferric orthophosphate (mean absorption 1.1%), and 95% for hydrogen-reduced iron (mean absorption 8.6%). The absorption of ferrous sulphate varied widely from 0.9 to 48.9% of the administered dose and the mean absorption, 3.9, 6.6, and 9.1% in the different assays, was roughly one-quarter of that found when feeding ferrous sulphate as a solution of inorganic iron.

General Conclusion

It would appear that commercial sources of elemental iron, ferric orthophosphate, and ferric pyrophosphate vary considerably in their bioavailability. In order to assist the food manufacturer in the control of supplies, there is a need for more information on the relationship between a standardized *in vitro* solubility test and particle size with relative biological availability in rats and humans for all three iron sources. However, considering current information, even with careful control, it is doubtful whether food manufacturers can find a suitable source for addition to infant cereals which has more than 30 to 50% the bioavailability of ferrous sulphate. Elemental iron powders, both hydrogen-reduced and carbonyl, have been reported with higher bioavailability but they have also been reported to cause organoleptic problems. Much information is still lacking on the bioavailability in humans of saccharated iron oxide and of the different forms of iron pyrophosphate. Fortunately, there are other ways of improving the bioavailablity of iron in cereals which appear promising. Firstly, there is encapsulation of a highly available iron source such as ferrous sulphate to isolate it from the food environment. This should prevent fat oxidation problems while hopefully still maintaining high bioavailability. Secondly, and maybe the simplest approach, is to add an absorption enhancer such as ascorbic acid along with a mediocre iron source. Ascorbic acid, by way of its reducing and chelating properties, can significantly increase iron absorption (33).

FACTORS INFLUENCING IRON ABSORPTION FROM INFANT FOOD

Chemistry of Iron

This subject has been extensively reviewed by Forth and Rummel (34), Spiro and Saltman (35), and Lee and Clydesdale (7). To understand the behavior of iron in foods and during digestion, and the influence of various factors on its bioavailability, however, one must have some knowledge of its chemical properties.

Oxidation States

Iron has several oxidation states ranging from Fe^{6+} to Fe^{2-}, depending on its chemical environment. Ferrous (Fe^{2+}) and ferric (Fe^{3+}) are the only states that occur naturally in foods since they are the only ones that are stable in an aqueous environment. Elemental iron is rarely found in biological systems but it does occur as a common food additive. Ferrous iron is rapidly oxidized to ferric iron in the presence of oxygen. Alternatively, ferrous iron may be formed by the reduction of ferric iron or the oxidation of elemental iron, i.e., $Fe^{3+} + e \rightleftharpoons Fe^{2+}$; $Fe^{2+} + 2e \rightleftharpoons Fe^{0}$.

Solubility of Ferrous and Ferric Iron

Ferrous iron is far more soluble than ferric iron, especially as the pH of the system is increased. In acidic aqueous solutions, ferrous and ferric irons do not occur in the free state but are hydrated as $Fe(H_2O)_6^{3+}$ and $Fe(H_2O)_6^{2+}$. As the pH is raised, they split off protons, in a process known as hydrolysis, to form the corresponding iron hydroxides: $Fe(OH)_2$ and $Fe(OH)_3$. These hydroxides become more insoluble with increasing pH and tend to be irreversible. Spiro and Saltman (35) indicate that the ferrous ion has a solubility of about 10^{-1} M at pH 7 and 10^{-3} M at pH 8, whereas the ferric ion has a solubility of about 10^{-3} M at pH 2 and only 10^{-18} M at pH 7. This is of considerable nutritional importance since, although both ferrous and ferric ions are readily soluble in the acid conditions of the stomach (about pH 2), the ferric ion is not soluble in the slightly alkaline conditions of the small intestine where the iron absorption takes place.

Formation of Complexes

In general, a metal ion can react with more than one ligand. The number of possible bonds with the ligands depends on the coordination number of the metal, which in the case of iron is six. If six ligands form one bond each with one iron atom, it would be a monodentate complex. Complexes formed by the participation of two or more ligand atoms from the same complexing agent are called chelates. Thus three ligands each forming two bonds would give a bidentate chelate and two ligands each forming three bonds would give a tridentate chelate and so on. Different ligands may also react with the same metal atom to form mixed complexes.

During digestion, the stability of the iron-ligand complex is governed by its thermodynamic and kinetic stability constants and by interfering reactions with other ligands and other metals. In general, the stability of the metal-ligand complex increases with the concentration of the ligand. Chelates are the most stable complexes and multidentate chelate has a much greater stability than a complex formed from several monodentate ligands.

Figure 2 summarizes the physicochemical factors that influence iron availability. Solubility of the iron source is extremely important; as some fortification iron sources are insoluble in gastric juice, they never enter the common iron pool. Most iron, however, is released from the iron complexes in the food by the acid pH of the stomach and enters the common iron pool. Ferric iron is reduced to ferrous iron (75–98%), depending on the presence of reducing agents (34). It is at this stage that reducing agents, such as ascorbic acid, would appear to have a big influence on iron availability. The elemental iron which dissolves in the gastric juice is transformed into ferrous iron.

As the common pool of ferrous and ferric iron plus the ligands leave the stomach and enter the intestine, there is a rise in pH to between 7 and 8. This favors a reformation of the complexes and there is competition between the different ligands

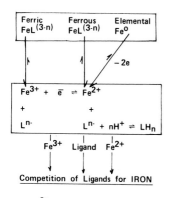

Competition of Ligands for IRON

— Fe^{3+} combines with ligands more strongly than Fe^{2+}

FOOD IRON

— entry of elemental iron and ferric fortification iron into common iron pool may be limited by solubility

STOMACH (PH 2 - 3)

— most iron is released from complexes into common iron pool

— Ferric iron is reduced to ferrous depending on reducing agents

INTESTINE (PH 7 - 8)

— re-formation of complexes, solubility and affinity influence bioavailability

INFLUENCE OF OH⁻

— Fe^{3+} precipitates as $Fe(OH)_3$
— Fe^{2+} much more soluble
— ligands dissociated

ABSORPTION INHIBITORS

— ligands which chelate iron to form insoluble complexes or very high affinity complexes

— iron is not released from chelate for absorption

— phosphate, oxalates, dietary fibre, tannins, phytate

ABSORPTION ENHANCERS

— ligands which form soluble chelates with iron and prevent precipitation (especially Fe^{3+})

— iron released from chelates for absorption

— amino acids, citrate, ascorbate

FIG. 2. Physicochemical factors influencing the absorption of food iron.

to complex iron. Bioavailability of iron is then determined by the solubility of the complexes which form and the strength of the affinity of the ligand for iron. If it is too strong, iron will not be released for absorption. In general, ferric iron binds with ligands more strongly than ferrous iron.

There are three competing phenomena in the intestine. The influence of hydroxide itself can precipitate the ferric iron. It can also dissociate the ligands, and which ligand then combines with iron depends both on its concentration and the magnitude of its affinity for iron. Absorption inhibitors are those ligands that chelate iron to form insoluble complexes or complexes of very high affinity so that iron is not released from the chelate for absorption. Examples are phosphates, oxalate, dietary fiber, tannins, and phytate.

Absorption enhancers are those ligands that form soluble chelates with iron (especially Fe^{3+}) and prevent its precipitation. Iron is released from the chelates for absorption. Amino acids, citrate, and ascorbate are in this category. It should be added that any ligand that forms stable chelates at the more acid pH of the stomach—ascorbic acid, lactoferrin, and ethylenediaminotetraacetic acid (EDTA) are possible examples—would complex iron before competing with other ligands in the intestine.

Inhibitors of Absorption

Hallberg (17) has reviewed the major inhibitors of nonheme iron absorption. The two major components of infant foods that contain inhibitors are cereals and soya products. The latter are often mixed with cereals as a weaning food or used to replace the milk protein in formulas. The exact nature of the inhibition is still unclear, although phytate, phosphates, and dietary fiber have been suggested for cereals. A less important inhibitor could be polyphenolic substances such as the tannins of chocolate or sorghum.

Cereals

The iron from cereal products is poorly available for absorption by humans. Various inhibitors have been suggested, including phytate and dietary fiber. Data concerning the role of phytate are confusing, with some studies finding an inhibitory effect and others not. According to Rotruck and Luhrsen (36), all studies which have shown an inhibitory effect have used purified sodium phytate, whereas those studies which have failed to show an effect have investigated naturally occurring phytate. The synthetic compound should more easily ionize and more readily form insoluble complexes with iron from the common pool.

The inhibitory effect of wheat bran on iron absorption was thought to be due to phytate; however, bran has been reported to maintain its inhibition of iron absorption even after its phytate had been destroyed (37), although the phosphate was not removed. In addition, monoferric phytate, which is the major form of iron in wheat bran, has been shown to be highly available to rats (38), dogs (39), and humans (37). It would now seem that the influence of bran or cereals on iron absorption is at least partly due to its fiber component (40). Absorption studies with various constituents of dietary fiber, including pectin and cellulose, have yielded negative results, however (41).

One recent finding is that the magnitude of the inhibitory effect is different for different cereals (41). Iron absorption is highest from wheat, intermediate from rice, and lowest from maize. These differences appear to be due in part to the influences of the different starches and to the different levels of phytate.

Soya

Many reports on the bioavailablity of iron from soya products have appeared in literature. Most studies with iron-deficient rats or iron-deficient humans have demonstrated a reasonably good bioavailability. Recent studies (42,43), however, using the extrinsic tag method with iron-replete adults, differ considerably from the earlier results and indicate that soya products may be a strong inhibitor of iron absorption.

Cook et al. (42) reported that when egg albumin in a semisynthetic meal was replaced with full fat soya flour, texturized soya flour, or soya isolate, the iron absorption fell from 5.5 to 1.0, 1.9, and 0.4%, respectively. The iron of the same soya isolate was found to have 59% of the availability of ferrous sulphate when fed to anemic rats (44).

Morck et al. (43) measured the iron absorption from an infant food supplement containing a mixture of soya with either wheat or maize. Forty-five to 74% of the protein content of the supplements was from soya protein. They were fortified with ferrous fumarate at the level of 15.6 mg/100 g and the level of ascorbic acid relative to iron was approximately 2:1 when fed. In iron-replete males, the iron absorption was only 0.6 to 1.4% which, when related to the reference dose absorption, was calculated to represent an absorption of 1.7 to 4.1% for iron-deficient infants. It was concluded that if these supplements were fed as recommended, they would supply only half of the daily requirements of iron-deficient children between 6 months and 3 years of age. These results, suggesting that the presence of soya is at least partially responsible for the poor iron availability, are in direct contrast to a previous study on infant formula by Rios et al. (8). Using the radioactively labeled compounds, these workers showed that the absorption of ferrous sulphate in a soya isolate formula was 5.4% as compared to 3.9 and 3.4% for two milk-based formulas.

The influence of soya on iron availability has recently been reviewed (41). It was concluded that soya-based infant formulas appeared to be adequate as a source of iron for infants under 1 year of age. The differences between the availability of iron from soya-based formulas and cereal-soya blends were suggested to be at least partly due to a higher level of ascorbic acid in the formula which is also more stable during storage of the product in hermetically sealed containers.

There are clearly some contradictory results in the literature on the influence of soya on iron absorption. These differences could be due to methodology; iron-replete adults may also not be a good model for young infants. However, as well as its content of other antinutrients (trypsin inhibitors, hemaglutinins, goitrogens) it now appears that soya may also have an iron-binding factor. The exact nature of the proposed inhibitor is as yet unknown; it has been observed with soya flours (~50% crude protein) and soya isolates (~90% crude protein). It does not appear to be due to phytate (~2% in the isolate) (20) nor to dietary fiber or carbohydrates since the highest inhibition was observed in the isolate (42), which contains very little or none of these substances. This inhibition was marginally reduced by baking at 200°C for 1 hr (iron absorption increased from 0.6 to 1.3%) and partially overcome by the addition of ascorbic acid (25:1, ascorbic acid:iron, wt/wt) when absorption was increased from 0.6 to 3.2%. One explanation could be that an insoluble iron-binding peptide is produced during the partial hydrolysis of soya protein in the stomach.

Tannins

One of the most potent inhibitors of nonheme iron absorption is Indian tea (45). When Indian tea was fed with a variety of meals there was a marked reduction in iron absorption which was shown to be due to the formation of soluble iron tannates (46). Although tea is not normally added to infant foods, other possible sources of polyphenols such as cocoa and sorghum may be, and could similarly inhibit iron absorption.

Enhancers of Iron Absorption

Ascorbic Acid

The ability of ascorbic acid to enhance nonheme iron absorption in humans has long been recognized. When ingested with a highly available iron salt such as ferrous sulphate, an increase in absorption of 33% was observed when 200 mg or more was given with 30 mg iron (6). When added to foodstuffs, the effect is even more dramatic because ascorbic acid also lessens the inhibitory effect of other ligands. Layrisse et al. (47) reported an almost sixfold increase in iron absorption (1.4–7.9%) by adult peasants in Venezuela, from 100 g of cooked maize containing 2.8 mg iron when 70 mg of ascorbic acid was added. Crystalline ascorbic acid or natural ascorbic acid from papaya had the same absorption-promoting effect. The enhancing effect of ascorbic acid augments with increasing doses. Using radioiron absorption tests, Cook and Monsen (48) measured the iron absorption in young men fed a semisynthetic meal containing dextrimaltose, corn oil, ovalbumin, and 4.1 mg iron. The increase in iron absorption (0.77–7.1%) was directly proportional to the amount of ascorbic acid added over the range of 25 to 1,000 mg (Fig. 3).

The effect of ascorbic acid on iron absorption seems to be related to both its reducing effect, preventing the formation of insoluble ferric hydroxide, and to its effect of forming soluble complexes with both ferrous and ferric ions at low pH, which then preserves iron solubility at the more alkaline duodenal pH. It also

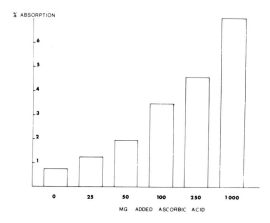

FIG. 3. Influence of ascorbic acid on iron absorption by young men (48). Ascorbic acid was added to a semisynthetic diet containing 4.1 mg Fe.

competes with other inhibitory ligands and has improved absorption of iron in the presence of inhibitors from cereals and soya (33,47,49) and the tannins from tea (45). Iron absorption is improved although inhibition is not removed completely. Morck et al. (33) fed young men meals of isolated soya protein containing 4 mg Fe; adding 100 mg ascorbic acid increased the iron absorption from 0.6 to 3.2%. This effect of ascorbic acid in the presence of inhibiting ligands could be explained by the fact that ascorbic acid complexes soluble food iron at a lower pH than do inhibitory ligands. Iron from the common nonheme pool complexes with ascorbate in the stomach and passes into the intestine as an iron-ascorbate complex, thus eliminating the influence of the inhibitory ligands which bind iron at the more alkaline intestinal pH.

From the work of Derman et al. (50), the absorption-enhancing effect of ascorbic acid is clearly demonstrated both in infant formulas and infant cereals. These workers measured the influence of ascorbic acid addition on the absorption of various radioactive iron sources added to infant formulas and infant cereals. Their results, summarized in Table 5, show that ascorbic acid similarly enhanced the absorption of the more soluble ferrous sulphate or ferrous ammonium citrate and the less soluble ferric pyrophosphate. They concluded that, irrespective of the iron source added, the absorption of iron from infant formulas or cereals can be increased threefold by an ascorbic acid to iron ratio of 5:1 (wt/wt) and sixfold by a 10:1 ratio. The influence of ascorbic acid on the absorption of elemental iron powders remains to be determined. The recommended ratios of ascorbic acid to iron of Derman et al. (50) compare favorably with the ratios of 5:1 normally found in infant formulas and in infant cereals when ascorbic acid is added. They are somewhat lower than what would be expected from other studies (47,48).

One potential problem with ascorbic acid addition is its instability during processing and storage. An overaddition by the manufacturer compensates for processing losses. Its instability during the storage of infant formulas is also easily

TABLE 5. *Influence of added ascorbic acid on iron absorption by multiparous women from infant formula and cereals*

	Iron source	Fe (mg) Added	Fe (mg) Final	Added ascorbic acid (mg)	Ratio ascorbic acid to Fe (wt/wt)	% Fe absorption
Infant formula (100 ml)	Ferrous sulphate	1.27	(1.27)	0	0	7.2
				8	6.2	20.8
				25	19.7	55.7
Infant cereal (30 g)						
A	Ferrous ammonium citrate	5	6.6	0	0	0.8
				50	7.6	10.3
B	Ferrous sulphate	6.9	8.3	0	0	1.0
				24	2.9	3.7
C	Ferric pyrophosphate	3.75	8.6	0	0	1.6
				10.5	1.2	2.8
				18.8	2.2	6.5
				37.5	4.4	7.5

From Derman et al. (50).

overcome by gassing the tins with nitrogen before closing; there is, then, virtually no loss under normal storage conditions. In stored cereals, however, ascorbic acid could be severely diminished during storage, depending on time, temperature, moisture content, and oxygen tension. One possible way of overcoming this may be the use of ethylcellulose-coated ascorbic acid, which costs only 3% more than the uncoated material (41).

Meat, Fish, Amino Acids, and Cysteine

The enhancing effect of meat and fish on iron absorption is well known. Unlike other enhancers, meat and fish increase the absorption of both heme and nonheme iron. The mechanism of absorption enhancement is not necessarily the same. For nonheme iron it does not appear to be due to protein per se, as egg albumin has no promoting effect. It could, however, be linked to amino acid composition. In human studies feeding black beans, Martinez-Torres and Layrisse (51) reported that the addition of either fish or an equivalent amount of synthetic amino acids almost doubled iron absorption. Absorption did not appear to be enhanced by any other amino acids except cysteine alone or in the presence of methionine. In rat experiments, however, histidine and lysine have also been reported to increase iron absorption (52).

The action of cysteine is presumably linked to its chelating and reducing powers, although its enhancing effect would seem to be far less than that of ascorbic acid. Martinez-Torres et al. (53) report that when 210 mg of cysteine was added to maize, soybean, or bean diets containing 2 to 3 mg Fe, it increased the absorption of the intrinsic iron 1.5 to 2-fold. The absorption of fortification iron (3 mg/Fe as ferrous sulphate, or ferric chloride) was similarly increased by 630 mg cysteine. The addition of cysteine to infant formulas or cereals appears impracticable because of its unpleasant smell; the addition of meat or fish similarly cannot be considered. As with ascorbic acid, cysteine loses its enhancing activity during cooking (53), presumably due to its conversion to cystine, or to other oxidation reactions.

Other Organic Acids

Moore (54), measuring the iron absorption from eggs, showed that whereas ascorbic acid, and to a lesser extent cysteine, increased absorption, citric acid, tartaric acid, and lactic acid were without effect. Succinic acid, on the other hand, appears to have powerful absorption-enhancing properties, at least in pharmaceutical preparations. Brise and Hallberg (6) (Fig. 4) added 30 to 500 mg succinic acid, 30 mg of iron as ferrous sulphate, and 10 mg ascorbic acid. They reported an increase in iron absorption from less than 5 to more than 50%. Other organic acids had no effect. Hallberg (17) reported that the addition of 150 mg of succinic acid to a hamburger meal increased nonheme iron absorption by 35%. Succinic acid is a chelator but has no reducing properties. It would appear to be much less active than ascorbic acid in enhancing iron absorption from meals.

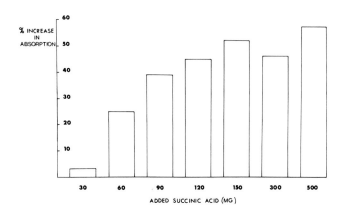

FIG. 4. Influence of succinic acid on iron absorption in humans (6). Succinic acid was administered with 30 mg Fe as ferrous sulphate and 10 mg ascorbic acid.

Sugars

The influence of sugars and fructose in particular has been much studied (7). Fructose, like other sugars, forms complexes with iron. Pollack et al. (55) found that fructose but not glucose or galactose increases iron absorption. The addition of large amounts of fructose to infant foods is not a practical proposition although the addition of the iron source ferric fructose, which contains about 20% iron, could be considered. In pharmaceutical preparations containing ferrous sulphate, sorbitol (about 12 mg/mg Fe) almost doubled the absorption of iron (56). In other studies on oral iron therapy (57), it was shown that sorbitol, mannitol, and xylose were the only carbohydrates with an absorption-promoting effect.

Synthetic Chelating Agents

These agents are not exactly absorption enhancers but more a way of adding iron in a reasonably strong complex which is little influenced by the inhibitory ligands present in some foods. Ethylenediaminotetraacetic acid is the most commonly used chelator, although others such as nitrilotriacetic acid (NTA) and lactobionate have also been used. The disodium salt of EDTA is a food additive permitted in the United States. It is used primarily as a preservative and in multivitamin preparations as a stabilizer for vitamin B_{12} (7). A highly stable iron chelate is formed by EDTA and direct feeding of NaFe EDTA showed impaired iron absorption when compared to ferrous sulphate (6). In a meal, however, more iron was absorbed from NaFe EDTA than from ferrous sulphate (58). MacPhail et al. (59) showed that the inhibitors of absorption present in cereals had less influence on the absorption of iron from NaFe EDTA, which was more than twice as well absorbed as ferrous sulphate when added to maize porridge. The subsequent addition of bran reduced the absorption of ferrous sulphate 11 times but had no influence on the absorption of iron form NaFe EDTA. The tannins of tea, a more potent inhibitor, did, however, cause some reduction in absorption and, as would be expected, ascorbic acid also had a lower absorption-enhancing effect. The use of NaFe EDTA seems very promising for populations subsisting largely on cereal-based diets where a high incidence of iron deficiency is due to a poor absorption of iron from foodstuffs. Its addition to infant cereals or soya-containing products could also prove extremely useful if it could be shown to be safe in long-term toxicology trials. It is interesting to note that ferric chelates of EDTA, NTA, and lactobionate produced significantly less lipid peroxidation than ferrous sulphate when added to liquid milk (60), indicating that they may cause less organoleptic problems.

Vitamin E

Vitamin E is a reducing agent which could help reduce ferric to ferrous iron in the stomach. In animal trials (2,61), vitamin E has been shown to enhance the effect of ascorbic acid, although its influence on iron absorption in humans has never been reported.

Food Processing and Storage

Food processing as well as product composition can affect the final bioavailability of iron in food. This seems to be due mainly to a transformation of ferric salts into the ferrous state.

Theuer et al. (9,10), using the hemoglobin repletion test in rats, determined the availability of iron salts in liquid soya or milk-based infant formulas, before and after commercial sterilization. Their results are shown in Table 6. In both types of formulas, processing substantially increased the RBVs of ferric pyrophosphate and ferric sodium pyrophosphate but had little influence on the RBV of ferrous sulphate. It is interesting to note that RBVs were lower in the soya products than in the milk products. Wood et al. (62) confirmed the beneficial effects of processing on ferric pyrophosphate and sodium iron pyrophosphate in liquid systems but found no effect on ferric orthophosphate or ferrous sulphate.

TABLE 6. *Effect of processing on the availability of iron added to infant formulas*

Iron source	RBV[a] before processing	RBV[a] after processing
Soya formulas		
Ferrous sulphate	90	106
Ferric pyrophosphate	39	93
Ferric sodium pyrophosphate	15	66
Milk-based formulas		
Ferrous sulphate	126	129
Ferric pyrophosphate	78	125
Ferric sodium pyrophosphate	42	60

[a]Ferrous sulphate = 100.
From Theuer et al. (9,10).

It seems probable that the increase in bioavailability of these ferric salts on processing is due to their transformation to the ferrous state. Lee and Clydesdale (63) reported that elemental iron, ferric orthophosphate, and ferric EDTA were solubilized to ferrous forms to a greater or lesser extent in an acid-type fruit beverage, with or without ascorbic acid undergoing ambient storage, spray-drying, or freeze-drying. Three days' storage at 25°C with added ascorbic acid converted 17% of the iron from ferric orthophosphate and 90% from elemental iron to the ferrous state. Hodson (64) similarly found that iron from ferric orthophosphate was converted to the ferrous form after 6 months' storage of a liquid dietary. The reduction potential of a food system affects the chemical state of the iron present (65) and conversion of ferric to ferrous iron is increased by the addition of reducing agents such as ascorbic acid (66) and by lowering the pH.

Processing poorly available iron salts into cereal products such as bread rolls (5) or mixed infant cereals (16), however, does not appear to increase their bioavailability. Similarly, Lee and Clydesdale (67) found that both soluble and relatively insoluble iron sources were largely insoluble after baking into biscuits.

It would appear that heat processing offers little assistance to the infant food manufacturer to improve the iron availability of the products. There is no improvement of the iron availability in cereals and, in most infant formulas, iron is added in the highly available forms that are largely unaffected by processing. There is some indication that processing of cereals does transform ferric to ferrous iron, since iron salts, wet-mixed with cereals and then heat-processed, often cause more organoleptic deterioration on storage than do the same iron sources dry-mixed with the final product. Although poorly available iron sources do probably improve in bioavailability on heat treatment in liquid products, if the products do not deteriorate organoleptically during storage then highly available ferrous salts presumably could have been added in the first place.

Other ways of improving iron availability from infant foods by processing are difficult to envisage unless there is some progress in identifying more clearly the inhibitory factors in cereals and soya so that selective extraction, destruction, or modification procedures could be developed. Phytates, for instance, could be largely removed. It is possible that different processing methods may change the way in which iron is bound within the product. Camire and Clydesdale (68), for example, showed that *in vitro* at pH 5 to 7, more iron was bound to wheat bran and lignin after toasting or boiling. It has never been demonstrated, however, whether this has any significance on its bioavailability. Once in the stomach, food iron may be released from its food-bound forms into a common iron pool where all food or endogenous ligands compete to complex it.

Increased Iron Level

One of the easiest ways of increasing the amount of iron absorbed would at first sight seem to be the addition of more iron. This is why infant formulas contain 12 mg Fe/liter as opposed to the 0.4 mg/liter present in breast milk. However, there are two problems. There is a question concerning the gastrointestinal tolerance of iron-fortified formulas. Iron plays an important role in the growth of microorganisms and it has been suggested that fortified formulas might increase the risk of gastrointestinal infection (69). Recent studies, however, indicate that supplemented iron does not provoke excessive gastrointestinal problems in infants (70). More importantly, iron has a number of demonstrated mineral-mineral interreactions with other divalent cations. A competitive reaction between iron and copper has been demonstrated in experimental animals (71). The inhibition of copper absorption by iron is believed to have been a contributary factor in a case of clinical copper deficiency on a premature infant fed an iron-fortified formula (72). Similar competitive reactions between zinc and iron have been shown in rodents (73) and in humans (74). The latter workers measured the influence of both heme and nonheme iron on the absorption of zinc in human subjects by measuring the change in plasma zinc concentration. These results demonstrated that zinc absorption was already greatly inhibited by inorganic iron at an iron to zinc ratio of 2:1. Heme iron had little influence on zinc absorption.

Iron-fortified formulas (about 12 mg Fe/liter) normally have an iron to zinc ratio of about 2:1, as has been recommended by Codex (75). Cereals, however, for which Codex makes no recommendations, are often fortified with iron (6–20 mg Fe/100 g) but seldom fortified with zinc. The significance is difficult to ascertain as cereals are not intended as a complete food but as a supplement to diets of infants and children. It would seem unwise, however, to increase the level of iron unconditionally in either formulas or cereals without considering the influence on zinc and copper absorption.

TECHNOLOGICAL PROBLEMS

Technological problems are not specific to iron but also concern other minerals commonly added to foods. The main problems concern color and off-flavor production. Other difficulties include the physical problems of precipitation of insoluble salts in liquid products and the even distribution of salts in dry products. Control of mineral fortification is also an important consideration as the consumer has the right to expect the product to contain the amount of nutrient claimed on the label. As part of the mineral is normally provided by the other ingredients of the foodstuff, natural variation in their composition is a complicating factor when formulating a product. Although expensive to set up and maintain, an in-house analytical capability is essential to detect under- or overadditions. This should be coupled with a sound sampling procedure for nonhomogenous products.

Color

As one might expect, many color problems result from the addition of iron to foods (76). In general, the more soluble the salt, the greater the problem. The addition of ferrous sulphate to liquid milk or soya products darkens their color and the higher the level of fortification the darker the product (77). Similarly, when we added ferrous sulphate or other soluble iron salts to infant cereals, a dark gray or green color developed when the products were made into a pap with milk. Douglas et al. (78) have reported that ferrous sulphate, ferrous lactate, ferrous gluconate, ferrous fumarate, ferric citrate, ferric choline citrate, and ferric ammonium citrate produced initial and persistent off-color when added to a chocolate milk drink.

Flavor

The addition of soluble iron sources to milk products can also cause changes due to fat oxidation (60). However, initial off-flavors have been shown to decrease after a storage period (78) and ferrous sulphate is often chosen as the fortification iron for milk-based formulas. In contrast, the addition of ferrous salts to cereal products, because of their higher level of readily oxidizable unsaturated fatty acids, can rapidly result in unacceptable off-flavor production (30).

The extent of the flavor problem depends mainly on the solubility of the iron salt; the less soluble salts give fewer problems. As an example, J. Burri *(personal communication)* added different iron salts to whole wheat flour (15 mg Fe/100 g) in aqueous suspension. The slurry was cooked by steam injection, roller-dried, packed into aluminum cans, and stored at 37°C for up to 7 weeks or for 1 year at 20°C. The extent of fat oxidation was estimated by measuring the level of pentane in the headspace. The double unsaturated fatty acids are known to be a major source of pentane during lipid oxidation. Off-flavors and odors were measured by an experienced taste panel. The results are shown in Figs. 5 and 6. Reduced iron, ferric pyrophosphate, iron saccharate, and ferric citrate generated less pentane than ferrous sulphate or ferrous gluconate. This correlated well with the taste panel who found that ferrous sulphate and ferrous gluconate gave unacceptable off-flavors after 4 to 6 weeks' storage. Ferric citrate was also judged unacceptable. Wheat flour fortified with reduced iron, pyrophosphate, or saccharate was judged to be similar to the unfortified control. A similar pattern of results was obtained after 1 year at 20°C. It is possible, of course, that some of the elemental iron or ferric iron could have been transformed to ferrous iron during the heat treatment, but this seems unlikely to have occurred to any great extent in view of the results. The duration and temperature of the heat processing, however, could play an extremely important role in regulating the shelf-life of the cereal products fortified with elemental iron or ferric salts before processing.

Attempts to Overcome Organoleptic Problems

Because of flavor and color problems, infant food manufacturers are forced to add poorly available iron compounds such as ferric pyrophosphate or reduced iron to their products instead of the more highly available ferrous sulphate. Attempts have thus been made to overcome the pro-oxidant nature of the highly available iron compounds while still maintaining their bioavailability.

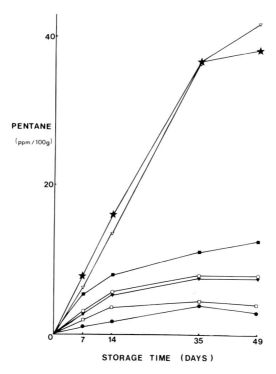

FIG. 5. Pentane production during storage at 37°C of precooked whole wheat flour containing various iron salts at 15 mg Fe/100 g (J. Burri, *personal communication*). *Open squares*, control; *closed squares*, ferric citrate; *open circles*, ferric pyrophosphate; *closed circles*, elemental iron; *open triangles*, ferrous sulphate; *closed triangles*, saccharated iron oxide; *star*, ferrous gluconate.

Iron Casein Complexes

Phosphoproteins such as milk caseins are strong natural chelators of transition metals such as iron. Their high affinity for metals is attributed to the presence in casein of clustered phosphoseryl residues (79). Iron binds more strongly than calcium so that, when added to a casein solution, it will replace calcium from the high-affinity binding sites. Forni et al. (80) prepared iron (ferric) caseinate by adding ferric lactobionate to a sodium caseinate solution and stirring for 1 hr at room temperature before concentrating and freeze-drying. The complex contained 0.31% iron. It was added at 6 mg Fe/100 g to a milk-based infant formula and 12 mg Fe/100 g to a precooked wheat flour. These products were placed in aluminum cans, stored at 37°C, and the lipid oxidation was followed by the analysis of pentane in the headspace. In the infant formula, pentane production as expected was very low with both iron sources. The levels of pentane generated by the stored cereal were much higher, even in the unfortified control sample, and although the iron casein generated less pentane than ferrous sulphate, it was still judged to be relatively pro-oxidative.

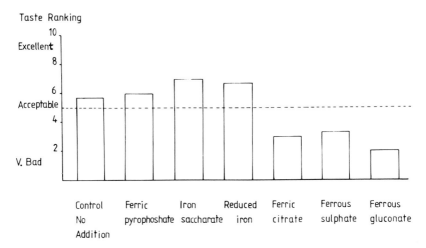

FIG. 6. Taste-testing of precooked whole wheat flour containing various iron sources (15 mg Fe/100 g) after 6 weeks' storage at 37°C. (J. Burri, *personal communication.*)

A preliminary bioavailability study with rats using radioactive ^{59}Fe showed that incorporation of ^{59}Fe from the iron-casein complex was 72% of that of iron from ferrous sulphate (F. Forni, M. J. Arnaud, and J. Hildago, *personal communication*). In the hemoglobin repletion test, the RBV was 90. The low iron content would mean that around 3% would need to be added to a cereal product. A possible advantage is that the absorption of iron from the iron-casein complex, like that from heme iron and ferric Na EDTA, would be less inhibited by other dietary constituents such as fiber or tannins. This still has to be investigated.

Encapsulated Ferrous Sulphate

In collaboration with Durkee Industrial Foods group, we have encapsulated anhydrous ferrous sulphate ($\sim 2H_2O$) with a variety of partially hydrogenated vegetable oils. We tested bioavailability and investigated organoleptic problems in a cereal flour. The products contained 40% capsule and 60% active substance. The coating materials, their melting points, and the relative bioavailability of the encapsulated ferrous sulphate compared to ferrous sulphate itself is shown in Table 7. The hemoglobin repletion test was used to measure bioavailability.

Encapsulation had little influence on the bioavailability of ferrous sulphate. The products encapsulated with partially hydrogenated soybean oil, partially hydrogenated palm oil, and mono- and diglycerides performed particularly well. In contrast, electrolytic iron and pyrophosphate had only about half the bioavailability of ferrous sulphate. The electrolytic iron (Glidden) was described as an extra fine powder (<44 μm) with a relative bioavailability of 72%.

When dry-mixed with a pre-cooked wheat flour (10 mg Fe/100 g) and stored at 37°C for 3 months, the encapsulated products did not cause any off-flavor problems

TABLE 7. *Relative bioavailability of encapsulated ferrous sulphate, ferric pyrophosphate, and electrolytically reduced iron as compared to ferrous sulphate*

Iron source	Melting point (°C)	Relative[a] bioavailability
Encapsulated ferrous sulphate 2H$_2$O		
partially hydrogenated soybean oil	65–66	101, 115
partially hydrogenated palm oil	57–58	95
mono- and diglycerides	54–55	101,116
partially hydrogenated soybean and cottonseed oil	51–52	79
maltodextrin	—	87
Ferrous sulphate 2H$_2$O	—	102
Ferric pyrophosphate	—	64,45
Electrolytically reduced iron	—	40

[a]As measured in the hemoglobin repletion test (ferrous sulphate 7H$_2$O = 100).

TABLE 8. *Discoloration of iron-enriched dried cereal-milk mixtures on addition of hot milk*

Iron source	Color reaction
Electrolytic iron	No discoloration
Iron pyrophosphate	No discoloration
Ferrous chloride	
Ferric chloride	
Ferrous citrate	Green coloration
Ferric citrate	
Ferrous acetate	
Ferric acetate	
Ferrous sulphate 2H$_2$O	Gray at low concentration
Ferrous sulphate 7H$_2$O	Green at high concentration
Ferrous sulphate 2H$_2$O encapsulated with partially hydrogenated soybean oil	Reactions similar to ferrous sulphate but slower at 50°C—no discoloration at 60°C—slow discoloration at 70°C—rapid discoloration

or excessive fat oxidation as measured by taste panel and pentane generation, respectively. They performed equally as well as electrolytic iron and the unfortified control. Unwanted color formation was investigated with the hydrogenated soybean oil capsule only. This capsule had the highest melting point (65°C) but provided little protection against unwanted color formation when added to the cereal (Table 8). The encapsulated product and a series of other iron salts at 7.5 and 40 mg/ 100 g were dry-mixed with a dried cereal-milk weaning food. The color problem did not occur during storage but during the preparation of the product for consumption. As with ferrous sulphate, various shades of gray and green appeared when hot milk was added. The color formation depended on the temperature of the milk and appeared at 60°C and above. This was perhaps to be expected as the capsule had a melting point of 65°C. Other soluble iron salts also exhibited green color formation, whereas electrolytic iron and pyrophosphate caused no discoloration.

We plan to investigate capsules of higher melting points; carnauba wax (melting point 82°C) and zinc stearate (melting point 121°C) are possibilites. Such capsules may well overcome color problems but their influence on bioavailabilty remains to be determined. For the moment, elemental iron, ferric pyrophosphate, and perhaps ferric orthophosphate and iron saccharate appear to be the most suitable iron sources with which to fortify cereals from an organoleptic viewpoint.

GENERAL CONCLUSIONS

The iron sources added to infant formulas are generally ferrous salts of high relative bioavailability. The amount absorbed from milk-based formulas would appear to be in the region of 4%, which is considered sufficient to meet the iron requirements of infants (81). The absorption of iron from soya-based infant formula would appear to be adequate (41).

Because of organoleptic problems, ferrous salts cannot be added to cereal products. Encapsulation of ferrous sulphate to prevent organoleptic deterioration would seem a worthwhile approach, provided a more heat-stable coating can be found which does not reduce bioavailability. The iron sources normally added to infant cereals are elemental iron, ferric pyrophosphate, and ferric orthophosphate. Another iron source which looks promising, but has been little investigated, is saccharated iron oxide.

As iron sources differ greatly in quality from batch to batch, the food manufacturer needs more precise information on the relationships between *in vitro* tests and bioavailability, so that an effective control system may be implemented. However, even with good control, it is doubtful whether the relative bioavailability of these sources will be much more than half that of ferrous sulphate. One exception may be carbonyl iron, but that too may cause organoleptic problems. Adding higher levels of iron sources in order to increase the absolute absorption must be balanced against a possible adverse effect on the absorption of copper and zinc.

In addition to being fortified with the less available iron sources, infant cereals also contain inhibitors of iron absorption. If the precise nature of the inhibitors in cereals (or soya) could be clearly identified, it might be possible to remove them technologically. Other technological treatments to modify the nature of food-bound iron may also be possible, although their influence on bioavailability is uncertain. For the moment, the addition of ascorbic acid seems to be the best and the simplest way to overcome inhibition partially and to produce satisfactory absorption values. The optimum ratios of ascorbic acid to iron, however, need to be confirmed or determined for the different iron sources commonly used. The use of other reducing agents such as vitamin E or chelating agents such as succinic acid also merits further investigation. By far the most promising chelator would appear to be EDTA.

Iron bound as ferric sodium, EDTA is much less influenced by inhibitors than other iron salts and would appear to be an extremely useful iron source for addition to infant cereals or even soya products, provided that it could be shown to be harmless.

REFERENCES

1. Codex Alimentarius Commission. Report of Codex Committee on Foods for Special Dietary Uses. Alinorm 81/26. Joint FAO/WHO Food Standards Programme. Rome, FAO, 1981.
2. Fritz JC, Pla GW, Roberts T, Boehne JW, Hove EL. Biological availability in animals of iron from common dietary sources. J Agric Food Chem 1970;18:647–51.
3. Fritz JC, Pla GW. Application of the animal haemoglobin repletion test to measurement of iron availability in foods. J Assoc Off Anal Chem 1972;55:1128–32.
4. Björn-Rasmussen E, Hallberg L, Rossander L. Absorption of "fortification" iron. Bioavailability in man of different samples of reduced iron, and prediction of the effects of iron fortification. Br J Nutr, 1977;37:375–88.
5. Cook JD, Minnich V, Moore CV, Rasmussen A, Bradley WB, Finch CA. Absorption of fortification iron in bread. Am J Clin Nutr 1973;26:861–72.
6. Brise H, Hallberg L. A method for comparative studies on iron absorption in man using two radio-iron isotopes. Acta Med Scand, 1962;171(suppl 376)7–73.
7. Lee K, Clydesdale FM. Iron sources used in food fortification and their changes due to food processing. Crit Rev Food Sci Nutr 1979;11:117–53.
8. Ríos E, Hunter RE, Cook JD, Smith NJ, Finch CA. The absorption of iron as supplements in infant cereal and infant formulas. Pediatrics 1975;55:686–93.
9. Theuer RC, Kemmerer KS, Martin WH, Zoumas BL, Sarett HP. Effect of processing on availability of iron salts in liquid infant formula products: experimental soy isolate formulas. J Agric Food Chem, 1971;19:555–8.
10. Theuer, RC, Martin WH, Wallander JF, Sarett HP. Effect of processing on availability of iron salts in liquid infant formula products: experimental milk-based formulas. J Agric Food Chem 1973;21:482–5.
11. Bothwell TH, Charlton RW, Cook JD, Finch CA. Iron metabolism in man. Oxford, Blackwell Scientific Publications, 1979.
12. McMillan JA, Oski FA, Laurie G, Tomarelli RM, Landaw SA. Iron absorption from human milk, simulated milk and proprietary formulas. Pediatrics 1977;60:896–900.
13. Saarinen UM, Siimes MA. Iron absorption from breast milk, cow's milk and iron-supplemented formula: an opportunistic use of changes in total body iron determined by haemoglobin, ferritin and body weight in 132 infants. Pediatr Res 1979,13:143–7.
14. Saarinen UM, Siimes MA, Dallman PR. Iron absorption in infants: high bioavailability of breast milk iron as indicated by the extrinsic tag method of iron absorption and by the concentration of serum ferritin. J Pediat 1977;91:35–9.
15. McMillan JA, Landaw SA, Oski FA. Iron sufficiency in breast-fed infants and the availability of iron in human milk. Pediatrics 1976;58:686–91.
16. Rees JM, Monsen ER. Absorption of fortification iron by the rat: comparison of type and level of iron incorporation into mixed grain cereal. J Agric Food Chem 1973;21:913–5.
17. Hallberg L. Bioavailability of dietary iron in man. Annu Rev Nutr 1981;1:123–47.
18. de Vet BJCM, Van Gool J. Lactoferrin and iron absorption in the small intestine. Acta Med Scand 1974;196:393–402.
19. Abernathy RP, Miller J, Wentworth J, Speirs M. Metabolic patterns in pre-adolescent children. XII. Effect of amount and source of dietary protein on absorption of iron. J Nutr 1965;85:265–70.
20. Hallberg L, Rossander L. Effect of different drinks on the absorption of non-haem iron from composite meals. Hum Nutr Appl Nutr 1982;36A:116–23.
21. Ranhotra GS, Gelroth JA, Torrance FA, Bock MA, Winterringer GL. Bioavailability of iron in iron-fortified fluid milk. J Food Sci 1981;46:1342–4.
22. Amine EK, Hegsted DM. Biological assessment of available iron in food products. J Agric Food Chem 1974;22:470–6.

23. Coccocrilli GD, Reussner GH, Thiessen R. Relative biological value of iron supplements in processed food products. J Agric Food Chem 1976;24:351–3.

24. Hinton JJC, Carter JE, Moran T. The addition of iron to flour. 1. The solubility and some related properties of iron powders including reduced iron. J Food Technol 1967;2:129–34.

25. Motzok J, Pennell MD, Davies MI, Ross HU. Effect of particle size on the biological availability of reduced iron. J Assoc Off Anal Chem 1974;58:99–103.

26. Pennell MD, Davies MI, Rasper J, Motzok I. Biological availability of iron supplements for rats, chicks and humans. J Nutr 1975;106:265–74.

27. Pla GW, Harrison BN, Fritz JC. Comparison of chicks and rats as test animals for studying the bioavailability of iron. J Assoc Off Anal Chem 1973;56:1369–72.

28. Shah BG, Giroux A, Belonje B. Specifications for reduced iron as a food additive. J Agric Food Chem 1977;25:592–4.

29. Fritz JC. Bioavailability of mineral nutrients. Chemtech 1976;6:643.

30. Harrison BN, Pla GW, Clark GA, Fritz, JC. Selection of iron sources for cereal enrichment. Cereal Chem 1976;53:78–84.

31. Shah, BG, Giroux A, Belonje B. Bioavailability of iron from iron phosphates in cereals and infant foods. J Agric Food Chem 1979;27:845–7.

32. Wade A, ed. Martindale. The extra pharmacopoeia. 27th ed. London, The Pharmaceutical Press, 1977.

33. Morck TA, Lynch SR, Cook JD. Reduction of the soy-induced inhibition of non-heme iron absorption. Am J Clin Nutr 1982;36:219–28.

34. Forth W, Rummel W. Iron absorption. Physiol Rev 1973;53:724–93.

35. Spiro TG, Saltman P. Inorganic chemistry. In: Jacobs A, Worwood M, eds. Iron in biochemistry and medicine. New York: Academic Press, 1974:1–26.

36. Rotruck JT, Luhrsen KR. A comparison study in rats of iron bioavailability from cooked beef and in soybean protein. J Agric Food Chem 1979;27:27–33.

37. Simpson KM, Morris ER, Cook JD. The inhibitory effect of bran in iron absorption in man. Am J Clin Nutr 1981;34:1469–78.

38. Morris ER, Ellis R. Isolation of monoferric phytate from wheat bran and its biological value as an iron source to the rat. J Nutr 1976;106:753–60.

39. Lipschitz DA, Simpson KM, Cook JD, Morris ER. Absorption of monoferric phytate by dogs. J Nutr 1979;109:1154–60.

40. Reinhold JG, Salvador-Garcia JL, Garzon P. Binding of iron by fibre of wheat and maize. Am J Clin Nutr 1981;34:1384–91.

41. International Nutritional Anaemia Consultative Group. The effects of cereals and legumes on iron availability. New York: The Nutrition Foundation, 1982.

42. Cook JD, Morck TA, Lynch SR. The inhibitory effect of soy products on non-heme iron absorption. Am J Clin Nutr 1981;34:2622–9.

43. Morck TA, Lynch SR, Skikne BS, Cook JD. Iron availability from infant food supplements. Am J Clin Nutr 1981;34:2630–4.

44. Steinke FH, Hopkins DT. Biological availability to the rat of intrinsic and extrinsic iron with soybean protein isolates. J Nutr 1978;108:481–9.

45. Disler PB, Lynch SR, Charlton RW, Torrance JD, Bothwell TH, Walker RB, Mayett FGH. The effect of tea on iron absorption. Gut 1975;16:193–200.

46. Disler PB, Lynch SR, Torrance JD, Sayers MH, Bothwell TH, Charlton RW. The mechanism of the inhibition of iron absorption by tea. S Afr J Med Sci 1975;40:109–16.

47. Layrisse M, Martinez-Torres C, Gonzalez M. Measurement of the total daily dietary iron absorption by the extrinsic tag model. Am J Clin Nutr 1974;27:152–62.

48. Cook JD, Monsen ER. Vitamin C, the common cold, and iron absorption. Am J Clin Nutr 1977;30:235–41.

49. Sayers MH, Lynch SR, Jacobs P, Charlton W, Bothwell TH, Walker RB, Mayett F. The fortification of common salt with ascorbic acid and iron. Br J Haematol 1974;28:483–95.

50. Derman DP, Bothwell TH, MacPhail AP, Torrance JD, Bezwoda WR, Charlton RW, Mayett FGH. Importance of ascorbic acid in the absorption of iron from infant foods. Scand J Haematol 1980;25:193–201.

51. Martinez-Torres C, Layrisse M. Effect of amino acids on iron absorption from a staple vegetable food. Blood 1970;35:669–82.

52. Van Campen D, Gross E. Effect of histidine and certain other amino acids on the absorption of iron [59] by rats. J Nutr 1969;99:68–74.

53. Martinez-Torres C, Romano EL, Layrisse M. Effect of cysteine on iron absorption in man. Am J Clin Nutr 1981;34:322–7.

54. Moore CV. The importance of nutritional factors in the pathogenesis of iron deficiency anaemia. Am J Clin Nutr 1955;3:3–10.

55. Pollack S, George JN, Reba RC, Kaufman RM, Crosby WH. The absorption on non-ferrous metals in iron deficiency. J Clin Invest 1965;44:1470–3.

56. Loria A, Medal LS, Elizondo J. Effect of sorbitol on iron absorption in man. Am J Clin Nutr 1962;10:124–7.

57. Hallberg L, Sölvell L, Brise H. Search for substances promoting the absorption of iron. Studies on absorption and side effects. Acta Med Scand 1966;181(suppl 459):11–21.

58. Martinez-Torres C, Romano EL, Renzi M, Layrisee M. Fe(III) EDTA complex as iron fortification. Further studies. Am J Clin Nutr 1979;32:809–16.

59. MacPhail AP, Bothwell TH, Torrance JD, Derman DP, Bezwoda WR, Charlton RW, Mayett FGH. Factors affecting the absorption of iron from FE (III) EDTA. Br J Nutr 1981;45:215–27.

60. Hegenauer J, Saltman P, Ludwig D, Ripley L, Bajo P. Effect of supplemental iron and copper on lipid oxidation in milk. 1. Comparison of metal complexes in emulsified and homogenized milk. J Agric Food Chem 1979;27:860–8.

61. Greenberg, SM, Tucker RG, Heming AE, Mathues JK. Iron absorption and metabolism. I. Inter-relationships of ascorbic acid and vitamin E. J Nutr 1957;63:19–31.

62. Wood RJ, Stake PE, Eiseman JH, Shippee RL, Wolski KE, Koehn U. Effects of heat and pressure processing on the relative biological value of selected dietary supplemental inorganic iron salts as determined by chick haemoglobin repletion assay. J Nutr 1978;108:1477–84.

63. Lee K, Clydesdale FM. Chemical changes of iron in food and drying processes. J Food Sci 1980;45:711–5.

64. Hodson AZ. Conversion of ferric to ferrous iron in weight control dietaries. J Agric Food Chem 1970;18:946–7.

65. Nojeim SJ, Clydesdale FM. Effect of pH and ascorbic acid on iron valence in model systems and in foods. J Food Sci 1981;46:606–16.

66. Nojeim SJ, Clydesdale FM, Zajicek OT. Effect of redox potential on iron valence in model systems and in foods. J Food Sci 1981;46:1265–8.

67. Lee K, Clydesdale FM. Effect of baking on the forms of iron in iron enriched flours. J Food Sci 1980;45:1500–4.

68. Camire AL, Clydesdale FM. Effect of pH and heat treatment on the binding of calcium, magnesium, zinc and iron to wheat bran and fractions of dietary fibre. J Food Sci 1981;46:548–51.

69. Strauss RG. Iron deficiency, infections and immune function: a reassessment. Am J Clin Nutr 1978;31:660–6.

70. Anonymous. Gastrointestinal tolerance of iron-fortified proprietary infant formulas. Nutr Rev 1981;39:210–1.

71. Smith CH, Bidlack WR. Inter-relationship of dietary ascorbic acid and iron on the tissue distribution of ascorbic acid, iron and copper in female guinea pigs. J Nutr 1980;110:1398–408.

72. Seeley JR, Humphrey GB, Matter BJ. Copper deficiency in a premature infant fed an iron-fortified formula. N Engl J Med 1972;286:109–10.

73. Flanagan PR, Haist J, Vallberg LS. Comparative effects of iron deficiency induced by bleeding and a low-iron diet on the intestinal absorptive interactions of iron, cobalt, manganese, zinc, lead and cadmium. J Nutr 1980;100:1754–63.

74. Solomons NW, Jacob RA. Studies on the bioavailability of zinc in humans: effects of heme and non-heme iron on the absorption of zinc. Am J Clin Nutr 1981;34:475–82.

75. Codex Alimentarius Commission. Recommended international standards for foods for infants and children. CAC/RS 72/74. Joint FAO/WHO Food Standards Programme. Rome, FAO, 1976.

76. Bookwalter GN, Black LT, Warner KA. Nutritional stability of corn-soy-milk blends after dry heating to destroy Salmonellae. J Food Sci 1973;38:618–22.

77. Hartman GH. Technological problems in fortification with minerals. In: Technology of fortification of foods. Washington DC: National Academy of Sciences, 1975:8–18.

78. Douglas Jr FW, Rainey NH, Wong NP, Edmondson LF, La Croix DE. Colour, flavour and iron bioavailability in iron-fortified chocolate milk. J Dairy Sci 1981;64:1785–93.

79. Osterberg R. Phosphorus linkages in α-casein. Biochim Biophys Acta 1961;54:424–31.

80. Forni F, Lambelet P, Löliger J, Jost R. Casein-oligoelement complexes: potential use in copper and iron supplementation of dietetic milk powders and cereals. Nestlé research report no. 1022. La Tour-de-Peilz, Switzerland: Nestlé Products Technical Assistance Co. Ltd., 1981.
81. ESPGAN Committee on Nutrition. Guidelines on infant nutrition. II. Recommendations for the composition of follow-up formula and Beikost. Acta Pediatr Scand [Suppl] 1981;287:1–24.

DISCUSSION

Dr. Dallman: I understand that some forms of fortification iron can settle to the bottom of the package with products such as cereals, so that the iron is unevenly distributed. One might expect that carbonyl iron, which is spherical, would be more likely to settle out than something like electrolytic iron, which has a rough surface. Do you know of any studies on this?

Dr. Hurrell: As far as I know there have been no published studies on this phenomenon, but I agree that carbonyl iron would be more expected to fall through to the bottom of the package than electrolytic iron, which could be more easily held by its flat, jagged structure.

Dr. Hallberg: All flour in Sweden has been fortified with carbonyl iron for many years. The sedimentation of the iron particles has been studied by the milling industry and as far as I am informed it is no practical problem.

Dr. Dallman: I think that this problem may apply to infant cereals.

Dr. Fomon: I had been under the impression that the electrolytic iron powder currently used for fortification of instant cereals in the United States was of small particle size (I believe 95% passes through a 325-mesh sieve) and therefore of high bioavailability. From Dr. Hurrell's discussion, I suspect that bioavailability of this iron may actually be rather low. I wonder what is known about the bioavailability of this form of electrolytic iron powder.

Dr. Hallberg: I don't think that particle size distribution is a good parameter of the bioavailability of reduced iron. We found that surface area per unit weight and rate of dissolution were better related to the bioavailability in humans.

Dr. Stekel: One aspect that concerns me is that most data are based on experience with foods that are available in developed countries. For instance, you say that we have no problems with milk formulas because we fortify the formula with ferrous sulphate with adequate results, but these formulas are sophisticated in their composition and especially in their packaging. They come in sealed cans, oxygen free, and so on. When one considers taking the regular milk powder available in a developing country and fortifying it with iron, which would be in principle a simple matter and not very expensive, the problem of packaging comes up and this may be a limiting factor. A factor that then needs to be discussed is what are the alternatives to good packaging conditions. I think that one alternative might be to protect the vehicle in some way from interaction with the iron salt. Would you like to comment on this?

Dr. Hurrell: Do you still use ferrous sulphate in Chile even though the products go rancid?

Dr. Stekel: We have told the manufacturers that when the iron fortification program starts they have to switch to oxygen-tight containers, but that is the problem. This has been one of the limiting factors in going from a successful pilot study to a national program.

Dr. Hurrell: Packaging is something that I did not consider in my talk although it is undoubtedly important. All soluble iron salts would presumably promote rancidity if the milk powders were not packed in air-tight containers. In a nonair-tight container I suppose one could consider using one of the less soluble iron salts, encapsulated iron or maybe iron saccharate, which may well overcome the organoleptic problems. Of course, the problem may then be one of bioavailability.

Dr. Stekel: I think that when you make calculations of the costs involved, in a program like the one in Chile where about 13 million kg of dry milk are distributed each year to infants, it turns out that to switch from unfortified to a fortified milk means an increase in price of about 13 to 14%. Of this, about 1% is ferrous sulphate and the ascorbic acid and 13% is the increased cost of packaging. So, this really becomes a very important limiting factor.

Dr. Hurrell: I agree, but air-tight packaging is also necessary to protect certain vitamins, such as A, C, and folic acid, in the product. It is not just for organoleptic reasons but also for nutritional reasons.

Dr. Stekel: I can see that, but you must realize that the product that is currently used is aimed primarily at the prevention of protein-calorie malnutrition, so that it is really dry milk without any vitamins or minerals added to it.

Dr. Hallberg: There is a great variation in the bioavailability of the iron phosphates. Even among ferric orthophosphate preparations on the market, the variation in rate of dissolution and in bioavailability is very marked. We produced ferric orthophosphate preparations with different physicochemical properties and found that preparations with the highest rate of dissolution had a relative bioavailablity of about 40% compared with ferrous sulphate.

The main requirements of a reduced iron preparation are that the relative bioavailability in humans is known, including the effect of food preparation (e.g., baking), that it is fairly high and does not vary from one batch to another.

Dr. Hurrell: I should like to ask how much iron we can add. If we add more iron we can increase the amount of iron absorbed, but just how high can we go from a nutritional or toxicological point of view, until we influence the absorption of other trace elements such as zinc, for instance. Increasing the amount of iron would seem to be by far the simplest method of getting more iron absorbed.

Dr. Fomon: In the United States a product fortified above a specified limit becomes officially designated as a supplement and may no longer be advertised as a food. For children under 4 years of age this limit for iron is 7.5 mg in a serving of average size. A serving is declared (by the manufacturers) to be 15 g of dry cereal. After dilution, this will amount to about 100 g or more of cereal as fed: a very large serving for a small infant. I doubt that manufacturers would like to advertise their infant cereals as nutritional supplements rather than cereals so I do not believe that the level of iron fortification will be increased unless the declared size of an average serving is reduced.

Dr. DeMaeyer: When planning a fortification program, one has also to take into consideration the cost and the commercial availability of the iron compounds that may be used in the fortification process. It would be interesting to have some information on the subject.

Dr. Hurrell: Ferrous sulphate is by far the least expensive and the most easily available.

Dr. DeMaeyer: Could you comment on the different forms of reduced iron?

Dr. Hurrell: As I mentioned, there are four types of elemental iron: hydrogen reduced, carbon monoxide reduced, electrolytic, and carbonyl. I believe that the hydrogen-reduced form is the most widely available and the least expensive. Electrolytic is perhaps the least easily obtained. Carbonyl iron is available in Europe from manufacturers of magnetic tape (such as BASF). I cannot comment more on the relative cost. I think that as far as price is concerned, Dr. Stekel has pointed out that the price of the iron compound itself is always a very small part of the overall price of the product.

Dr. Stekel: Dr. Hurrell, I wonder whether you would like to comment on the use of hemoglobin as a food fortificant.

Dr. Hurrell: I think the main problem with hemoglobin is that it contains only 0.3% iron, so that one would have to add 5% of hemoglobin to have 15 mg of iron. That would certainly turn the product a different color. You said yourself that you could only add it to chocolate-colored biscuits because that was the only place where the additional color was not too important. Also, I think ethical problems of adding blood to infant foods will be difficult to overcome, and there would be microbiological problems. I don't think one can foresee the addition of hemoglobin to commercially produced infant foods.

Dr. Stekel: I think you are right that the iron concentration is very low, but you have to consider that you are using not only the iron but also the protein.

Dr. Hurrell: Another problem with hemoglobin which should be borne in mind is that it contains little isoleucine, although it does have a high level of lysine.

Dr. Stekel: It is short on isoleucine, but when you add it to products that are cereal based—infant cereals, for instance, or wheat cookies—because of the high amounts of lysine and other essential amino acids in hemoglobin, and because of the low amino acid scores of these vegetable products, despite the fact that it is short in isoleucine, the amino acid score of the final product is increased. I agree that the microbiological and other problems are such that we probably do not have many reliable sources of hemoglobin available at this time, but I think it is certainly something that can be shown to work and it should perhaps be considered.

Dr. Hallberg: I think that dried blood (hemoglobin iron) can be used to fortify foods under certain conditions. Attempts were made in Sweden to fortify bread with dried blood; the bioavailability was fairly good, but there were problems with the shelf-life of the bread and it is no longer used. I think the best use of dried blood as an iron fortificant is in meat products such as sausages and hamburgers, especially when soya protein has been used as a partial substitute for meat and therefore the heme iron content of the product is reduced. The reason for using dried blood in meat products is that meat for unknown reasons promotes the absorption of heme iron; it is about 25% in meals containing meat but only 10% in other meals.

Dr. Garby: What about heme? That would solve the problem of the low iron content, but is heme difficult to handle chemically?

Dr. Hallberg: I think there are two patented processes I know about which both produce hemoglobin iron with good bioavailability and good shelf-life. In most meat products I think that the blood can be used as such.

Dr. Stekel: It is not always the case that purified heme is poorly absorbed. If you do the studies in a water solution this is the case, but we have some studies adding heme to milk, for instance, where absorption was very good. Apparently, the protein media in the milk had a protective effect on the formation of the large heme macromolecules, thus the heme in the milk was as well absorbed as the hemoglobin.

Iron Nutrition in Infancy and Childhood,
edited by A. Stekel. Nestlé, Vevey/Raven Press,
New York © 1984.

Prevention of Iron Deficiency

Abraham Stekel

*Institute of Nutrition and Food Technology, University of Chile,
Casilla 15138, Santiago 11 Chile*

Infants and children need to absorb about 1 mg of iron per day. This is a disproportionate requirement, compared to adults, that derives from growth. Children consume less food than adults and their diet often consists of foods with little iron content and poor iron availability. This is the challenge that needs to be met in the prevention of iron deficiency in early life.

Evidence is accumulating that iron deficiency may be associated with impaired function of various tissues (1). In the light of this knowledge, the objective of prevention during infancy and childhood should be not only to avoid the occurrence of anemia, but also to assure an adequate supply of iron to all tissues during this critical period of development.

Ideally, prevention of a nutritional deficiency should be attained by the consumption of a good diet. Unfortunately, in the case of iron, this is not always possible, and it may be necessary to fortify the diet or give iron as a supplement. In this chapter, I shall briefly review the various interrelated approaches to the prevention of iron deficiency in infants and children. The importance of adequate dietary practices and of avoiding excess iron losses will be emphasized; the options of food fortification and iron supplementation will then be discussed.

DIET

There are marked geographic (2) as well as socioeconomic (3) differences in the prevalence of iron deficiency that indicate the importance of the quality of the diet. Due to the high iron requirements in infancy and the relative monotony of the infant diet, with milk being the main source of calories, iron deficiency tends to be prevalent even in developed countries, especially in lower socioeconomic populations. After the first year of life, the child starts consuming the regular household food and, at this time, the marked differences in iron content and iron availability between different diets become apparent. Nutritional iron deficiency in preschool and school-age children in developed countries is relatively uncommon but is still highly prevalent in the poorer population groups of Latin America, Africa, and Asia.

The bioavailability of iron from different foods and diets varies considerably. Of great importance is the chemical form in which iron is presented to the intestinal mucosal cell. Several studies (4,5) have demonstrated that iron enters into two "common pools" that behave differently in terms of absorption, the so-called heme-iron and nonheme iron pools. Heme iron, present in hemoglobin and myoglobin, is well absorbed and is relatively unaffected by diet composition (6–8). Nonheme iron, the form of iron present in vegetables, cereals, and in some foods of animal origin that are of importance in infantile nutrition, such as milk and eggs, generally is poorly absorbed and is greatly affected by enhancing or inhibiting substances in the diet (7). Some of these are listed in Table 1. Since most food iron is nonheme, the presence or absence of these substances plays a vital role in the availability of dietary iron.

An important advance in our knowledge of the contribution of the diet to iron nutrition is the role of breast-feeding. Even though the iron content of human milk is low, it is much more available than the iron in cow's milk (9,10). As a consequence, infants that are breast-fed have an advantage over artificially fed infants in the initial few months of life (11). However, after 4 to 6 months, even breast milk cannot supply the needed iron and the infant must rely on the introduction of other foods and on supplementation to meet requirements.

It is not possible to prevent iron deficiency in all cases with diet alone, at least in infancy. However, in the light of the preceding discussion, a few recommendations can be made. First, breast-feeding should continue in all infants for at least 6 months. Second, when solid foods are introduced, proper consideration should be given to our present knowledge of dietary factors affecting iron absorption and, when possible, foods containing heme iron and/or enhancers of nonheme iron absorption (meat, ascorbic acid) should be offered. Third, foods that markedly inhibit absorption, such as tea, should be avoided.

AVOIDING EXCESS IRON LOSSES

Physiological iron losses are relatively fixed and unaffected by the iron status of the individual. However, pathological conditions, some of which are very common in many areas of the world, can markedly increase the loss of iron, particularly via the gastrointestinal tract.

The most studied and best documented cause of excessive iron loss is parasitic infection, a condition frequently occurring in preschool and school-age children in tropical areas (12). Infants with acute diarrhea may also lose significant amounts

TABLE 1. *Factors affecting the bioavailability of nonheme food iron*

Enhancing	Depressing
Meat, fish, chicken	Carbonates, oxalates, phosphates
Ascorbic acid	Phytate
	Bran, vegetable fiber
	Tea
	Egg yolk

of blood. The cumulative loss of iron resulting from repeated episodes of gastrointestinal infection can be very significant (13). Improvement of sanitary conditions in areas with a high prevalence of diarrhea and parasitic infection will obviously contribute to the prevention of iron deficiency.

Another factor contributing to excessive blood loss in infancy is the use of fresh or pasteurized cow's milk (14,15). This phenomenon decreases with heat treatment of the milk and seems to be of importance only in the early months of life. Present recommendations are to avoid the use of fresh cow's milk in the feeding of infants at least during the first 6 months of life (16,17).

FOOD FORTIFICATION

Food fortification is the preferred way of preventing iron deficiency in infants and in those children whose regular diet does not provide enough available iron.

The principles behind successful food fortification with iron have been extensively reviewed in recent publications (18–20).

A suitable vehicle must first be chosen. Ideally, the food vehicle should be regularly consumed by the target population in amounts that do not vary considerably between different individuals so that a level of fortification that is adequate for most of the population can be selected. It should, at some stage, be centrally processed so that iron can be added to it, and the organoleptic characteristics and shelf-life should not be noticeably changed by the fortification process. The iron preparation used for fortification should be relatively inexpensive and easy to incorporate. Most importantly, it should have a good bioavailability, an obvious fact that was not always considered in the past. Several soluble ferrous salts and reduced iron of small particle size seem to conform to these requirements (19).

The iron bioavailability from the fortified product must be studied in humans. Its efficacy should next be demonstrated in pilot field studies. Finally, if the product is to be used in a program (local, regional, national), its effectiveness must be demonstrated under the regular operating conditions of the program.

Infants

Milk-based formulas and especially prepared infant cereals are the most commonly used iron-fortified products in infancy.

There are many commercially prepared iron-fortified infant formulas on the market. They are basically cow's milk that has been modified to resemble human milk. Most contain about 12 mg iron per liter of formula, in the form of ferrous sulphate (21).

The first demonstration in the field of the effectiveness of iron-fortified milk is the study by Marsh et al. (22). These authors gave a small number of term and preterm infants from 0 to 9 months of age a milk-based, commercially prepared formula, containing 12 mg/liter of elemental iron as ferrous sulphate. This formula also contained 55 mg/liter of ascorbic acid. Two additional groups received the same formula without iron, and evaporated milk. No solid foods were recommended until 9 months, but some infants did receive a cereal preparation without iron. Mean hemoglobin concentration at 9 months in term infants was 12.69 g/dl in the fortified group versus 10.46 g/dl and 9.67 in the groups receiving the unfortified formula and the evaporated milk, respectively. Corresponding figures in prematures were 12.49 g/dl for the fortified-formula group and 9.40 and 8.55 g/dl for the other two groups, respectively. There is no information on the distribution of hemoglobin values in this study, therefore the incidence of anemia in the different groups cannot be calculated.

Andelman and Sered (23) used the same product in a large number of predominantly nonwhite infants of very low socioeconomic condition in the city of Chicago. The fortified formula was given from discharge from the hospital or from the first clinic visit until 6 to 9 months of age. A control group received evaporated milk. Both groups were given strained foods at 3 months and cereals, eggs, meat, vegetables, and fruits at 6 months. At about 1 year of age, mean hemoglobin concentration was 11.9 g/dl in 321 infants who had received the fortified formula and 10.4 g/dl in 143 infants in the control group. A very high percentage (76%) of the infants in the control group developed anemia during the study. In the fortified group, about 15% of the infants were anemic at 12 months of age and 22% at 15 months, indicating that the product, used for only 6 to 9 months, could not control anemia in this very underprivileged group of infants.

Saarinen (11) used a proprietary infant formula containing 11 mg iron/liter as ferrous gluconate in 47 term Finnish infants, starting before 1 month of age and continuing the administration until 1 year of age. Cooked vegetables were started at 3.5 months, meat and eggs at 6 months, and table food at 9 months of age. They also received an iron-fortified cereal (0.1 mg/g of dry cereal) starting at 5 months. Essentially none of these infants had any sign of iron deficiency during the first year of life as measured by hemoglobin concentration, transferrin saturation, mean corpuscular volume, or serum ferritin. In contrast, at 9 and 12 months of age, a low serum ferritin existed in about 15% of the 29 infants fed cow's milk and unfortified cereal.

There are very few studies of this nature in developing countries. In Chile, two different iron-fortified formulas have been the subject of investigations in recent years (24,25). Since a large program of free distribution of dry milk to infants or their lactating mothers exists in this country, covering 80% of the infantile population, it was thought that fortification of this milk with iron could reduce the high prevalence of iron deficiency. Under this program, 3 kg of dry milk are given each month from 0 to 6 months of age and 2 kg from 6 to 24 months of age. Mean duration of breast-feeding in Chile is about 3 months. Solids are usually introduced at 4 months of age.

The first fortified product was studied between 1972 and 1975. It was low-fat (12%) dry milk fortified with 15 mg elemental iron per 100 g of powder or 1 liter of reconstituted milk as ferrous sulphate. Geometric mean iron absorption from this formula in primarily iron-deficient infants was 3 to 4% (25). About 300 infants received the fortified milk from 3 months to 15 months of age. Controls received the same milk without iron fortification. At the end of the trial, anemia had been reduced from 34.6% in the control group to 9.9% in infants known to be receiving fortified milk consistently. Differences in transferrin saturation and free erythrocyte protoporphyrin were small.

These results, although significant, were less than optimal due to the relatively low absorption of iron from this unmodified milk and to the fact that some of the product was consumed by other family members. The 0.3 to 0.4 mg of extra iron that was probably absorbed from the fortified milk was not enough to prevent iron deficiency in infants receiving no other fortified foods.

A second fortified formula was developed in the laboratory in 1975 as a result of studies demonstrating the importance of ascorbic acid on the bioavailability of fortification iron in milk (26). This was a full-fat (26%) dry milk fortified with 15 mg iron (as ferrous sulphate) and 100 mg of ascorbic acid per 100 g (1 liter of reconstituted formula). The product was slightly acidified in order to discourage consumption by other family members. Iron absorption from this milk in predominantly iron-deficient infants was 10 to 12% (24,25), 2.7 times higher than that from fortified milk without ascorbic acid given to the same infants (Fig. 1).

A pilot field trial was conducted with this formula between 1976 and 1978. The fortified milk was given from 3 to 15 months of age to 280 spontaneously weaned infants attending three National Health Service clinics in the city of Santiago. The regular unfortified full-fat dry milk powder was given to 278 infants. In both groups, eggs and fruits were given at 4 months, vegetables and meat soup at 5 months, unfortified cereals and legumes at 6 to 7 months, and regular table food

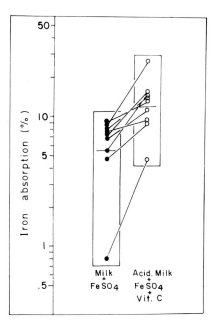

FIG. 1. Absorption of fortification iron from two different milk formulas as compared in the same subjects by a double isotope technic. Infants received on day 1 low-fat milk fortified with ferrous sulphate and on day 2 acidified milk fortified with ferrous sulphate and ascorbic acid. (From Stekel et al., ref. 25.)

at 9 to 12 months. Although these infants were of low socioeconomic condition, diarrhea was relatively uncommon and protein-calorie malnutrition affected less than 10% of the population.

The milk fortified with iron and ascorbic acid had a marked effect on iron nutrition, producing significant differences with the control group in all measured laboratory parameters at 9 and 15 months of age (Fig. 2). At 9 months, a hemoglobin concentration below 11 g/dl was present in 7.5% of the cases receiving fortified milk versus 34.7% in the control group. At 15 months, anemia existed in only 1.6% of the infants receiving the fortified product versus 27.8% of those

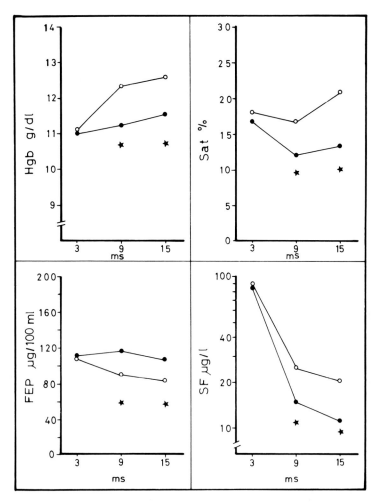

FIG. 2. Mean values of hemoglobin (Hgb), transferrin saturation (Sat), free erythrocyte protoporphyrin (FEP), and serum ferritin (SF) at 3, 9, and 15 months of age in infants receiving acidified milk fortified with iron and ascorbic acid *(open circles)* or unfortified milk *(closed circles)*. *Asterisks* indicate that differences are significant at $P < 0.001$. (From Stekel et al., ref. 25.)

receiving unfortified milk. Occurrence of anemia in the control group at 15 months would have been higher if cases with a hemoglobin concentration below 9 g/dl at 9 months had not been removed for treatment.

The same product was subsequently tested in a large regional field trial, under the normal operating conditions of the Chilean milk distribution program. At seven large clinics in the city of Santiago, infants born after 1 August 1978 received acidified milk fortified with iron and ascorbic acid after weaning; infants born before then received the regular unfortified program milk. The rest of the health care was identical in the two groups. A random sample of 400 infants born immediately before or immediately after the fortified milk was instituted was selected for detailed laboratory studies. Prevalence of anemia at 15 months of age was markedly reduced from 29.9% in the infants born in June/July to 5.5% in infants born in August/September. Enough iron was absorbed from the fortified formula to produce an increase in iron stores, as measured by serum ferritin (Fig. 3).

It is thus apparent that the use of adequately fortified milk formulas during the first year of life can prevent the development of iron deficiency in artificially fed infants. However, it must be emphasized that the iron bioavailability from these products may vary considerably. Ascorbic acid plays a critical role in this respect.

Iron-fortified cereals are also an effective and relatively inexpensive way of providing fortification iron to infants. They have the advantage that they can be

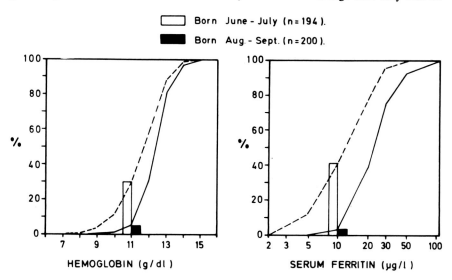

FIG. 3. Regional field trial of acidified milk fortified with iron and ascorbic acid. Cumulative frequency distribution of individual values of hemoglobin and serum ferritin at 15 months of age in infants born on June/July 1978 receiving unfortified milk *(broken line)* and on August/September 1978 receiving fortified milk *(solid line)*. The height of the columns indicates the percentage of infants with hemoglobin <11 g/dl **(left)** and serum ferritin <10 μg/l **(right)** in each of the two groups.

used in both breast-fed and artificially fed infants. In the United States, especially prepared iron-fortified cereals for infants have been available for many years. For a long time, they were fortified with iron salts, such as sodium iron pyrophosphate, that are almost completely unavailable for absorption (27). This is probably why, despite their widespread use in infant feeding, they had little impact on the prevalence of iron deficiency (28).

The best demonstration of the effectiveness of fortified cereals in preventing iron deficiency in infants is the work by Moe (29). This author gave Norwegian infants from 3.5 months until 1 year of age a cereal fortified with ferrous saccharate at two different levels: 12.5 and 5 mg/100 g. As controls, he studied a group receiving an excessive amount of iron (more than 20 mg/day) in the form of fortified cereal plus oral medicinal iron and a group fed the regular Norwegian infant diet, which, at 12 months of age, provided a calculated daily iron intake of 3.4 to 7.0 mg. Infants given the 12.5 mg cereal had hemoglobin concentrations similar to those receiving more than 20 mg iron, whereas those receiving the 5-mg cereal had significantly lower values at 9 and 12 months. Anemia (Hb <11.0 g/dl), which was very prevalent in the group receiving the unfortified diet (42.5% at 12 months), existed in 27.7% of the cases in the 5-mg cereal group but only in 4% of the infants in the 12.5-mg cereal group (Fig. 4). The author concluded that this cereal, fed regularly, twice a day from the age of 3.5 months, and providing a total daily dietary iron intake of about 10 mg at the age of 8 to 12 months, will produce an optimal hemoglobin concentration in almost all infants.

Dry cereals in the United States contain a much higher iron concentration (30). Since 1972, most of these products are fortified with reduced iron of small particle size. Two regular servings of 7 to 14 g/day of fortified dry cereal (45 mg iron/100 g of cereal) will provide 6 to 12 mg iron, of which about 4% is absorbed (31).

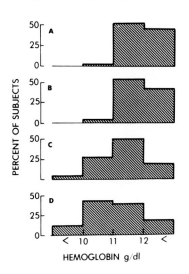

FIG. 4. Distribution of hemoglobin concentration at 1 year of age in infants receiving from the age of 2.5 months a cereal fortified with 12.5 mg iron/100 g (group **B**), the same cereal fortified with 5 mg iron/100 g (group **C**), and an intake of more than 20 mg iron/day in the form of fortified cereal plus oral medical iron (group **A**). Infants in group **D** received the regular diet with no extra iron (29). (From Dallman et al., ref. 24.)

This, according to the Committee on Nutrition of the American Academy of Pediatrics, is a sufficient supply of supplementary iron for most infants (16).

In areas of the world where breast-feeding is prolonged, cereals could represent a very good way of providing needed supplementary iron starting at about 4 to 6 months of age. At about the same age, infants that are exclusively breast-fed require calorie and protein supplementation. Cereals, fed as a gruel with a spoon, do not compete with suction from the breasts, thus contributing to the prolongation of breast-feeding.

Unfortunately, cereals traditionally used to supplement breast-fed infants in developing countries have several limitations: iron bioavailability is low, the quality of the protein is suboptimal, and the energy density is low when prepared as a gruel.

In our laboratory (E. Calvo, *unpublished data*) an extruded rice flour cereal fortified with 5% bovine hemoglobin concentrate has been prepared in an attempt to overcome some of these limitations. This cereal gives a suitable gruel preparation at 20% dilution and has an improved protein quality. It provides 14 mg of hemoglobin iron per 100 g with a mean absorption of the heme iron of 14.2%. It can be calculated that two servings a day of 20 g of this cereal will provide about 0.8 mg absorbed iron. The effectiveness of this product in prolonging breast-feeding and preventing iron deficiency is presently being investigated in a longitudinal field trial in Santiago.

Children

Theoretically, fortified milk and fortified cereals could also be used to provide extra iron to preschool children. In practice, however, preschool and older children must rely on the regular household diet. As already discussed, iron nutrition in these children will depend on the content and availability of iron from the different diets. Children will also benefit from iron fortification of products aimed at the general population.

In many countries, wheat flour is fortified with iron, thus increasing the iron intake from products such as bread and pasta. The impact of the consumption of fortified wheat flour on the iron nutrition of children has not been determined. The use of sugar fortified with sodium iron EDTA in the general population is presently under investigation in a large community study in Guatemala. This iron salt has special characteristics in its absorption behavior when mixed with food (32,33), which makes it a promising food fortificant. Preliminary results of the field studies seem to indicate a positive effect in children (F. E. Viteri, *personal communication*).

Common salt fortified with ferric orthophosphate and sodium acid sulphate (1 mg iron/g salt) has recently been tried in India as a means to provide extra iron to the general population (34). The product is reported to have good organoleptic characteristics and a good shelf-life. Large-scale field trials were conducted in three rural areas and one urban area located in different parts of India, each covering a total population of 4,000 to 6,000. Hemoglobin levels were determined before and at 6, 12, and 18 months after the introduction of iron-fortified salt. Prevalence of anemia at the beginning of the trial was extremely high, particularly in the rural areas. In Calcutta, for example, 94.6% of the population was anemic. A highly significant increase´in hemoglobin concentration occurred in all centers in essentially all age and sex groups. In Calcutta, at 12 months, hemoglobin had risen 3.3 g/dl in the 1- to 5-year-old group and about 3.2 g/dl in the 6- to 14-year-old group. Prevalence of anemia in the 1- to 5-year-old group (Hb <11 g/dl) was reduced from 96.3 to 38.8% in Calcutta, from 66.3 to 28.2% in Hyderabad, and from 19.1 to 9.1% in the urban center of Madras. Changes in the prevalence of anemia of a similar order of magnitude occurred in the 6- to 14-year-old group and also in essentially all other groups. The iron-fortified salt was acceptable to the population and its consumption was, reportedly, without any untoward effects.

Other products that are extensively used and provide extra iron to preschool children are the special food supplements supplied to developing countries by the Food for Peace Program of the U.S. Department of Agriculture. They include products such as corn-soya milk, corn-soya blend, wheat-soya blend, wheat protein concentrate blend, and whey-soya drink mix, all of which are fortified with iron, as ferrous fumarate, in the proportion of 15.6 mg iron/100 g. Iron absorption from these mixtures is quite low (35). However, based on their absorption studies, Morck et al. have calculated that when consumed in the recommended amounts, they can supply about half of the daily iron requirement of iron-deficient preschool children (35).

School lunch programs also provide an opportunity to supply extra iron to schoolchildren, where needed. In Chile, 6.7% of school-age children are anemic and 31.8% have a transferrin saturation below 15% (36).

The School Lunch Program in Chile includes, at breakfast or at tea time, three 10-g wheat flour cookies per child. The fortification of these cookies with a 6% bovine hemoglobin concentrate, resulting in a product with improved protein quality and good organoleptic characteristics and shelf-life has been proposed (J. A. Asenjo, *unpublished data*). Thirty grams of cookies provide about 5 mg of hemoglobin iron. Heme iron absorption from the cookies is about 20%, which should result in the absorption of 1 mg of iron per child on each school day. The effect of using these fortified cookies in the school lunch program is presently being measured in longitudinal studies in Santiago.

IRON SUPPLEMENTATION

When adequately fortified foods are not available, as is the case in many parts of the developing world, iron requirements in infants should be met by supplementation of the diet with medicinal iron.

Oral Iron

The effectiveness of oral supplementary iron in preventing iron deficiency was demonstrated a long time ago (37,38). Iron supplementation should start at about

4 months of age in term infants and no later than 2 months in preterm infants, and should continue at least through the remainder of the first year of life. The Committee on Nutrition of the American Academy of Pediatrics recommends that the dose of supplementary iron should not exceed 1 mg/kg/day for term infants and 2 mg/kg/day for preterm infants, up to a maximum of 15 mg/day (16).

Ferrous sulphate is the standard preparation for oral iron supplementation. It is inexpensive and well absorbed. Several other soluble ferrous salts are equally well absorbed (39). Preparations containing other "hematinics" should be avoided. Ascorbic acid, which has a marked effect on the absorption of nonheme dietary iron, is probably not justified in combination with medicinal iron (40). Tolerance in infants is usually good. In one careful study, definite symptoms associated with preventive doses of oral iron were no different from those associated with placebo (41).

The main obstacle in achieving effective prevention with oral iron medication is compliance. The daily administration of a medicine to an apparently healthy infant for several months is very difficult to obtain, even from educated mothers. This is well exemplified by the work of Ríos *(personal communication)* in our laboratory. He studied prospectively 130 preterm infants from birth until 1 year of age. At 3 months, oral iron supplementation, 2.5 mg/kg body weight, was prescribed to 65 of the infants who were receiving unfortified whole milk powder. The iron preparation, a commonly used liquid containing ferrous sulphate (FER-IN-SOL, Mead Johnson) was delivered every 3 weeks to each infant's house by a nurse who motivated the mother and checked for unused medicine. The other 65 infants received the same powdered milk fortified with 15 mg iron and 100 mg ascorbic acid per liter of reconstituted product. At 6, 9, and 12 months of age, hemoglobin concentration was significantly lower in infants on iron medication (Fig. 5). Anemia at 12 months existed in 23.9% of these subjects versus only 4.2% of those receiving fortified milk. The most likely explanation for the poorer results in the infants receiving medicinal iron was poor compliance, despite the very high motivation of the mothers and the careful supervision by professional personnel.

Parenteral Iron

In theory, parenteral iron is an attractive alternative for the prevention of iron deficiency in infancy. The full requirements for the first year of life can be administered in a single visit, avoiding the problems of interfered absorption of fortification iron by food and lack of compliance or intolerance to oral iron supplementation. It would be particularly useful as a preventive measure in situations where susceptible individuals are reached only sporadically by health services and are usually thereafter lost to follow-up.

Based on these types of considerations, we performed in 1975 a study in which 250 normal term newborns were given 150 mg of iron dextran (IMFERON, Fisons) intramuscularly before discharge from the hospital (M. Olivares, *unpublished data*). These infants were followed prospectively until 15 months of age. The results in

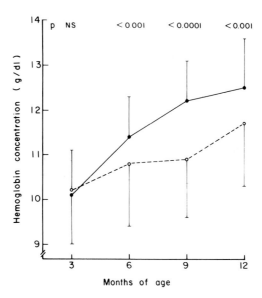

FIG. 5.   Mean values ± 1 SD of hemoglobin concentration at 3, 6, 9, and 12 months of age in preterm infants who received, starting at 3 months of age, oral iron supplementation *(broken line)* or a milk formula fortified with iron and ascorbic acid *(solid line)* (E. Ríos, P. Chadud, V. Vega, and A. Stekel, *unpublished observations*).

relation to prevention of iron deficiency were highly satisfactory. Only 1.3% of infants had a hemoglobin concentration below 11.0 g/dl at 15 months of age. Adverse reactions, occurring in 2.5% of the cases, were mild—skin rash, low-grade fever, and polypnea—in a 48-hr observation period. Other authors (42,43) have obtained similar results.

In 1977, Barry and Reeve (44) in New Zealand reported that parenteral administration of iron dextran was associated with an increase in the incidence of serious bacterial infections in the neonatal period. The study, however, was based on retrospective analysis of epidemiological data without controls run in parallel. A newer preparation of parenteral iron, iron-poly (sorbitol gluconic acid) complex, is claimed to have less adverse reactions than iron dextran (45). This product has not been studied in infancy.

Although further studies need to be carried out in order to clarify the issue of parenteral iron in the newborn, the possible risk of infection plus the possibility of severe anaphylactic reactions make its use, at present, unadvisable in young infants.

ACKNOWLEDGMENTS

The following investigators participated in the Chilean milk fortification studies: Mirna Amar, Marisol Cayazzo, Patricia Chadud, Gloria Heresi, Eva Hertrampf, Sandra Llaguno, Manuel Olivares, Fernando Pizarro, Ernesto Ríos, and Tomás Walter. The expert secretarial help of Adriana Vargas is acknowledged.

This work was supported in part by grants from the United Nations University, The Consejo Nacional para la Alimentación y Nutrición (CONPAN), Chilean Ministry of Health, and the Departamento de Desarrollo de la Investigación, University of Chile.

REFERENCES

1. Dallman PR, Beutler E, Finch CA. Effects of iron deficiency exclusive of anaemia. Br J Haematol 1978;40:179–84.
2. World Health Organization. Nutritional anaemias. Report of a World Health Organization Scientific Group. Geneva: World Health Organization; 1968. Technical report series no. 405.
3. Owen GM, Kram KM, Garry PJ, Lowe JE, Lubin AII. A study of nutritional status of preschool children in the United States, 1968–1970. Pediatrics 1974;53:597–646.
4. Cook JD, Layrisse M, Martínez-Torres C, Walker R, Monsen E, Finch CA. Food iron absorption measured by an extrinsic tag. J Clin Invest 1972;51:805–15.
5. Hallberg L, Bjorn-Rasmussen E. Determination of iron absorption from whole diet: a new two-pool model using two radioiron isotopes given as haem and non haem iron. Scand J Haematol 1972;9:193–7.
6. Callender ST, Mallet BJ, Smith MD. Absorption of haemoglobin iron. Br J Haematol 1957;3:186–92.
7. Layrisse M, Cook JD, Martínez-Torres C, Roche M, Kuhn IN, Walker RB, Finch CA. Food iron absorption: a comparison of vegetable and animal foods. Blood 1969;33:430–43.
8. Turnbull AL, Cleton F, Finch CA. Iron absorption. IV. The absorption of hemoglobin iron. J Clin Invest 1962;41:1897–907.
9. McMillan JA, Landaw SA, Oski FA. Iron sufficiency in breast-fed infants and the availability of iron from human milk. Pediatrics 1976;58:686–91.
10. Saarinen UM, Siimes MA, Dallman PR. Iron absorption in infants: high bioavailability of breast milk iron as indicated by the extrinsic tag method of iron absorption and by the concentration of serum ferritin. J Pediatr 1977;91:36–9.
11. Saarinen UM. Need for iron supplementation in infants on prolonged breast feeding. J Pediatr 1978;93:177–80.
12. Fleming AF. Haematological manifestations of malaria and other parasitic diseases. Clin Haematol 1981;10:983–1011.
13. Elian E, Bar-Shani S, Liberman A, Matoth Y. Intestinal blood loss: a factor in calculations of body iron in late infancy. J Pediatr 1966;69:215–9.
14. Wilson JF, Lahey ME, Heiner DC. Studies on iron metabolism. V. Further observations on cow's milk-induced gastrointestinal bleeding in infants with iron deficiency anemia. J Pediatr 1974;84:335–44.
15. Woodruff CW, Clark JL. The role of fresh cow's milk in iron deficiency. I. Albumin turnover in infants with iron deficiency anemia. Am J Dis Child 1972; 124:18–23.
16. Committee on Nutrition, American Academy of Pediatrics. Iron supplementation for infants. Pediatrics 1976;58:765–8.
17. Fomon SJ, Filer LJ, Anderson TA, Ziegler EE. Recommendations for feeding normal infants. Pediatrics 1979;63:52–9.
18. Baker SJ, DeMaeyer EM. Nutritional anemia: its understanding and control with special reference to the work of the World Health Organization. Am J Clin Nutr 1979;32:368–417.
19. International Nutritional Anemia Consultative Group. Guidelines for the eradication of iron deficiency anemia. Washington, DC: The Nutrition Foundation, 1977.
20. World Health Organization. Control of nutritional anaemia with special reference to iron deficiency. Report of an IAEA, USAID, WHO Joint Meeting. Geneva: World Health Organization, 1975; Technical report series no. 580.
21. Fomon SJ. Infant nutrition. 2nd ed. Philadelphia: WB Saunders, 1974:376–9.
22. Marsh A, Long H, Stierwalt E. Comparative hematological response to iron fortification of a milk formula for infants. Pediatrics 1959;24:404–12.
23. Andelman MB, Sered BR. Utilization of dietary iron by term infants. Am J Dis Child 1966;111:45–55.

24. Dallman PR, Siimes MA, Stekel A. Iron deficiency in infancy and childhood. Am J Clin Nutr 1980;33:86–118.
25. Stekel A, Olivares M, López I, Amar M, Pizarro F, Chadud P, Llaguno S, Cayazzo M. Prevention of iron deficiency in infants by milk fortification. In: Underwood BA, ed. Nutrition intervention strategies in national development. New York: Academic Press, 1983.
26. Stekel A, Olivares M, Amar M, Pizarro F. Effect of ascorbic acid on the absorption of supplementary iron in milk. Kyoto, Japan: 16th International Congress of Hematology, 1976:Abst. 3–12.
27. Cook JD, Minninch V, Moore CV, Rasmussen A, Bradley WB, Finch CA. Absorption of fortification iron in bread. Am J Clin Nutr 1973;26:861–72.
28. Smith NJ, Ríos E. Iron metabolism and iron deficiency in infancy and childhood. In: Schulman I, ed. Advances in pediatrics. Vol 21. Chicago: Year Book Medical Publishers, 1974.
29. Moe PJ. Iron requirements in infancy: longitudinal studies of iron requirements during the first year of life. Acta Paediatr 1963; [Suppl]150;1–67.
30. Fomon SJ. Infant nutrition. 2nd ed. Philadelphia: WB Saunders, 1974:410–1.
31. Ríos E, Hunter RE, Cook JD, Smith NJ, Finch CA. The absorption of iron as supplements in infant cereal and infant formulas. Pediatrics 1975;55:686–93.
32. Layrisse M, Martínez-Torres C. Fe (III)–EDTA complex as iron fortification. Am J Clin Nutr 1977;30:1166–74.
33. Viteri FE, García-Ibañez R, Torún B. NaFe EDTA as an iron fortification compound in Central America: absorption studies. Am J Clin Nutr 1978;31:961–71.
34. Working Group on Fortification of Salt with Iron. Use of common salt fortified with iron in the control and prevention of anemia. A collaborative study. Am J Clin Nutr 1982;35:1442–51.
35. Morck TA, Lynch SR, Skikne BS, Cook JD. Iron availability from infant food supplements. Am J Clin Nutr 1981;34:2630–4.
36. Ríos E, Olivares M, Amar M, Chadud P, Pizarro F, Stekel A. Evaluation of iron status and prevalence of iron deficiency in infants in Chile. In: Underwood BA, ed. Nutrition intervention strategies in national development. New York: Academic Press, 1983.
37. Mackay HMM. Nutritional anaemia in infancy with special reference to iron deficiency. London: His Majesty's Stationery Office, 1931.
38. Sturgeon P. Studies of iron requirements in infants and children. IV. Recommended daily dietary allowances. In: Wallerstein RO, Mettier SR, eds. Iron in clinical medicine. Berkeley: University of California Press, 1958.
39. Brise H, Hallberg L. Absorbability of different iron compounds. Acta Med Scand 1962;171(suppl 376):23–37.
40. Grebe G, Martínez-Torres C, Layrisse M. Effect of meals and ascorbic acid on the absorption of a therapeutic dose of iron as ferrous and ferric salts. Curr Ther Res 1975;17:382–97.
41. Burman D. Haemoglobin levels in normal infants aged 3 to 24 months, and the effect of iron. Arch Dis Child 1972;47:261–71.
42. Cantwell RJ. Iron deficiency anaemia of infancy: some clinical principles illustrated by the response of Maori infants to neonatal parenteral iron administration. Clin Pediatr 1972;11:443–9.
43. Tonkin S. Maori infant health: trial of intramuscular iron to prevent anaemia in Maori babies. NZ Med J 1970;71:129–35.
44. Barry DMJ, Reeve AW. Increased incidence of gram-negative neonatal sepsis with intramuscular iron administration. Pediatrics 1977;60:908–12.
45. Fielding J. ed. Ferastral: proceedings of a conference. Scand J Haematol 1977; (suppl):32;1–399.

DISCUSSION

Dr. Siimes: I wonder why so much unsupplemented formulas are sold in areas where iron deficiency is common in infancy?

Dr. Fomon: In the United States, the major infant formula manufacturers produce formulas "with" or "without" iron, generally at the same price. Formulas "with" iron generally provide about 1.8 mg/100 kcal, whereas those "without" iron generally provide about 0.15 mg/100 kcal. Many physicians believe that the formulas with iron are responsible for adverse reactions—diarrhea, constipation, regurgitation, fussiness—and therefore prefer formulas without iron. There are few studies on this point. A study by Oski [*Pediatrics* 66:168,

1980] with 93 infants enrolled soon after birth and the majority studied until 6 weeks of age failed to detect any difference in manifestations between those fed formulas with and without iron. However, additional studies should be carried out.

Dr. Hallberg: I think that in this important review, there should be a summary included on the findings you have made of diarrhea and infection in these two groups.

Dr. Stekel: We have measured specific signs of gastrointestinal intolerance and especially diarrhea, and we have found that there is no increase in these in the group receiving the fortified formula, and that in certain periods of the summer there has been a significant decrease in the prevalence of diarrhea in the group receiving the fortified milk. There are some problems of interpretation because the fortified milk was acidified and the unfortified control was not, but at least we can say very clearly that there are no increased signs of intolerance.

Dr. Dallman: There is another reason why the use of unfortified formulas has persisted. Pediatricians have justifiably tended to be very conservative about having formula constituents that deviate markedly from the composition of breast milk. Certainly, the iron-fortified products deviate markedly in respect to iron. As we have discussed, some deviation can be justified on the basis of the poorer bioavailability of iron from cow's milk formulas as compared to breast milk.

Dr. Stekel: There is certainly a need for more documentation of the possible side effects of iron in formulas and, particularly, of medicinal iron. As I was reviewing material for my paper, I could find very few good studies. The one that I quote, which is the one by Burman [ref. 41], is probably one of the best ones—and I am not sure that the interpretation that I gave to the findings in that paper is really accurate. I said that the author found no important differences between infants given oral iron and the ones given placebo. Dr. Fomon commented the other day that if one looks carefully at the data there may be some differences. Side effects may be related to which iron preparation is given, or to the dosage. We know infants are often prescribed many times the recommended doses. These sort of things need to be studied.

Dr. Finch: One possible cause of bowel symptoms may be a change in bacterial flora. It would be expected that an altered iron content might favor some bacteria over others. Is there any evidence relating to changes in bacterial flora in infants given high-level iron supplements or fortified formulas?

Dr. Stekel: Not that I am aware of, and these studies are quite difficult to perform. We have done some studies on stool cultures, but these are probably not very relevant because we are studying the flora at a level of the gut where it is not really important. In order to sample the areas of the gut that need to be studied we need quite sophisticated techniques and I am not aware of any studies of this kind.

Dr. DeMaeyer: Is there any information concerning the effect of repeated gastrointestinal infections on iron absorption, especially in young children?

Dr. Chandra: The question of nutrient absorption in relation to diarrhea was discussed at a workshop in Bellagio recently. There was little information on iron or other minerals.

Dr. Stekel: Isn't there information that even mild inflammatory states will impair iron absorption? I think this information is available.

Dr. Cook: As I recall there was only one study published in the *Lancet* a number of years ago from Jamaica showing that fever impairs iron absorption in infants.

Dr. Dallman: Another study by Bender-Götze and co-workers [*Mschr Kinderheilk* 124:305, 1976] came to the same conclusion. Iron absorption was decreased by about 50% in children with acute febrile infections but returned to control values after recovery from the fever.

Dr. Guesry: I would like to return to the ascorbic acid question since Dr. Stekel has raised the point. The recommendation for ascorbic acid is 50 mg/day, but since you have shown that with a higher amount of ascorbic acid it is possible to increase the iron absorption, would you recommend increasing the level of ascorbic acid up to 100 or 200 mg?

Dr. Stekel: One is always hesitant to recommend the increase of a nutrient in a product based not only on a direct nutritional need for that nutrient, but, as it would be in this case, because of a pharmacological effect. However, knowing the wide safety range that we have with this particular vitamin, I have not hesitated to recommend in my country a concentration of 100 mg/liter.

Dr. Hallberg: I would like to comment on the suggestion of making several studies with different levels of iron fortification. Sometimes it is too easy to ask for more studies without considering the tremendous amount of work involved in making a *good* study. We need a few, but very good studies, designed so that interpolations can be made. It is not necessary to repeat studies in every country; there is then always a risk that confounding results are obtained because of poor experimental design, insufficient number of subjects, and so on.

Dr. Fomon: Although I agree that the number of clinical studies must be limited, I am not willing to retreat from my position that it is of considerable importance to determine whether fortification of an infant formula with ferrous sulfate at 0.9 mg/100 kcal (the calculated advisable intake) is as effective in achieving desirable iron nutritional status as the current fortification level of 1.8 mg/100 kcal.

Dr. Stekel: Coming back to the question of possible modifications of the intestinal flora, I wanted to ask Dr. Chandra if he thinks that some kind of information of this sort can be obtained from regular stool cultures, or if you really have to go into more sophisticated studies.

Dr. Chandra: Assessment of fecal flora is of limited value. Next best to the invasive procedure of duodenal aspiration, one may use the string test, which is employed for the diagnosis of Giardia infection.

SUBJECT INDEX

Subject Index